HARVARD ORIENTAL SERIES

Edited by MICHAEL WITZEL

VOLUME SIXTY-NINE

RAI MYTHOLOGY

Kiranti Oral Texts

by

Karen H. Ebert
&
Martin Gaenszle

PUBLISHED BY THE DEPARTMENT
OF SANSKRIT AND INDIAN STUDIES,
HARVARD UNIVERSITY

DISTRIBUTED BY
HARVARD UNIVERSITY PRESS
CAMBRIDGE, MASSACHUSETTS
AND LONDON, ENGLAND
2008

For information write to Editor, Harvard Oriental Series,
Department of Sanskrit and Indian Studies,
1 Bow Street, Cambridge MA 02138, USA
617-495 3295; email: witzel@fas.harvard.edu

Library of Congress Cataloguing in Publication Data

Rai Mythology: Kiranti Oral Texts

(Harvard Oriental Series; v. 69)
ISBN 978-0-674-03272-9
I. Karen H. Ebert 1945-
Martin Gaenszle 1956-
II. Title
III. Series: Harvard Oriental Series; 69

CIP

CONTENTS

Map of Rai Groups

N
↑

✶ MT.EVEREST

Khaling   **Mewahang**   *Yamphu*

Kulung Saam   Lohorong

Sunwar **Thulung** Nachereng

Hayu   *Bahing*   Dumi Koi   Sangpang   *Yakkha*

Lumba

Umbule   Dungmali *Mugali*   *Limbu*

Phangduwali

Camling   **Bantawa**

Jerung

Puma

Athpare

Belhare

Chintang   *Chulung*

bold: languages represented in this volume
plain: other Rai languages
italics: other Kiranti languages

Abbreviations

A	actor		LW	loan word integrating suffix
ABL	ablative		MAN	manner subordinator
ALL	allative		MIR	mirative
AMB	ambulative		NEG	negator
AP	agentive participle		NML	nominalizer
APP	suffix of appeal		NPT	nonpast
APPL	applicative		ns	non-singular
AUX	auxiliary		P	patient
CAUS	causative		p	plural
CL	classifier		PART	particle
COM	comitative		PERF	perfect
CONV	converb		PFV	perfective
d	dual		POSS	possessive
DAT	dative		PP	patientive participle
DIST	distal		PROG	progressive
e	exclusive		PROX	proximative
EMPH	emphatic		PT	past
ERG	ergative		PURP	purposive
EVI	evidential		QUOTE	quote marker
FOC	focus		REC	reciprocal
GEN	genitive		REFL	reflexive
HAB	habitual		REL	relational prefix (=3sPOSS)
hiLOC	locative for higher location		REP	report particle
HUM	human		S	intransitive subject
i	inclusive		SEQ	sequential
IDEO	ideophone		SIM	simultaneous
IMPER	imperative		TEL	telicizer
INCH	inchoative		TEMP	temporal subordinator
INF	infinitive		TOP	topic
INST	instrumental		VB	verbalizer
INTJ	interjection		V2	second verb in compound
INV	inverse			
IPFV	imperfective			
levLOC	loc. for same level location			
LINK	linker			
LOC	locative			
loLOC	loc. for lower location			
LP	locative participle			

I. Rai Mythology

Martin Gaenszle

The Rai, the largest subunit of the Kiranti in East Nepal, are a heterogenous group which consists of more than twenty linguistically and culturally distinct subgroups (commonly termed 'subtribes'). In spite of the historical contingency of what is today an ethnic group, the Rai have all rich mythologies which possess a high degree of family resemblance. Before I give a general introduction to the structure and content of these mythologies, it will be useful to take a look at the role of mythology in Rai society. Myth is generally defined as a "sacred" narrative, differentiating it from other genres such as folk stories and legends. However, such a classification follows our own criteria and not that of the culture studied. So first of all, one has to understand the place and meaning of mythology in the traditional worldview of the Rai themselves.

1. The Tradition

Mythology among the Rai is an integral part of their religious tradition, known by a term which is cognate in the various Rai languages. Among the Mewahang Rai, for example, it is known as *muddum*, among the Yakha Rai as *mintum*, among the Kulung as *ridum*, or among the Camling simply as *dum*: thus there is apparently a common root (**dum*) which points to a shared conceptual base.[1] All these terms designate the essentially oral tradition of the group, including both the spoken „texts" as well as their ritual performance. The Tradition (written with a capital initial letter this is perhaps the best translation of the indigenous designations) thus includes, for example, ritual invocations of the ancestors during funerals or harvest festivals, ceremonial dialogues on occasions such as weddings, or complex shamanic séances for the purpose of healing. These ritual performances, which typically require the use of a distinct ritual language, generally presuppose knowledge of the mythic deeds of the ancestors. Thus myth and ritual are intrinsically linked as a way to both commemorate the achievements of the ancestors in the past and to communicate with them to secure their continuing

---

[1] Among the Limbu, who beside the Rai are the second major Kiranti group, the Tradition is known as *mundhum*.

blessing in the present. With the help of their mythological and ritual Tradition the Rai maintain their link to the ancestral world: it is the foundation of their cultural order and the source of their ethnic identity.

There is evidence that at one time the major myths of origin where fully embedded in ritual action and possibly were only performed in this context in the ritual language. However, the mythology today is part of ordinary narrative practice, i.e. the myths can be told in non-ritual contexts and may be recounted even in the Nepali language. Yet there are still traces of the ritual embeddedness of myth. For example, among the Mewhang the funerary rites of those who have died an inauspicious death, i.e. either a *hillasi* (victim of accidental death, murder etc.), *ma:maksi* (mother who died in childbed or during pregnancy) or *chanu* (unborn child) require a special shamanic séance called *selewa*, which can only be performed by a highly knowledgeable shaman, a *selemi*.[2] In this séance the shaman, in order to safely escort away the unfortunate and dangerous spirit, goes on a verbal journey along a special route, usually towards the south or west, and as he chants he recounts parts of the myths of origin, namely the episode of Tiger and Bear (see BR1.41-104, Jh1.50-95, Nir1.143-231). In the Mewahang myth these spirits originate from the dead protagonists, and it is said that the ritual retelling "reminds" the inauspicious spirit of the way it came into being.

This example clearly illustrates that mythic stories among the Rai, even if they appear as pastime narratives, are still an important interpretive frame for cultural practice. As it will become plain in the following, the myths deal with the creation and foundation of cultural institutions, such as marriage, agriculture, house-building, kinship relations, village rituals by recounting a long history of ancestral events. The myths about the past thus give meaning to life in the present, they are charters, to use Malinowski's well-known term, for the living.[3] In the following we will give a short outline of the structure and content of the major Rai myths and their relation to ritual practice. Since there is much variation a general account is bound to be biased in one way or another, but the purpose is simply to give an idea about basic and recurrent themes, without any claims of completeness.

2. Structure and content of Rai mythology

The mythology can be divided into roughly four major parts or cycles: the myths of creation, the myths about the culture hero, the myths of ancestral migration and the myths about the first settlements and village foundations. Though the mythology is usually not recounted as a whole, i.e. from beginning to the end, and the cycles are not always clearly connected, one can nevertheless say that there is an inherent chronological order which is expressed in a genealogical order: the protagonists in the mythology are related through kinship – they are ancestors of the living. Therefore the mythic actors can be schematically represented in a complex genealogical tree which originates from the first living being and goes all the way to the present day Rai descendants (see Gaenszle 2000: 310). Foreigners are seen as the descendants of lines which have branched off earlier and thus are in principle part of this segmentary structure.

---

[2] A similar situation holds among the Camling, where the special priest is called *surlima*.

[3] See Malinowski 1954.

2.1. Creation myths

The creation myths recount how the first living creatures, the variety of species, came into being. Generally emphasis is given to the duality of earth and sky, or the soil and water, which combine to produce life. Among the Thulung, for example, Heaven rained and a lake formed on Earth into which leaves were swept by the wind: from these moistened leaves sprang the first plant, and this again produced the creator goddess (Allen 1976: 37). In some cases, the snake is regarded as the first living being which moves between the upper and lower domains and from which all further life has originated. Whereas there is considerable variance, and often uncertainty, concerning these primordial events, with the appearance of the creator goddess one reaches firmer ground. This figure, known by various names (Somnima, Naima, Miyapma, etc.), is depicted as a woman who - living in a world without men (only mothers, grandmothers, and the wind) - is desperately in search of a husband. Eventually she hears about a male person living up in the sky (Salapa, Paruhang, Ruwasila, etc.) and sends out intermediaries to bring him down (Nir1.14ff., BR1.22f.). But seeing him she is struck by his ugliness (in some versions because of a huge goitre) and rejects him (Nir1.97-98, Jh1.17-19, BR1.24). The would-be groom then resorts to a trick: he dries out the earth and leaves his semen as the only liquid on a leaf. When the woman is about to die of thirst she is forced to drink the urine/ semen (unknowingly) whereupon she becomes pregnant (Nir1.122-124, Jh1.38-44, BR1.25-61). In due course she gives birth to the variety of species: tiger, bear, monkey or dog (and other creatures) - and the First Man.[4] Evidently this myth about the creator couple combines images of a primordial marriage with those of divine creation. Though the initiative comes from the woman's side (inverting present social practice), the match is arranged by an intermediary, just as it is done today, and thus establishes a precedence. At this point, however, culture and nature are not yet distinguished. This changes in the subsequent episode, which introduces the topic of hunting. After some quarrels in the familiy the divine mother's offspring, namely Tiger, kills their mother and decides to bury her in a kind of failed funeral (Jh1.74-95, Nir1.197-231, BR1.62-104). In the process Bear eats parts of the corpse, which raises the anger of Man. Such cannibalism can not be tolerated and the two wild animals are killed or sent back to the jungle. As indicated above, this episode is in some cases given as the reason for the existence of various kinds of death spirits, introducing death – and religion (culture).

The creation myths are at the base of various ritual activities. Because of their descendence from the divine snake (cf. Nir1.232ff.) the respective Rai groups are obliged to pay reverence and do regular sacrifices to this apical ancestor, as he continues to exert positive as well as negative influence. In terms of cults there is not only one *nāgi* but several, as many Rai subtribes have their own ritual: the Mewahang have the the *Bhārte nāgi* and *Lùkwamaŋ*, the Sampang Rai have the *Waya nāgi*, the Khaling have their own *nāgi*, and there are various Kulung *nāgi*s. Obviously the cults have gone their separate ways, just as the ancestors have, and in fact the migration myths recount how the cults have been "divided up", not only among subtribes, but later on even among clans (see below).

The mythic creator couple (Somnima and Salapa, Naima and Paruhang, Miyapma and Ruwasila etc.) are the source of all the life and variety of the natural world. However, neither is the object of any cult. Though the husband is often said to be *Śiva* (or *Mahādew*), a deity of the Great Tradition that plays some role in the local cults, there is no identification of the two in ritual practice. Nor is there any identification of the wife with any of the *dewi*s which are locally worshipped. But both creators do sometimes figure in Rai ritual. During the harvest celebrations of the Mewahang, on the day of the offering

---

[4] The sequence and kind of species born varies, though in all cases tiger is senior to man.

of the first rice to the (more immediate) ancestors (N. *nuwāgi*),[5] a dancer enacts various species from among those generated by Somnima, such as different birds and forest animals,[6] and eventually brings to life Paruhang as an old man with a goitre and Somnima as a weaving woman through the performance. In the Mewahang ritual texts there are certain expressions alluding to these creator ancestors, as, for example, the term "*somnikhoŋ pa:rukhoŋ*" (M* 'the wooden plates of Paruhang and Somnima'). So these deities are prototypes of the ancestral order. As a description of the first - cosmic - marriage, the myth is not only a social model for courtship and marriage in general, but at the same time contains biological metaphors of fertility, the duality of the seasons (rain and dryness) etc. Hence the myth emphasizes the roots of the social world in the wider natural or cosmological framework. It seems that on this plane the ancestors are still too "divine" and too remote to become effective agents in the present who require worship (this is quite common in "tribal" religions, cf. Sahlins 1968: 104f.).

It has already been pointed out that the subsequent episode of Tiger and Bear, which recounts the origin of the various kinds of evil death spirits, is evoked in ritual to remind the spirits of this origin. At the same time it can be seen as a neat mythical foundation of the origin of death, including the well-known distinction between spirits resulting from inauspicious deaths and the ones resulting from ordinary deaths, even though the latter are not specially mentioned here. It seems to be no coincidence that the differentiation between a "good" and "bad" death takes place at this particular stage. Before, the ancestors had the cosmic power to create the **natural** order, but now, because some ancestors (i.e. Tiger and Bear) have behaved in a "wild" or uncivilized manner, a **cultural** order – which requires rituals - is imposed on the unruly results of the creation.

2.2. The culture hero (orphan story)

The next cycle recounts the origin of Rai cultural institutions, such as hunting, agriculture, house-building, and ritual.[7] The major actor is the culture hero known by rather similar names among the different Rai groups (Khakculukpa, Khocilipa, Khakcilik etc.). Again there are numerous different version with different episodes, but the general plot is much the same. While the culture hero is seen as a descendant of the First Man, he is always depicted as an orphan who lived with his two elder sisters in a time of hardship. After he seems to have died - having eaten too much or too little and fallen asleep - the sisters bury their little brother and separate, going in two different directions: one up into the mountains, the other down to the plains. This is another important precedent: the fate of sisters in Rai society is to move away and live in different villages than their parents and male siblings. After waking up the hero, now completely on his own, has to make a living in the jungle, equiped only with a knife and a banana seedling, which the sisters had left as a funeral gift. The boy, now a young man, faces many dangers, but through his cunning he survives. One episode recounts how he is captured by a cannibal jungle woman, whom he tricks into eating her own daughter (Bant2.61ff., Ha2.33ff.). This story full of violence and cleverness is usually recounted with great amusement and may appear like a

---

[5] The *nuwāgi* is a major occasion to commemorate the ancestors. On this day the ascending lineage ancestors who have died in an ordinary way are fed with the newly harvested rice.

[6] Among others, the following creatures are enacted: fish (unspecified), whistling thrush (N. *kalcūṛe*, *Myiophoneus caeruleus*), brown hill prinia (N. *cipurke*, *Prinia criniger*), fly (unspecified), crane (N. *karyāṅ kuruṅ*, *Anthropoides virgo* ?), deer (N. *mirga*, *Muntiacus muntjak*), tiger and bear.

[7] For an interpretation of the Mewahang cycle see Gaenszle 1991: 271-291.

folk tale. Yet the episode also concludes with etiological motifs: the creation of rivers, rocks and paths, in other words: the landscape (Ha2.63ff.).

After these trials in the wilderness, the hero eventually establishes various cultural practices. One day, as he is fishing he repeatedly catches a stone (Ha2.75ff., Thul2.33ff.). At first he throws it back, but it turns out that it is his would-be spouse, who, while at home, does his cooking and cleaning. This episode may be read as the foundation of the once common practice of marriage by capture (Nep. *cori biha*). Now the couple begins to do agriculture, growing millet. After their first child is born they decide to build the First House. Again this story is a detailed template for contemporary practice: it provides an instruction of how a proper Rai house is to be constructed, for example it "explains" why a certain kind of beam must be used, and gives reasons why this requires certain blood sacrifices (Thul2.62-75, Khal2.38ff.).

When the house is finished the hero plans to hold a grandiose house-inauguration ritual – until today a highly important event. He remembers his lost sisters and, by sending various animals as messengers, eventually manages to find them and bring them back (Ha2.91ff., Thul2.77ff.. They all reunite in a big festive celebration which resembles both, a house inauguration as well as a wedding. In fact, even today a marriage is often ritually finalized only after the birth of children and the building of a house.This myth, then, can be seen as founding, or setting the precedent for, present day Rai cultural institutions and traditions. It recounts the coming of age of the hero as a process of leaving wilderness (or: nature) behind and establishing culture.

Not surprisingly, it is on the occasion of house inaugurations and weddings that this myth is evoked: The reappearance of the two sisters is ritually enacted during the house- inauguration while elders sing songs relating to the myth, and the "sisters'" dancing around the life-tree is an important part of the marriage ceremonies, during which the groom is identified with the culture hero. Thus he is a founding ancestor with very human qualities: he is rather a figure of self-identification than an object of worship. His wife, to the contrary, is of more superhuman origin: she is often depicted as a descendant of the snake deity (though in some versions this is a distinct episode, see Nir1.232ff.). It is said that because of this marriage the Rai have to sacrifice regularly not only to the *nāgi* (snake deity) of their patriline but also to the *nāgi* which is inherited from the mother's side.

The culture hero is not the object of a sacrificial cult, yet there is an important deity which appears to be closely linked to this divine ancestor, the house deity which inhabits the most sacred corner of the house. The origin of this deity is not stated in the myth explicitly, but as the orphan brother is the builder of the first house he also established the first house altar. Still today, only after this deity has been invoked at its altar for the first time during the house inauguration ceremony does a newly built house become inhabitable. At least for the Mewahang an analysis of ritual shows that this deity is associated with domestic prosperity, the solidarity between brothers and sisters, and also with the affinal bond of husband and wife (Gaenszle 2002: 235-250).

That the culture hero is particularly associated with the house may be seen as indication of the symbolic significance of domestic space. In Rai culture, where villages are generally not compact settlements but widely dispersed, the house is a central social and spatial unit. What Sagant (1981: 149) has said about the Limbu's view applies to the Kiranti in general: for them "the village, that's already almost the jungle", i.e. beyond domestic space wilderness begins. In some cases the culture hero is also associated with shamanism (cf. Hardman 2000: 129), i.e. ritual expertise for the protection of the house. The shaman is the typical mediator between domestic space and the untamed forces of the "outside".

2.3. Migration myths

The migration myths of the third cycle are of special importance for an understanding of the social system. These myths are very prominent among all Kiranti groups. In the Rai narratives the migration begins at the Place of Origin situated down in the plains, „where all the waters drain" (Gaenszle 1991: 292-305). This place is described as a hole in the ground, or a primal lake; today it is often said to be close to Barachetra, the Hindu pilgrimage site located near the confluence of the Seven Rivers (Saptakosi), which form the drainage system of East Nepal. From there four brothers, whose names differ according to the teller's group identity, migrated up towards the mountains. Among the Mewahang Rai, for example, they are Khambuhang, Mewahang, Limbuhang and Mece Koce (in order of seniority). For the Camling the eldest is Limbu, then follow Bantawa(or Sunwar /Bahing), Camling and Tharu (cf. Noc3, though this version is a bit confused). Along with the four brothers travelled their four sisters. However, the youngest brother and the youngest sister were left behind and stayed in the plains. The elder siblings crossed the river near Barachetra with the help of blood offerings (BR5, Nir3). But at this point a quarrel erupted among the brothers, because the eldest one had tricked the younger ones. They decided to split and divide up the territory, and each of the remaining three brothers eventually migrated up along one of the three big rivers in Kirat country, the Dudh Kosi, the Arun and the Tamur. There, in the course of time, they settled down and further split up in different valleys.[8]

These migration stories are typically cited to explain the difference among the various subtribes, and thus they can be regarded as the underlying pattern for the indigenous conception of ethnic differences. Generally these mythic episodes are seen as the reason for the division of different cults: when the brothers had crossed the river and divided up the land they also took up different ritual traditions, as well as different dietary habits.

But there is also another link between the myth and ritual practice. The ancestral journey up the rivers is often evoked in the verbal journeys of ritual specialists. Though the routes of these journeys, which are undertaken for the search of lost souls, are often different ones, there are some cases where the ritual experts travel along the ancestral paths. For example the Mewahang priest, when escorting away the harmful spirit of women who died in childbed, travels down to the Place of Origin, which is said to be the place where the spirits earlier originated (e.g. Gaenszle 1994). In some cases funerary priests escort the soul of the deceased back along the path of ancestral migration (Allen 1974: 7; Forbes 1998). Thus again the myths establish an order which is at the base of present-day cultural practice.

2.4. Village foundations

The myths eventually recount how one's forefathers' group found the territory of present day settlement and established a legitimate link with its spirit. This is the precedent of contemporary village rituals for the fertility of the soil. The myths further narrate how the first settlers interacted with other groups, in particular "brothers", i.e. other subtribes, with whom there are conflicts over the control of

---

[8] Among the Limbu, it may be added here, migration myths are equally prominent. The migration also begins at a Place of Origin, but here this place - called *co-lung* - is located in the hills: it is the place where one of the ancestral being fell from the sky and the earth opened (Sagant 1976b: 79f.). Departing from this Place of Origin the "Ten Limbus" split, and five of them migrated to the north, to Lhasa in Tibet, and the other five migrated to Kashi (i.e. Benares) in the South. Later on, however, they migrated back to the Nepalese hills and settled on their present territories.

the land. These stories typcially lead to a description of how the present day clans evolved from the village founder and end up with an account of the narrator's own genealogical affiliation, thus positioning him/her within the grand genealogy of Kiranti mythical ancestry.

Some of these latter stories have more the character of legends, as certain episodes may have a historically authentic background. However, in a comparative perspective many stories are strikingly similar in their plots and draw on the same imagery, such as the stories about one brother tricking the other into getting the bigger share of land (BR5, TH4, also see Gaenszle 1991: 302f., Allen 1976: 151-158). In any case, these stories do not generally figure in ritual practice. Apparently this is due to the fact that the events are not taking place in a distinct ancestral time, but rather are events which happened just a short time ago.

To sum up, it can be observerd that Kiranti mythology is a grand genealogical account of the origin of life, the variety of the species, mankind, Kiranti culture and the diversity of Kiranti social groups: it is an account of continuous differentiation in time and space. The migration of the ancestors represents the fissiparous tendencies of the segmentary kinship system as well as the all-important territorial linkages. As the ancestors migrate up the rivers they split up and appropriate their respective share of land. It emerges that the myths reflect the various levels of the social structure: the migration stories depict the division of subtribes, the first settler stories describe the division of village territories and eventually lead to an account of the division of kin groups. And the origin stories, among other things, highlight the significance of the house and the institution of marriage. Thus the mythology of the Tradition may be seen as a comprehensive template - or charter - for cultural institutions and social divisions.

3. Comparisons

As already indicated the mythologies of the various Rai groups share many common features, but there are also a lot of differences. A comparative mythology of the Kiranti is still very much in the beginning, due to the lack of comprehensive data. But there are already some tentative forays into this field, and the present book is another modest step in this direction. My own study of Mewahang myths has drawn sporadically on comparisons with the Thulung material collected by N. Allen (Gaenszle 1991/2000), and Karen Ebert, applying a kind of motif index approach, has ventured into a comparison of the culture hero cycle among seven Rai subtribes (Ebert 2000: 9-11). The latter exercise shows quite clearly that the myths in different groups (though some are represented only by one version) share many of the episodes including small details in imagery and metaphor. But at the same time some tellings omit complete episodes which are elaborate in others. This may in some cases be coincidental, as even narrators from one group have their preferences and omissions, as is evident from the comparison of three Camling narrators (Ebert 2000: 8). Lacking a large corpus of myths told by various persons, it is difficult to say whether the lack of an episode in one telling is a feature of the local tradition or simply the result of the narrator's mood of the day.[9] Nevertheless, in the case of the Thulung, for example, which are represented by eight versions, it is possible to come up with the observation that here the episode of the cannibalistic forest woman is apparently unknown,[10] whereas in

---

[9] It should be emphasized, however, that some of the narrators (like the Camling Lal and Ha) were not entirely spontaneous in there tellings but had prepared themselves, even with some written notes.

[10] The same seems to be the case for the Dumi and Khaling.

other groups, such as the Camling, the Mewahang and the Lohorung, it is common. The mythic cycles among different groups display nothing more and nothing less than a family resemblance.

But comparison is not restricted to Rai or even Kiranti mythologies. N. Allen has suggested to proceed towards "a comparative mythology of the Bodic speakers" (this is the subtitle of an article, Allen 1979). As in his unpublished monograph Allen points out structural parallels in the Thulung stories with Tibetan ones. Similarly in later articles he has pursued this path, focusing, for example, on the motif of drought in myths of creation (Allen 1986) or the role of animal guides (Allen 1997a), showing that certain themes which are found among the Rai are also present in regions several thousand miles away (such as Nuristan and Arunachal Pradesh). Later he calls it, more cautiously, a "Himalayan comparative mythology", as it has become clear that "the divides recognised by linguistic taxonomy cannot be relied on in the study of other parts of culture." (Allen 1997b: 435).

In any case, it is especially among the Tibeto-Burman speaking groups of the Himalayas that we find traces of a common mythological heritage. In the following I will give a few examples, somewhat rhapsodically, just to illustrate the kinds of resemblance.

Among the Kham Magar, where the myths of origin are transmitted in shamanic songs, we find the story of Pudaran (male) and Biselme (female), the first hunters who in the beginning have a relationship as fictive siblings. At one point Pudaran dries out all water sources, thus forcing Biselme to drink the only remaining water – Pudaran's urine which he had left in a water hole (Oppitz 1991: 187). Though the whole context is rather different and Biselme does not get pregnant from this, the story is surprisingly similar to that of the Rai creator couple. As to Biselme and Pudaran, quasi-siblings who turn incestuous, they eventually introduce the first grains, wheat and rye (a similar combination of the themes of incest and creation is found in Nir1.32ff.).

In the mythological chants of the Gurung, whose shamanic tradition displays considerable family resemblances with that of the Magar, we also find stories distantly reminiscent of the Rai creator couple myth. As Strickland points out, the myth of the demon called Sirapi, though quite different in its general character, is similar to the Rai myth in that it tells of a "rejected spouse who takes away some substance vital to the rejecting partner" (Strickland 1982: 225). Here it is the husband, the shaman, who rejects the demon as his wife (though the sex is unclear); subsequently she takes revenge by stealing his soul. This structural similarity is rather abstract and not entirely convincing. But there are other themes inviting other possible comparisons in the myths. In one version the demon magically does harvest work for two brothers, who hide in order to find out who it is: Eventually they find out that it is a woman who comes down from the sky ("I am the daughter of the sun and the moon"), and the elder brother instantly marries her (Strickland 1982: 210, 216). This myth clearly evokes the cycle of the Rai culture hero, who likewise marries a woman who magically works for him and who, appearing as a stone, has also a "foreign" origin. In some versions this is further qualified as a divine origin: in Mewahang myth she is the daughter of the snake king. Generally, these Gurung myths deal with the dangerous "otherness" of marriage partners. Some passages are reminiscent of the Rai episode in which the culture hero fights with the forest demoness and her daughter (also demonic beings), a fight which contains certain sexual overtones (Gaenszle 2000: 255). These examples show that similarities are far from straightforward. What in one tradition is found in several different episodes may appear in condensed form in the myth of another.

There are even more striking similarities with Rai myths among various groups in the northeastern Himalayas (the former Northeastern Frontier Area, NEFA), some of which the Rai explicitly regard as "brother tribes", i.e. belonging to the Kiranti family. Among the Taraon Mishmis, for instance, a myth tells of a young orphan who meets a beautiful girl while fishing. She is the daughter of a serpent that lives in the river and changes to human when on land. The young man wants to marry her, but there is extensive opposition to this unusual marriage (Elwin 1958: 336ff.). In a quite similar myth of the Hrusso (Aka), the girl is the daughter of the "lord of the river" (Elwin 1958: 169). The motif of the prepared meals is found, among other places, in a Minyong variant (Elwin 1958: 114f.). A systematic comparison of the Rai myths with those of these groups from Assam and Arunachal Pradesh appears to be a promising undertaking. Unfortunately, there is still little useful material on the subject.

But even among groups not belonging to the Tibeto-Burman speaking category we find some parallels. A unique case are the Tharu, who today speak an Indoeuropean language but regard themselves as belonging to the Kiranti – with good reasons. Their myths are – like those of the Magar – highly sanskritised, but still we find traces of a Kiranti heritage. The creator god called Guru Baba has one daughter (McDonaugh 1989: 195-196). Apparently for lack of other men she wants to marry her father who takes on the appearance of a leprous ascetic in order to put her off. Eventually, however, after overcoming a number of obstacles, she succeeds, and Guru Baba changes his form into the splendid incarnation of Mahadeo (Shiva). The girl becomes Gauri-Parbati, and so the couple is identitfied with the famous Hindu god and goddess. It is interesting in this context that also among the Rai the creator ancestor (Paruhang etc.) is often identified with Shiva, and likewise his frightening appearance as an ascetic is given as the reason why the creatrix (Somnima etc.) is reluctant to marry him. This is a typical case of Sanskritisation, a process of cultural assimilation in which tribal groups all over South Asia have often shown a preference for the figure of Shiva.

The Tharu also have migration myths which tell about four (sometimes five) brothers who came to the present place of settlement and divided up the ancestral land. A central theme is the principle of seniority which defines the relationship among the brothers and consequently the relationship of the descending clans (Krauskopff 1989: 88-89). However, this myth deals only with the ancestors of priestly clans and so a central issue is the division of functions among these. Beyond these general features there seem to be few similarities in detail with the Rai myths. It may be added at this point that among the Dhimal, another group residing in the Tarai (the plains) which claims Kiranti heritage (and which indeed speaks a Kiranti language), there is a migration myth which fits into the Rai pattern (though here are only two brothers): the Dhimal claim to be descendants from the youngest brother who according to the myth was left down in the Tarai at the time of migration because he could not follow the fast pace of his senior (Bista 1980: 142). This episode, like the Rai ones, contains the detail about the fast growing bananas on the trail being the reason for the brothers to lose contact (BR5.1ff.).

In this way the Kiranti myths display often startling family resemblances with other Himalayan mythologies, sometimes in the broad patterns of a "deep structure", sometimes in little details. The present situation is evidently the result of centuries of migration and fission but also of borrowing and assimilation.

4. Conclusion

Rai mythology may be regarded as a body of foundational narratives which recount how the world became what it is. In the classic sense of the term mythology establishes the "sacred" order – "sacredness" (which does not exist as an explicit concept among the Rai) understood as the quality of unquestionable validity derived from the authority of ancestral beings. Therefore the myths are intrinsically bound up with ritual, the sphere of sacred performance, even if not always in a straightforward manner. The myths, as was pointed out, are part of a more complex mytho-ritual Tradition which is the root of Rai identity.

Just as the myths display a certain family resemblance with other non-Kiranti groups in the central Himalayas, so, it should be added, does the concept of the Tradition (i.e. what is known as *muddum* or other cognate terms). Among the Gurung, who like the Rai have an elaborate ritual language, the equivalent concept is *pe-da lu-da*, which Strickland (1987: 71n.) renders as "principle word example word". The term refers to the body of ritual recitations which recount mythic events (see above) while performing shamanic action. The ethnographers of the Gurung derive the term *pe* from Tibetan *dpe*, 'pattern', 'model', 'parable' (Jäschke 1987: 327), a term also used in reference to the mythic past as evoked by traditional Tibetan bards (Tucci 1980: 233). This etymological link is corroborated by the fact that the Lohorung Rai call their Tradition *pe-lam* (< *lam* 'path'), which in this comparative perspective is not as odd as it first may appear.

The mythology of the Rai is distinct in its imagery, narrative plots and general structure, yet it is not an isolated phenomenon. There are a number of basic themes which recur in related form in other regions of the Himalaya, and even beyond. Of course, creation myths which play on the duality of earth and sky, soil and water, and the duality of the seasons (rain and drought) are rather common, especially in a landscape marked by a monsoon climate. But the particular link which is made with marriage and affinity among the Rai is more unique. In fact, this is a theme which appears to be of central importance: as long as there is no proper marital union, there is no fertility, even if the partners have to overcome a certain reluctance and repulsion. The bond between brothers and sisters is always depicted as strong, so strong even that incest appears as a "natural" attraction which has to be overcome. But once a proper marriage link has been established, it brings about domestic prosperity and peace. The remaining myths, which deal with the ancestors' migration and settlement, can be seen as expressing an ethos of hunters and slash-and-burn agriculturalists. The link to a territory is important, but may also be temporary.

Clearly, the core of Rai or Kiranti religion is an ancestral religion. The Tradition is basically a way to keep intact the crucial link with the world of the ancestors. Mythological narratives keep up the memory of ancestral creations, deeds and migrations, reminding the living of the origin of the natural and cultural order. Ritual performances make use of an ancestral speech (it is both the speech of the ancestors and for the ancestors), and by communicating with the ancestors in a pleasant idiom, presenting offerings of good food (rice, meat) and other coveted items (beer, liquor) the ancestors are made and kept happy, so that they „look benevolently" (as, for example, a ritual expression among the Mewahang goes) on their descendants, refrain from making trouble but ensure the prosperity of the living.

References:

Allen, Nicholas J. 1974. The ritual journey: a pattern underlying certain Nepalese rituals. In: Christoph von Fürer-Haimendorf (ed.), *Contributions to the Anthropology of Nepal*. Warminster: Aris and Philipps, pp. 6-22.

Allen, Nicholas J. 1976. *Studies in the myths and oral traditions of the Thulung Rai of east Nepal*. Oxford (unpublished PhD thesis).

Allen, Nicholas J. 1979. Tibet and the Thulung Rai: Towards a Comparative Mythology of the Bodic

Speakers. In: M. Aris & Aung San Suu Kyi (eds.), *Tibetan Studies in Honour of Hugh Richardson*. Warminster: Aris & Phillips Ltd., pp. 1-8.

Allen, Nicholas J. 1986. The Coming of Macchendranath to Nepal: Comments from a comparative point of view. In: R. Gombrich N. Allen, T. Raychaudhuri and G. Rizvi (eds.), *Oxford University Papers on India, Vol. 1*. Delhi: O.U.P., pp. 75-102.

Allen, Nicholas J. 1997a. Animal guides and Himalayan foundation myths. In: Samten Karmay & Philippe Sagant (eds.), *Les habitant du toit du monde*. Paris: Société d'ethnologie, pp. 375-390.

Allen, N.J. 1997b. 'And the lake drained away': an essay in Himalayan comparative mythology. In: Alexander W. Macdonald (ed.), *Mandala and landscape*. New Delhi: D.K. Printworld, pp. 435-451.

Bista, Dor Bahadur. 1980. *People of Nepal*. Kathmandu: Ratna Pustak Bhandar (orig. 1967).

Ebert, Karen. 2000. *Camling texts and glossary*. München: LINCOM Europa (Languages of the world/ Text collections, 11).

Elwin, Verrier. 1958. *Myths of the North East Frontier of India*. Shillong: North East Frontier Agency.

Forbes, Ann Armbrecht. 1998. Sacred geography on the cultural borders of Tibet. In: Anne-Marie Blondeau (ed.), *Tibetan Mountain Deities: Their Cults and Representations*. Wien: Verlag der Österreichischen Akademie der Wissenschaften, pp. 111-121.

Gaenszle, Martin. 1991. *Verwandtschaft und Mythologie bei den Mewahang Rai in Ostnepal. Eine ethnographische Studie zum Problem der 'ethnischen Identität'*. Stuttgart: Franz Steiner Verlag Wiesbaden.

Gaenszle, Martin. 1994. Journey to the origin: a root metaphor in a Mewahang Rai healing ritual. In: Michael Allen (ed.), *The anthropology of Nepal: peoples, problems, processes*. Kathmandu: Mandala Book Point, pp. 256-268.

Gaenszle, Martin. 2000. *Origins and migrations: kinship, mythology and ethnic identity among the Mewahang Rai of East Nepal*. Kathmandu: Mandala Book Point & The Mountain Institute.

Gaenszle, Martin. 2002. *Ancestral voices: oral ritual texts and their social contexts among the Mewahang Rai in east Nepal*. Münster, Hamburg, London: LIT Verlag.

Hardman, Charlotte E. 2000. *Other worlds: notions of self and emotion among the Lohorung Rai*. Oxford, New York: Berg.

Jäschke, H.A. 1987 (1881). *A Tibetan-English Dictionary*. New Delhi: Motilal Banarsidass.

Krauskopff, Gisèle. 1988. *Maîtres et Possédés. Les rites et l'ordre social chez les Tharu (Népal)*. Paris: Editions du CNRS.

Malinowski, Bronislaw. 1954. *Magic, science and religion. And other essays*. Garden City, New York: Double Day Anchor Books.

McDonaugh, Christian. 1989. The mythology of the Tharu: aspects of cultural identity in Dang, West Nepal. *Kailash* 15 (3-4): 191-205.

Oppitz, Michael. 1991. *Onkels Tochter, keine sonst*. Frankfurt: Suhrkamp Verlag.

Sagant, Philippe. 1976a. Les Limbu, population du Népal oriental. *L'Ethnographie, Nouvelle Série* 72 : 146-173.

Sagant, Philippe. 1976b. Becoming a Limbu Priest - Ethnographic Notes. In: John Hitchcock & Rex Jones (ed.), *Spirit Possession in the Nepal Himalayas*. Warminster: Aris & Phillips Ltd., pp. 56-99.

Sagant, Philippe. 1981. La tête haute. Maison, rituel et politique au Népal oriental. In: Gérard Toffin (ed.), *L'Homme et la Maison dans l'Himalaya*. Paris: CNRS, pp. 149-175.

Sahlins, Marshall D. 1968. *Tribesmen*. Englewood Cliffs: Prentice-Hall.

Strickland, Simon S. 1982. *Belief, practices, and legends: a study in the narrative poetry of the Gurungs of Nepal*. Cambridge: Unpublished PH.D. Dissertation.

Strickland, Simon S. 1987. Notes on the language of the Gurung Pe. *Journal of the Royal Asiatic Society* 1 : 53-76.

Subba, Chaitanya. 1995. *The culture and religion of Limbus*. Kathmandu: K.B. Subba.

Toba, Sueyoshi. 1983 Khaling Texts, Yak (Tokyo: Institute for the Study of Languages and Cultures of Asia and Africa (ILCAA).

Tucci, Giuseppe. 1980 (1970). *The religions of Tibet*. London: Routledge and Kegan Paul.

II. Rai languages

Karen H. Ebert

1. Introduction

The Kiranti people and languages between the rivers Likhu and Arun, including some small groups east of the Arun, are usually referred to as "Rai", which is a somewhat vague geographic rather than a genetic grouping (cf. map).[1] Most Rai languages have less than 10,000 speakers and are threatened by extinction. Some are spoken only by elderly people. Practically all speakers of Rai languages are also fluent in Nepali, the language of literacy and education and the national language of Nepal.

---

[1] The term Rai is usually confined to those groups which share the Rai culture (including the mythology). However, the term is not clearly marked off against other Kiranti groups; thus the (non-Rai) Athpare are often referred to as "Athpare Rai".

There is no valid genetic subgrouping of Kiranti or of Rai languages. Glover's (1974) evaluation of the Swadesh hundred word list for seven languages yielded only 26 per cent of cognates for the Rai group. Khaling, Kulung, and Bantawa come out as a subgroup with 42 per cent shared cognates. This result is at odds with Winter's comparison of 85 basic verbs in twelve Rai languages (Winter 1991-92). Northwestern languages (e.g. Khaling) turned out to share less than 20 cognates with central (e.g. Kulung) and southeastern languages (e.g. Bantawa). Application of the methods of historical linguistics to data from the Linguistic Survey of Nepal does not yield neat bundles of isoglosses for specific phonological, morphological or lexical features.

I find it useful to distinguish broadly between southeastern Kiranti, including Rai languages like Bantawa and Camling[2] and Non-Rai languages like Limbu and Athpare, and northwestern languages like Khaling and Thulung. For certain features it seems useful to distinguish also a central group. This is not meant to be a genetically valid grouping, nor is it relevant for all features. Some traits are, for example, found only in eastern and southeastern languages, including Mewahang, others only in central languages, including Camling and Bantawa.

Some traits that distinguish SE from NW Rai (and Kiranti in general) are:
1. no initial consonant clusters,
2. agentive participles formed with *ka-*,
3. intransitivized 1st patient forms,
4. prefixes for 2nd person and 3rd person plural on the verb,[3]
5. agglutinative morphology with long suffix chains,
6. preference for finite-marked forms in subordination.
The isoglosses for the first three features run right through the Camling area, distinguishing NW-Camling from SE-Camling.

SE features like prefixed person markers and the participle formation with *ka-* are found also in Tibeto-Burman languages further east, e.g. in Naga and Chin languages. The highly agglutinative morphology of SE languages is characteristic of North Munda languages, and so is the preference for finite-marked subordinate clauses (cf. Ebert 1993).

In the following, I shall chose examples from the languages and preferably from the texts represented in this volume.

---

[2] The spelling of Camling is a notorious problem. In Nepal "Chamling" is more common, but the initial affricate is not aspirated. Consequently this spelling would require *chha* (for *cha*) 'child', *chham* (for *cham*) 'song', as practiced in the English transliteration of Nepali and other languages of South Asia. Apart from aesthetic considerations, this spelling ignores parallels with other regular oppositions, like *j : jh, b : bh* etc.

[3] 2nd person is represented by a prefix also in the NW language Khaling; see 2.2 and appendix.

2. Verbal systems

2.1. Simple and extended stems

Most Rai languages have two stems for each verb. In SE languages the full stem occurs before vowels, the reduced stem before consonants and word-finally: Camling *lod-yu* 'he told him', *lo-na* 'I told you'. Stem alternations are more complex in NW languages; Thulung and Khaling stem I and II are dependent on tense and on the shape of the suffix; cf. 'die' and 'go' in Khaling:

(1) KHAL   mis-tä   'he died' (2.2)[4]
             i-mây[5]   'you will die' (2.6)
             mâyh-khâ-pä   'dead [person]' (2.19)
             die-V2:GO-AP

             khös-tä   'he went' (2.11)
             mu-khöc-e   'don't go!' (2.4)

Simple verb stems have the structure C(r/l)V(C), or C(r/l)VCC. Initial consonant clusters (Cr/l) are found only in NW Rai; cf. the mythological name Khliyama (NW-Camling) vs. Khiyama (SE-Camling and Bantawa, text 2).

The causative stem formants *-t* and *-s* are partially productive. A few transitive or causative verbs allow a secondary causative or applicative.

		intrans.		trans./causative		applicative	
(2) a.	BANT	i-	'laugh'	is-	'make laugh'	itt-	'laugh at'
		par-	'shout'	pays-	'make shout'	patt-	'shout at'
				choŋs-	'send'	chokt-	'send to'
b.	CAM			hors-	'throw'	hord-	'throw at'
				chuŋs-	'send'	chod-	'send to'

---

[4] References to texts in this volume and sentence numbers. A few examples are from the texts in Ebert 1994, 2000.

[5] Khaling *â* is a back vowel, written *a* by Toba; his *aa* is [a]. The Thulung front rounded vowels *ö, ü* are written *eo, iu* in the sources (Allen 1975, 1976). I use *ë* for [ə].

Camling and Bantawa stems are often identical, but Camling has an extended base in -*a*, which is the basis for finite forms, but behaves like the Bantawa past marker -*a* (see 2.4). Thulung derives some causative stems by devoicing and aspiration: *get*- 'come up' / *khet*- 'bring up'.

In the more frequent analytic causatives the verb 'make' is either attached to the stem in root serialization, or it follows the preconsonantal stem as an independent verb: Khaling *sey-mât-t-ü* (see-make-PT-3sP) 'he showed him', Bantawa *khaŋ ti-mett-u* (see 2-make-3P) 'you showed him'.

2.2 Person-number affixes

The Rai finite verb is characterized by a complex system of person and number affixes (cf. appendix). Some widespread Tibeto-Burman suffixes are well preserved: -*ŋa* 1st singular, -*na* 2nd singular, -*i* 1st and 2nd plural, -*ci*, -*si* dual. SE languages also have prefixes with parallels in other Tibeto-Burman languages, like *ta*- for 2nd person, *mi*- for 3rd plural.

In principle both actants of a transitive scenario are marked on the verb, but the two markers cannot always be identified in a straightforward way. SE languages typically use both the 1st and the 2nd person affixes in 2→1, whereas the old 2nd person marker -*na* serves as a portmanteau for 1→2. In the NW language Thulung -*na* is a second person marker only, whereas 1→2 is -*ni*. Person markers, especially that of 2nd person, are often independent of role (3b).

(3)	a.	2s→1s			1s→2s	
	BANT	**ti-chir-ŋa**	'you push me'		chir-**na**	'I push you'
		2-push-PT-1s(:PT)			push-1→2(:PT)	
	THUL	ghro-**ŋ**-di	'you pushed me'		doaa-**ni**	'I want you'
		push-2→1-PT			want-1→2	
	b.	2→3s			3→2s	
	BANT	**ti-khaŋ-u**	'you see him'		**ti-khaŋ**	'he sees you'
		2-see-3P			2-see	
	THUL	loaa-**na**	"		loaa-**na**	"
		see-2			see-2	

In spite of common principles the paradigms are arranged quite differently, especially in the configurations involving speech act participants (cf. appendix). The verb forms of NW languages are generally shorter than those of SE languages, some of which produce lengthy suffix chains with copied suffixes. NW languages are less agglutinative.

Third person nonsingular animate patients are usually marked in Bantawa and Camling (but cf. (46b)). The 3nsP suffix -ci is followed by a copy of the preceding person marker. It does not occur together with a dual marker, which is also -ci (but follows the stem or the base). Thulung and Khaling usually do not mark nonsingular patients.

(4)   marked nonsingular animate patient

    CAM   rhok-ãi-**c**-ãi   'I will chase them'
             chase-1s:IPFV-3nsP-[copy]

    unmarked nonsingular animate patient

    THUL   upiyã-ka khreḍḍ-ü   'the flea bit them [the sisters]...' (2.82)
            flea-ERG   bite:PT-3s>3

    nonsingular inanimate patient unmarked on verb

    BANT   yɨwatiŋ-ci tar-u   'she brought the bones' (2.47)
            bone-ns   bring-3P

The verbal affixes contain more information than the pronouns. The role of 1st or 2nd person is often understood only from the verb.

(5)   CAMLING
    a. (kaini)   khat-**i**   'we went'
        we$_{pi}$ go-1pS/P

    b. (kaini)   lod-u-**m**   'we told him'
        we$_{pi}$ tell-3P-1/2pA

    c. (kaini)   pa-lod-**i**   'he/they told us'
        we$_{pi}$ INV-tell-1pS/P

In (5a) the suffix -i excludes an interpretation as a transitive agent, which would need the 3P marker -u. As there is no prefix ta-, the form cannot refer to a 2nd person, which also has plural -i (cf. ta-khat-i 'you$_p$ go'), and finally the absence of an exclusive suffix narrows the interpretation to inclusive 'we'. In (5b) the suffix -m (following -u) can only be an agent marker; and in (5c) the inverse marker pa- indicates that -i marks a patient.

2.3. Inverse and "marked scenarios"

Some languages show traces of direction marking. Camling has an inverse-marking paradigm in the NW dialect, based on the person hierarchy 1 / 2 > 3s > 3p. But the SE dialect has a 1st person patient prefix *kha-*, with subject marked as in intransitive forms (for details see Ebert 1997:38ff).

(6)

	NW-CAMLING			SE-CAMLING	
3s→1di	**pa**-loda-ci		3s→1	**kha**-loda	'he told me/us'
	INV-tell-d			1P-tell	
3p→1di	"		3p→1	**kha**-mi-loda	'they told me/us'
				1P-3pS-tell	
2s→1s	ta-lod-uŋa		2s→1	**kha**-ta-loda	'you told me/us'
	2-tell-1s			1P-2-tell	
3p→3s	**pa**-loda		3p→3s	**pa**-loda	'they told him'
	INV-tell			INV-tell	

Whereas the Camling data exhibit a dialectal split, the distribution of the Bantawa inverse marker is unclear. The data show not only individual and dialectal variation, but also some inconsistencies in the same text.[6] In most sources Bantawa inverse *i-* combines with a 3p agent marker (*i-m-*), but not in 3p→3s, which has only *i-*. In both languages the inverse prefix does not combine with second person marker. But whereas Bantawa has an inverse prefix with 3ns→2 (and no second person marker), Camling lacks an inverse marker in all 3→2 forms.

---

[6] In Bantawa text 2 we find for 3d>3s

     khaŋ-a-**c-u**   'they$_d$ saw him' (2.27)

     i-khumt-a-**c-u**   'they$_d$ buried him' (2.27)

     INV-bury-PT-d-3P

     i-ser-khais-a   'they$_d$ killed it off' (2.112f)

     INV-kill-V2:SEND-PT

N. K. Rai has *i-m-* also in 1p→2, which can hardly be interpreted as inverse, and in a few non-inverse negated forms (see (18)). Gvozdanovic (1985:121) presents a paradigm from South Bhojpur with a different distribution from that represented in the appendix (p. 48), in which moreover inverse marking sometimes differs in the two basic tenses:

NPT ɖhaṭ-ŋa-cɯŋ   'they$_d$ beat me'

PT   **ʉ**-ɖhaṭṭ-a-ŋ-cɯŋ   "

     INV-beat-PT-1s-d:1s

(These forms are odd, as normally the 1s marker is copied after 3nsP *-ci* only if it stands for an agent; cf. example in fn. 12.) In a second paradigm from North Bhojpur (Gvozdanovic p. 124) there are no prefixes at all.

(7)   BANTAWA   NW-CAMLING
        3s→1pe   **i**-khaŋ-in-ka   **pa**-khaŋ-im-ka   'he saw us$_{pe}$'
                    INV-see-1p-e   INV-see-1p-e

        3p→1pe   **i-m**-khaŋ-in-ka   "   'they saw us$_{pe}$'
                    INV-3p-see-1p-e

        3p→3s   **i**-khaŋ-a   **pa**-khaŋa   'they saw him'
                    INV-see-PT   INV-see

        3s→2s   **ti**-khaŋ-a   **ta**-khaŋa   'he saw you$_s$'
                    2-see-PT   2-see

        3ns→2s   **i-m**-khaŋ-a   "   'they saw you$_s$'
                    INV-3p-see-PT

Khaling has one and the same prefix in all 2nd person and in inverse configurations, thus 2s *i-mây* 'you will die', 2s/3s→1s *i-grök-a-ta* (2/3A-throw-1sP-PT) 'you/he threw me' (2.35), with the exception of 1s→2s *grök-tä-ni* 'I threw you'. A very similar system is found in Dumi, which excludes 1→2 generally from the "marked scenarios" (van Driem 1993:123).[7]

2.4. Tense-aspect forms

Most Rai languages have two basic tense-aspect forms. The simplest situation is found in Bantawa, which has the past marker *-a* and leaves the nonpast unmarked. Camling stem + *a* constitutes a finite base, whereas the nonpast/imperfective is marked by *-e* (*-ne* after vowels), following the person-number markers. The 3P marker *-u* (~ *-yu* ~ *-yi*) becomes *-yo* in the nonpast/ imperfective.

   Camling and Bantawa look superficially very similar, but the systems differ in intricate ways. In both languages *a* following the stem is elided by a vowel; as a result only half of the verb forms are tense-marked in Bantawa (cf. Ebert 1994:144). Bantawa marks 3P after the dual, Camling does not. Camling has generalized *-uŋ(a)* as a 1s marker, in Bantawa it is *-ŋ(a)*, and *-u* is always a 3P marker.

---

[7] The Dumi system thus resembles that of Rawang/Dulong, which has a prefix if 1st person is a participant, but it is not the actor. In the wider Tibeto-Burman area there seems to be a continuum in marking 2nd person, non-1st-person and inverse, individual languages and dialects making somewhat different distinctions.

(8)   BANTAWA   CAMLING
3d→3   PT   i-khaŋ-**a**-c-u   pa-khaŋa-ci   'they_d saw it'
             INV-see-PT-d-3P   INV-see-[a]-d
       NPT   i-khaŋ-c-u   pa-khaŋa-c-**e**   'they_d see it'
             INV-see-d-3P   INV-see-[a]-d-IPFV

2s→1s PT   ti-khaŋ-**a**-ŋ   ta-khaŋ-uŋa   'you saw me'
             2-see-PT-1s   2-see-1s
       NPT   ti-khaŋ-ŋa   ta-khaŋ-uŋ-**e**   'you see me'
             2-see-1s   2-see-1s-IPFV

3s→3s PT   khaŋ-u   khaŋ-u   'he saw him'
             see-3P   see-3P
       NPT   "   khaŋ-**yo**   'he sees him'
                                       see-3P:IPFV

1pi→3s PT   khaŋ-u-m   khaŋ-u-m   'we saw him'
             see-3P-1/2pA   see-3P-1/2pA
       NPT   "   khaŋ-u-m-**e**   'we see him'
                                       see-3P-1/2pA-IPFV

The Mewahang past marker is -*a*, nonpast /-K/ (-*k*, -*ʔ*, -*uk*) between stem and person suffixes. As in Bantawa and Camling, -*a* is elided by the following vowel of a suffix.

(9)   MEWAHANG
1pi   PT   en-in   'we_pi returned'   NPT   en-**k**-in   'we_pi will return'
2s   dab-**a**-na   'you_s came'   dab-**uk**-na   'you_s will come'
2p-1s   lom-aŋ-ni   'you_p beat me'   lom-**ʔ**-aŋ-ni   'you_p will beat me'
             beat-1s-2p   beat-NPT-1s-2p

Thulung and Khaling mark past by a suffix /-T/, which is often assimilated to the stem. The position of /-T/ is sometimes before, sometimes after person-number suffixes. /-T/ takes the vowel of the preceding suffix in the latter case. The past and nonpast forms are not always predictable, and it may be more adequate to set up two stems, e.g. Thulung NPT *sen-* (*ser-*), PT *set-* (*seḍ-*).

(10)   THULUNG
3s   PT   lësta   /lëks-T/   'he went'
                         go-PT

3p→3	PT	bemḍi	/be-mi-T/	'they made [it]'
			make-3p-PT	
2s→1s	PT	ghroŋḍi	/ghro-ŋi-T/	'you threw me'
			throw-2→1-PT	

b.

3d→3	NPT	senci	/sen-ci/	'they_d will kill [it]'
			kill:NPT-d	
3d→3	PT	secci	/set-ci/	'they_d killed [it]'
			kill:PT-d	
3s→3	PT	seḍḍü	/set-ü/	'he killed it'
			kill:PT-3s>3	

Table 1: Basic tense markers					
	BANT	CAM	MEW	THUL	KHAL
PT	√-**a**-PN	√-**a**-PN	√-**a**-PN	√-**T**-PN	√-**T**-PN
				√-PN-**T**	
NPT	Ø	√-**a**-PN-(**n**)e	√-**K**-PN	Ø	Ø

The simple finite verb forms are usually described as past and nonpast. At least in Camling they are aspecto-temporal forms. The imperfective/nonpast is used with habitual meaning in past contexts (see Nir1.7, Nir1.261, Ha2.77ff). In periphrastic tense-aspect forms two formations prevail. Progressives, iteratives, habituals are usually based on two finite verbs, which can be contracted to different degrees. Perfects consist of participles or nominalized equivalents followed by an existential verb (see also Bantawa (32), Thulung (33a)).

(11) BANT   ti-pi-ci-**ŋ**-ci   'they_d (usually) give to you' (2.8)
              2-give-d-IPFV-d

      BANT   low-a-**yakt**-a-c-u   'they_d kept telling him' (2.9)
              tell-PT-CONTV-PT-d-3P

      THUL   lës-ta-**m bay-ra**   'she had/was gone' (2.23)
              go-PT-PP be-PT

      CAM   khim   m-uŋ-**ko**   **hiŋ-e**   'I have built a house' (Lal4.30)
              house   make-1s-NML be-IPFV

2.5. Compound verbs

In compound verbs of SE languages both verbs are finite marked, but prefixed person-number markers and outer suffixes appear only once.

(12) BANT   chir-a-da-c-u   'they$_d$ left it' (2.24)
                leave-PT-V2:PUT:PT-d-3P

                ti-ca-khat   'he will eat you' (2.37)
                2-eat-V2:TAKE

    CAM   mi-pora-saŋa   'they grew up' (Nir1.50)
                3pS-grow-V2:COME.UP

                lod-u-m-chuŋs-u-m-c-um-ka   'we$_{pe}$ sent them away, telling them ...'
                tell-3P-1/2p-V2:SEND-3P-1/2p-3nsP-[copy]-e

In the other languages the two verbs are connected in root serialization. In Thulung a syllable closing nasal of the suffix is copied after the first verb (see also (16)).[8] There is no tense marker after V1.

(13) KHAL   mis-khös-tä   'she died' (2.2)
                die-V2:GO-PT

    MEW   thuu-khä-k-ci   'they have intercourse' (1.54)
                mix-V2:GO-NPT-d

    THUL   par-jöll-ü   'she left her behind' (2.6)
                leave-V2:PUT:PT-3s→3

    THUL   goa-**m**-jöl-mu   'give (to sb.)' (2.97)
                give-[m]-V2:PUT-INF

The postverbs 'die/kill' and directional motion verbs are constructed with a linker in Thulung and Khaling, but as compound verbs in SE languages.

---

[8] Vowels are copied with verbs in stem final *e/o*: *p-ü-leaḍ-ḍ-ü* 'he ate it up' (2.13; *pe-/po-* 'eat'). This process is not restricted to compound verbs: *büü-r-ü* 'he made/said it', *b-i-yi* 'we make' (2.73). It is also applied to verbs borrowed from Nepali: *khij-ü-r-ü* 'she mocked him' (2.7).

(14) THUL   khrecci   **ma**   secci   'they_d bit it [the louse] to death' (2.83)

             bite:PT:d   LINK   kill:PT:d

    KHAL   khlo-tä   **na**   mis-tä   'it was crushed to death' (2.81)

             be.crushed-PT   LINK   die-PT

but: BANT   datt-u-ser-u   'he beat her to death' (2.76)

             beat-3P-V2:KILL-3P

    CAM   pa-bila-seta   'they squeezed it to death' (Ha2.92)

             INV-rub-V2:KILL

Compound verbs fulfill similar functions as in Indo-Aryan languages; i.e. most postverbs ("explicators", "aspectivizers") are telicizers while keeping some of their full verb meaning (otherwise one postverb would suffice). The telicizers are either directional (GO, COME, FALL, RISE) or manner characterizing (THROW, PUT, KILL). Note that in compounds like Bantawa *dattu-seru* and Camling *pabila-seta* it is the postverb that is modifying. The beating and squeezing is done in a 'killing' way.

    The V2 'give' is benefactive/malefactive. Bantawa has a self-benefactive postverb EAT, which — together with Athpare — it shares with Munda languages.

(15) KHAL   pher-sä-tä   'he sewed for her' (Toba 1983:9)

             sew-V2:GIVE-PT

    BANT   hoptaŋ   kiŋs-u-pɨ-ci   'he hung up a bacon for them' (2.129)

             bacon   hang-3P-V2:GIVE:3P-3nsP

    BANT   wadin   kup-ca-yaŋ-sa   'picking up the eggs (to eat/for herself)'

             egg   pick-V2:EAT-IPFV-SIM   (2.89)

Reflexives seem to originate in two verbs in NW languages. As with compound verbs, the initial nasal of a suffix marker is copied after V1.

(16) THUL   tayaar   ba-m-si-m-ḍi   'they got ready' (4.26)

             ready   make-[m]-REFL-3p-PT

    THUL   pe-pa   li-n-siṭ-ni   'pretend to be eating!' (4.17)

             eat-AP   lie-[n]-REFL-2p

There is a great variety of reflexive forms in Bantawa and Camling (cf. Ebert 1994:52f). Camling has the finite base *a* after the reflexive marker *-ãic-*, thus also suggesting a verbal origin: *dhas-ãica-ci* 'they descended'.

2.6. Negation

There are many different patterns of negation. Most verb forms are negated by a prefix *ma(n)-* or *mi-*, but some have a negative suffix or both. There is no exact correspondence between negated and asserted tenses.

Bantawa and Mewahang have a negative prefix in the past and a suffix *-n/-na* in the nonpast. Camling has a negative infix *n* only in 1s→3 (see (18)) Bantawa forms that are identical in assertions are thus always different in negation. In Camling, on the contrary, negated forms are sometimes not differentiated in the two basic tenses (with dialectal and individual variation; cf. Ebert 1997:29ff).

(17)

		NPT	PT
BANT	ASS	nett-u	=
		tease-3P	
	NEG	net-u-**n**	**man**-net-**do**
		tease-3P-NEG	NEG-tease-AUX:3P
		'she will not tease him'	'she did not tease him'
CAM	ASS	cit-yo	cit-yu
		tease-3P:IPFV	tease:3P
	NEG	pa-cit-ãi(na) / pa-cit-õ	pa-cit-ãi(na)
		NEG-tease-NEG -3P(:NEG)	
		'she will not tease him'	'she did not tease him'

Note that the Camling negative prefix is identical with the inverse marker. Bantawa also uses the (otherwise inverse) prefix *i-* in negated 1s→3 (i.e. non-inverse).

(18) BANT   **i**-sin-**ni**-ŋ (< ni+u-ŋ)   'I don't know' (2.38)
              NEG-know-NEG:3P-1s

      CAM   **pa**-chai-**n**-uŋ   'I don't know'
              NEG-know-NEG-1s

Thulung and Khaling have a negative prefix in all tenses; an irrealis marker *-wa ~ -ba* replaces past /T/; cf. with asserted Thulung *theḍ-ḍ-ü* 'he understood':

(19)

	NPT	PT
THUL	me-theṭ-pu	mi-theḍ-**ba**
	NEG-understand-1s→3:NPT	NEG-understand-IRR
	'I do not understand' (2.66)	'he did not understand' (2.70)
KHAL	mu-câkt-u	mu-câkt-u-**wa**
	NEG-know-1s→3	NEG-know-1s→3-IRR
	'I do not know it' (2.43)	'I did not know it' (2.37)

2.7. Nonfinite forms

The nonfinite forms of Rai languages are
- participles
- infinitives
- purposives
- converbs

All Rai languages have an active participle; NW languages also have locative participles. Participles are much more frequent in NW than in SE languages. They are used mainly as nouns, rarely as attributes, as in (20).

Table 2: Nonfinite forms					
	BANT	CAM	MEW	THUL	KHAL
		SE NW			
AP	-kaba	ka- -pa	-kapa	-pa	-pä
	ka- (-pa/-ma)				
PP	?	—	?	-ma	[-pä]
LP	—	—	—	-khom	-de
INF	-ma	-ma	-ma	-mu	-nä
PURP	-si	-si	-si	-ḍa	-bi
SIM.CONV	-sa	-sa	-sa, -loŋ	-to	-to
SEQ.CONV				-saka	
NEG.CONV	man- -paŋ	ma-	?	mi- -saka	mi- -sa

(20) THUL   mö   lëk-**pa**   mücü-mim   'the people who went' (4.13)
             that   go-AP   person-p

     KHAL   bhaya-bi khway-**de** läm   'a path leading to that place' (5.5)
             place-LOC go-LP   path

Camling participles differ in the two main dialects. SE-Camling has the prefix *ka-*, NW-Camling the suffix *-pa*.

(21) SE-CAM   dõsi   **ka**-sõ   'the later-comer'
              behind   AP-come.up

     NW-CAM   dõsi   sõ-**pa**   "
              behind   AP-come.up

Bantawa mostly has a suffix formation: *dak-mɨ-**kaba*** 'loom-doer = weaver' (2.51), but cf. *cha **ka-ca-ma*** 'child eater' (2.85; with the female suffix *-ma*). A separate patientive participle is attested only for Thulung.[9]

Infinitives are used as nouns or as complements to modal, phasal or cognitive verbs. Some languages allow a nonsingular animate patients to be indicated by a number suffix after the infinitive (22b). Others indicate a patient by a possessive prefix (22c).

(22) a. CAMLING
         m-sikha   la nâ   naci   mu-**ma**   puis-yu.
         3sPOSS-happiness VB and dance   do-INF   start-3P
         'He became happy and started to dance.'

     b. KHALING
         äci   beŋmä-su   uŋ-a   biha   bi-**n-su**   äy-ŋa.
         you(d) sister-d   I-ERG   marriage give-INF-d   say-1sS
         'I was thinking to give you two sisters in marriage.' (2.59)

---

9 Khaling uses the same suffix as for the AP, but the participles seem to be based on different stems; cf. *inpo käm **mü-pä*** 'the one who does your work' (2.32) and ***mün-pä*** *go-tä* 'it was made' (2.27 =(38b)).

c.   CAMLING
    Salapa-lai **m**-dei-**si**   m-khum-**si**...   mi-khata.
    Salapa-DAT 3sPOSS-make.appear-PURP   3sPOSS-wake-PURP 3pS-go
    'They went in order to make Salapa appear, to wake him up ...' (Nir1.20)

Converbs function as modifiers of verbs. All Rai languages I know have a simultaneous converb, which is restricted to same subject contexts and typically reduplicated.

(23) THUL **mal-to mal-to**   lës-ta   'searching, searching she went' (2.13)
           search-SIM search-SIM go-PT

      CAM   **khõ-sa khõ-sa**   khata   'looking, looking he went' (Nir1.232)
           look-SIM   look-SIM   go

All Rai languages also have a negative converb, which can refer to actions previous or simultaneous to that of the finite verb.

(24) BANT **man**-cep-**paŋ** yuŋa-yakta-ci   'they remained without speaking' (2.126)
           NEG-speak-CONV stayed-CONTV-d

      THUL **mi**-rep-**saka**   lëër-a   'go without looking !' (Eb1994:258)
           NEG-look-CONV go-IMPER

3. Noun phrases

3.1. Personal pronouns and possessive prefixes

Pronouns distinguish dual vs. plural and inclusive vs. exclusive (Table 3). As participants are marked on the verb, pronouns are not obligatory. The third person pronouns listed below are only used for animate referents (see (40) for a Camling text example using *khu*). Most often the distal demonstratives are used instead (see Table 8).

Table 3: Personal pronouns

	BANT	CAM	MEW	THUL	KHAL
1s	iŋka	kaŋa	aka	go	uŋ
1di	iŋkaci	kâcka	icin	guci	ici
1de	iŋkaca	kaici	iciga	gucuku	ocu
1pi	iŋkan(ci)	kai	ikin	guy	ik
1pe	iŋkanka(ci)	kaika	ikka	guku	ok
2s	khana	khana	ana	gana	in
2d	khanaci	khanci	anci	gaci	eci
2p	khananin	khani	anin	gani	en
3s	kho(ko)	khu	oo	gu	âm
3d	khoci	khuci	ooci	guci	âmsu
3p	"	"	"	gumi	âmhäm

Table 4: Possessive prefixes

	BANT	CAM	MEW	THUL	KHAL
1s	iŋ-	a-	ak-, aŋ-	a-	a-
1di	anco-	ic-	icim-	ici-	is-
1de		âc-	?	aci-	os-
1pi	an-	i-	ikim-	iki-	ik-
1pe		(i-)	?	aki-	ok-
2s	am-	kap-	ap-, am-	i-	i-
2d	amco-	?	?	ici-	es-
2p	an-	kai-	?	ini-	en-
3s	i-	m-	op-, om-	u-	u-
3d	unco-	kic-	oocim-	uci-	us-
3p	"	"	"	uni-	un-

The reduced inventory of possessive prefixes in SE languages is surprising, given that the prefixes are very frequent.[10] Camling uses *i-* also with 1st plural possessors excluding the hearer, and *ic-* (1di) and *âc-* (1de) are not always distinguished; a 2d prefix does not occur in the texts and

---

[10] There is no overlap between possessive prefixes and person markers on the verb. Only Khaling *i-* serves as both.

could not be elicited. Prefixes can be replaced by possessive pronouns, which are formed in a variety of ways:

a) genitive of the personal pronouns
b) genitive of the possessive prefixes
c) possessive prefix or pronoun + nominalizer
d) irregular

(25) a. CAM   khu-mo   'his, hers'
          KHAL   âm-po   'his, hers'

      b. CAM   i-mo   'ours$_{pi}$'

      c. BANT   iŋ-ko[11] 'mine'
          THUL   i-ma   'yours$_s$'
          MEW   ooci-m   'theirs'

      d. CAM   aŋa   'mine'
                   amka   'ours$_{pe}$'

Often the possessive pronouns are used together with the prefixes: Bantawa ***moci-wo unco-makanchi*** (they-NML/GEN 3nsPOSS-stepmother) 'their stepmother' (2.6), Khaling ***in-po i-beŋmä-häm*** (you$_s$-GEN 2sPOSS-sister-ns) 'your sisters' (2.40).

Possessive prefixes are usually obligatory with inherently relational nouns, which include — besides the usual kinship terms, names for parts etc. — also terms for emotions (26) and for order (Camling *m-bhusi* 'before, in front', *m-selam* 'the next day' (*selam* 'tomorrow')).

(26)   CAM   m-sikha   la   'he was/became happy' (cf. (22a))
                   3sPOSS-happiness VB:3s

          BANT   unco-laja   kara   'they felt ashamed' (2.126)
                   3nsPOSS-shame   VB:3sPT

          THUL   uci-laaji   lüürü   'they$_d$ felt ashamed' (2.90)
                   3dPOSS-shame   VB:3s→3

---

11 The Bantawa genitive marker is identical with the nominalizer (cf. Table 7).

3.2. Case markers

All Rai languages have a combined ergative-instrumental and a genitive case marker. Most have a comitative, which is also used to coordinate nouns (with optional repetition after the second noun, e.g. Khaling *soroli-kolo ut-kolo* 'jackal and camel'; Bantawa *layo-nin wadin* 'fried rice and eggs' (2.88).

Rai languages are morphologically ergative. Thulung and Camling exhibit a split between speech act participants and non-participants, only the latter being marked (Ebert 1997:46). Bantawa, Mewahang and Khaling allow an ergative marker with all persons (for Khaling see 2.23, 2.29).

(27) BANT   iŋka-**a**   i-net-ni-ŋ.[12]   'I shall not tease her.' (2.38)
              I-ERG   NEG-tease-NEG:3P-1s

     MEW   aka-**ʔa**   dibuŋwa muu-ʔ-aŋ.   'I will bring game.' (1.69)
              I-ERG   game   do-NPT-1s

Table 5: Case markers

	BANT	CAM	MEW	THUL	KHAL
ERG/INST	-ʔa	-wa	-ʔa	-ka	-ä
GEN	-ko ~ -wo	-mo	-mi	-kam, -ku	-po
COM	-ni	—	-loŋ	-nuŋ	-kolo
LOC	-da	-da	-pi	-ḍa	-bi
highLOC	-du	-dhi,-di	-tu	-la	-tü
lowLOC	-yu	-i	-mu	-yu	-yu
levLOC	-ya	-ya	-yu	-no	-yü
ALL	-nin	-ni	—	—	—
ABL	-ŋka	-ka	-paŋ	-ka,-m	-ka
MED	-lam	-la	-lam	-lam	-la

---

[12] But without ergative:

    iŋka   iŋ-kɨyaŋpa-ci   chemt-u-ŋ-yaŋ-cɨŋ.
    I   1sPOSS-mat.uncle-ns attract-3P-1s-IPFV-3nsP:1s
    'I am attracting my maternal uncles.' (2.84)

Possessor nouns are in the genitive case. The possessor can be cross-referenced by a possessive prefix on the head noun.

(28) KHAL   us-celpa-**po**   u-khâm   'their$_d$ brother's house'
                      3dPOSS-brother-GEN   3sPOSS-house

       CAM   kic-chala-**mo**   m-khim   'their$_{d/p}$ brother's house'
                      3nsPOSS-brother-GEN   3sPOSS-house

A dative marker -*lai* is sometimes borrowed from Nepali to mark animate patients. 'Dative subjects' are conspicuously absent; the experiencer is indicated by a possessive prefix (see (26)).

Double case marking can be found involving the comitative or a locative as the first element. Ablative and allative are suffixed to a locative (see also (30a,b)).

(29) a.   THULUNG
            Jaw-**nuŋ** Khliw-**nuŋ-ka** ...   roa-becci
            Jaw-COM   Khliw-COM-ERG   say-make:PT:d
            'Jaw and Khliw said ...' (2.2)

       b.   CAMLING
            syolãima-**da-ka**   ta-ris-yo ...
            gourd-LOC-ABL   2-predict-3P:IPFV
            'You will predict from the long gourd ...' (Nir1.273)

A unique trait of Rai languages are locational case markers which indicate a position higher or lower than the place of reference. This mirrors the importance of the dimension UP/DOWN in Rai mythology and everyday life (Ebert 1999, Gaenszle 1999). The 'altitude' markers are used instead of the general locative.

(30) a.   BANTAWA
            Hecchakuppa-ʔa mo yiŋ pakha-**ya-ŋka**   en-u-yakt-u-ŋ-u.
            Hecchakuppa-ERG   that word outside-levLOC-ABL hear-3P-CONTV-3P-IPFV-3P
            'Hecchakuppa constantly heard these words from outside.' (2.74)

       b.   CAMLING
            aŋa   a-gãu-**di-ni**   khat-ace!
            my   1sPOSS-village-hiLOC-ALL   go-d:IMPER
            'Let's go up to my village!' (Nir1.240)

The Mewahang altitude markers can either be used instead of a locative, or they are suffixed to the general locative.

(31)   MEWAHANG

  a.   berepookha.appookha-**yu**   ruwaŋ-ʔ-aŋ-lo
         (rit.:watering.place)-levLOC   come.over-NPT-1s-TEMP
         'when I come over to the watering place' (Gaenszle 1999:155)

  b.   na-**pi-tu**   Paruhaŋ cuʔa-neemo, kuʔmu Somnima   cuʔa-neemo.
         heaven-LOC-hiLOC Paruhang was-REP   DOWN Somnima   was-REP
         'Up in heaven Paruhang lived, down on the earth there was Somnima.' (1.1)

The locative case markers combine with deictic roots (see also Thulung *möla* in (42b)).

(32)   BANTAWA

         mo-ya   i-yɨwatiŋ-ci   bhukt-u-ŋ-do-ŋ-ko   yaʔa-ŋ.
         that-levLOC 3sPOSS-bones-ns   bury-3P-1s-V2:PUT:3P-1s-NML be-1s
         'I have buried her bones over there.' (2.46)

4. Pragmatic particles

Pragmatic particles are often borrowed from Nepali, but they can be used somewhat differently in Rai languages. Table 6 shows the most important ones.[13]

Table 6: Some pragmatic particles					
	BANT	CAM	MEW	THUL	KHAL
TOPIC	-lo	-lo,-na	-na	-ne	-ne
FOC	ye	mna		ḍe ~ re	
		cahi	*cahi*	*cahĩ*	*cây*
(=NML)	-ko~-wo	-ko		-m	
REPORT	nimaŋ	*raicha*	neemo	e, *rëcha*	e
		are, ni	*are*		
MIR	*rëchë*	*raicha*	*rahecha*	*rëcha*	*râycha*

---

[13] I have kept the spelling of the sources. Pronunciation depends on the familiarity of the speaker with standard Nepali, but all variants of e.g. *cahi* and *rahecha* sound more or less the same.

4.1. Topic and focus markers

Marking of the topic — what is talked about and assumed to be known to the hearer — is common in all Rai languages. A topic marker can occur several times in a clause. Topic markers are common with temporal adverbs and temporal clauses. They are also used with 1st and 2nd person pronouns (i.e. with referents that are trivially "given"), and they can follow a case marker. In (33b) the topic is Khliyama and not her bones.

(33) a.   THULUNG
            ici-ri-**ne**   guci-**ne**   secci-m   ho.
            1diPOSS-brother-TOP   we$_{di}$-TOP   kill:PT:d-NML be
            'Our brother, we have killed him.' (2.96)

  b.   CAMLING
            Khliyama-mo-**na**   m-saruwa   mâttrai hinga-ko   raicha.
            Khliyama-GEN-TOP   3sPOSS-bones   only   stay-NML   REP
            'Of Khliyama only the bones remained.' (Lal2.61)

Various focus markers occur in the texts; most of them are rare,[14] and it not always easy to determine their exact function. *cahi*, borrowed from Nepali, usually marks contrastive focus (see also Bantawa (35b), Thulung (39)).

(34)   KHALING
            câkâpe **cây** chito khös-tä, ser **cây** wätäka   khös-tä.
            flea   FOC fast go-PT   louse FOC slowly   go-PT
            'The flea went fast, but the louse went slowly.' (2.44)

Thulung marks contrast also by *pheri* (cf. 2.23). Further, in most languages the nominalizer can mark focus.

(35) a.   CAMLING
            uko   a-rõ-**ko**!
            this   1sPOSS-rice/food-NML
            'This is my food!'

---

[14] The Bantawa focus suffix -*wo* occurs only three times in text 2 — against 46 occurrences of the topic marker -*lo*. In the Thulung texts, the focus particle *re* (*de* after consonant) is somewhat more frequent.

b.   khoko khoko cama-khaima mi-dir-u-ŋas-yi-**ko**,   tyiko tyiko

which which   food-ECHO   NEG-finish-3P-V2:STAY-3P-NML that   that

cahi hiŋ-e   lod-yi-ko   raicha.

FOC be-IPFV tell-3P-NML REP

'Whatever part he had not finished eating, THAT he said "is there."' (Jh1.83)

It is very common in Rai languages — as in Tibeto-Burman in general — to nominalize the whole utterance (e.g. Camling Ha2.16, 17, 27; Thulung 2.17, 2.18). All Camling sentences are nominalized before the report particle *raicha.*

4.2. Evidentials

Rai speakers seldom end their sentences in a verb. Usually there is an evidential particle in sentence final position, i.e. an indication the speaker gives as to the source of his knowledge. The sentence-final report particles (Thulung and Khaling *e,* Mewahang *neemo,* Bantawa *nimaŋ)* characterize narrative texts and are often repeated sentence after sentence.

The Nepali mirative *rahecha* indicates that the speaker has just become aware of a fact, or that something turned out to be such-and-such. In Rai languages the particle has been adopted in this function, but in Camling and Thulung it is also a report particle. (36a,b) shows the mirative together with a focus marker (see also Thulung 2.61, Bantawa 2.27, 2.86).

(36) a.   THULUNG

a-krüm-kora   re-pa-ne   gana **re** **rëcha**!

1sPOSS-hunger-thirst look-AP-TOP you FOC MIR

'The one who cared for my hunger and thirst turned out to be you!' (2.53)

b.   BANTAWA

sit **ye**   **rëchë**!

louse FOC   MIR

'Oh, it is a louse!' (2.110)

In focussing first person, as in *go re* 'it is me!' (TH2. 45), *iŋka-wo* 'it is me!' (BANT2.34), the mirative is of course not possible.

Nepali *ni* marks facts that should not be doubted. Speakers of NW-Camling do not make a difference between *raicha* and *ni* (or *niko*).[15] *ni* seems to have lost much of its original function, so that it is sometimes even attached to a noun for emphasis. The weakening of pragmatic force also leads to several pragmatic particles — even of the same type — following each other.

(37)   MEWAHANG
         Makluŋ-mi **cahi** kalo jureli-ʔa   lu   bhok   pit-u-**neemorahecha are**.
         (name)-GEN FOC black (bird)-INST INTJ sacrifice give-3P-REP MIR   REP
         'Maklung's [elder brother], it turned out, had sacrificed with a black jureli bird,
         so it is told.' (3.20)

5. Clause combining

5.1. Subordination

All Kiranti languages have the basic word order SOV, which is the common order in all of South and Central Asia. But differently from the surrounding languages, the majority of subordinate clauses are finite in Kiranti. Not all of the nonfinite forms listed in Table 2 are used to subordinate whole clauses: participles are mainly used as nouns; simultaneous converbs do not allow separate subjects, but have the function of modifying adverbs.

Relative clauses are expressed by nominalized finite-marked clauses in all Rai languages. Clauses are sometimes subordinated by a case marker, which directly follows the finite-marked verb (Camling *khataci-daka* (go-ABL) 'after they$_d$ went'). Temporal clauses, the only type of subordinate clause that occurs frequently in narrative texts, are often topic-marked (see (38a,b)).[16] In Thulung (esp. in text 2) they are often nominalized and followed by a postposition or by *belaka*, a frozen ablative form from Nepali *belaa* 'time'. All three northern languages use temporal *-lo* optionally followed by a topic marker.

(38) a.   CAMLING
           rya-ci-**kona** borpa-mo-na   m-kuŋ-da-na   m-ma-mo
           laugh-d-TEMP bear-GEN-TOP   3sPOSS-tooth-LOC-TOP 3sPOSS-mother-GEN
           m-muse   bo   hapta-ŋasa-ko   raicha.
           3sPOSS-hair PART stick-V2:STAY-NML REP

           'When they laughed - think! - mother's hair was sticking in Bear's teeth!' (Jh1.88)

---

[15] Cf. text Ha2, in which the speaker starts with *raicha,* and then continues with *ni.*

[16] I do not separate the optional topic markers in temporal expressions, but gloss Bant. *-hidalo,* Cam. *-kona, -pana, -palyo,* Khal./Thul. *-lone,* Mewahang *-lona* as one morpheme (TEMP).

b. KHALING

mana pheri mesâŋ khös-tä na ho-tä-**lone** u-kâm-bi-ne yu-kway

then again thus go-PT and come-PT-TEMP his-house-LOC-TOP rice-vegetable

mün-pä go-tä e.

make-PCPL be-PT REP

'And when he again went and came back, a meal was prepared at his house.' (2.27)

c. THULUNG

gana ŋaddo lëks-a! roa-ŋɖo-**m-belaka** me-lëë-na-wa.

you first go-IMPER say-1sS:PT-NML-TEMP NEG-go-2s-IRR

'When I said 'Go first!' you did not go.' (2.20)

Table 7: Clause connectors with finite marked verbs

	BANT	CAM	MEW	THUL	KHAL
NML	-ko~-wo	-ko	-m	-m	-m
NPT:NML	-	-	-	-mim	-mim
TEMP	-hida(lo)	-kona	-lo(na)	-lo(ne)	-lo(ne)
	-talo	-pa(lo)(na)		-m+POST	
SIM/MAN	-lo	-lo	—	—	—
COND	[moloko]	-kho	-lapsu	-la	-kho
LINKER	—	nâ	maŋ	ma	na
		SE NW			
SEQ	kiya	ki —	—	—	—

5.2. Linking and sequence

Sequences of events that are connected with a linker or sequence marker are not subordinated. Rai languages lack a sequential converb ('conjunctive participle'), which is remarkable in the South Asian context. SE-Camling distinguishes a linker *nâ* and a strictly sequential marker *ki*; the other languages have only one or the other. The Thulung and Khaling linkers function also with simultaneous actions or in quasi-compounds (see *huɖɖa ma lësta* 'flew away' in (39)). For both, the linker and the sequential marker, there is no condition of subject identity.

(39)   THULUNG
         u-loak   mi-bi-si-wa   **ma** u-wa   caῆi
         3sPOSS-y.sibling   NEG-listen-REFL-IRR   and 3sPOSS-e.sibling   FOC
         huḍ-ḍa **ma** lës-ta.
         fly-PT and go-PT

'The younger sister did not obey, and the elder sister flew away.' (2.5)

The SE-Camling sequential marker *ki* is equivalent to Bantawa *kiya*. (40) exemplifies both, pure linking and sequence. Occasionally linkers introduce a new clause in a narrative. [17]

(40)   SE-CAMLING
         khana aso kholi-di   waŋa, lod-yi **nâ** phyabd-yi-chuŋs-yi-ko raicha
         you now jungle-hiLOC enter   tell-3P and slap-3P-V2:SEND-3P-NML REP
         borpa-lai. phyabd-yi **ki**   khu pani kholi-di   waŋ-khata-ko   raicha.
         bear-DAT [repet.]   SEQ he   PART jungle-hiLOC enter-V2:GO-NML REP

'"You go up into the jungle now," he said, and he slapped Bear and sent him
away. He slapped him and then he [Bear] went up into the jungle.' (Jh1.95-96)

6. Narrative discourse

6.1. Reference tracking

Animate participants are introduced with the numeral 'one' if they play a role in the following episode (41a,b).

(41) a. BANTAWA
         ikta wa   khara .... **moko wa**-lo ...
         one rooster went   that rooster-TOP
         'A rooster went ... The rooster ...' (2.117,118)

---

[17] A common way of connecting event sequences in a narrative is by anaphoric terms, which refer back to the preceding event. These terms are derived from the distal demonstratives: BANT *munkiya(lo)*, CAM *tyudaka(na)*, MEW *molmaʔa*, THUL *mömsaka, mömlo(ne), mökotima*, KHAL *mebena, mana(ne)*, all meaning 'then', 'and then'.

b.   KHALING

tu hâs-po u-cö   suhpu motnu e. **mä hâs** ... mis-tä.

one   person-GEN her-child three were REP that person   die-PT

'There was a person who had three children. That person... died.' (2.1-2)

Inanimates can be combined with 'one' (42a), but more often they are not, as in (42b). However, indefinite marking is far from regular even with animates. Participants that are mentioned a second time take the distal demonstrative, which is thus developing into a reidentifying article.

(42) a.   BANTAWA

ikta wabuk yukta-da-cu ... **moko wabuk** kera.

one   calabash kept-PUT-d:3P   that   calabash broke

'They kept a calabash [on his grave] ... The calabash broke ...' (2.28/32)

b.   THULUNG

chörcü-ra jüll-ü ...   **mö chörcü**-ra-m luk-ta...

basket-LOC   put:PT-3s>3 that   basket-LOC-ABL come.out-PT

pherile **mö chörcü**-la lës-ta ma   mö-la-ŋa   bay-ra.

again   that   basket-hiLOC go-PT and   that-hiLOC-EMPH stay-PT

'... he put it into a basket. [When he went off fishing again, the stone/girl] came out of the basket, [cooked food etc ...] Again she/it went up into the basket and remained up there.' (2.38-41)

The main characters of the mythological narratives are usually known and mentioned with their name when they appear on the scene. The reidentifying demonstratives are applied even to proper names and to possessive phrases. The referents of (43a,b) have been mentioned before.

(43) a. CAM   tyiko Salapa   'that Salapa'

    THUL   mö Khakcilik   'that Khakcilik'

    KHAL   mä Grom Las-su   'those two Grom and Las'

b. BANT   mo   unco-makanchi   'their stepmother' (2.23)

            that   3nsPOSS-stepmother

    CAM   tyiko m-nicho Simnima   'his little sister Simnima' (Nir1.12)

            that   3sPOSS-y.sibling S.

THUL	mö	u-ser-mim	'her bones' (2.15)
	that	3sPOSS-bone-PL	
KHAL	mä	us-wä	'their_d younger sibling' (2.4)
	that	3dPOSS-y.sibling	

There is no verb 'have'; a possessed referent is introduced by 'one' followed by a possessive construction.

(44) BANTAWA

ikta unco-cheŋgara yaŋa .... moci **mo cheŋgara** i-sera nimaŋ.

one their-goat was they that goat INV-killed REP

mo i-sera kiya **mosa**-ʔa dici i-metta.

that INV-killed and that-INST treatment INV-made

'They had a goat ... They killed the goat. They killed it and made a treatment with it.' (2.14, 2.20-21)

A reidentifying pronoun might seem necessary if the subject changes. But this is not the case in Rai languages. It is often up to the hearer to find out, which is the actor and which the patient. If a pronoun is used to refer to a 3rd person, it is usually a form derived from a demonstrative root. Table 8 lists only the singular forms; starred forms occur before ergative/instrumental case endings (cf. *mosa-ʔa* in (44)).

Table 8: Reidentifiers (distal demonstratives)					
	BANT	CAM	MEW	THUL	KHAL
adnominal	mo(-ko)	tyu(-ko)[18]	mo-ʔo	mö	mä
pronom.	mo-ko	tyu-ko	mo-ʔo	mö-ram	mä(-m)
	mosa-*	tyukopa-*			
place	mo-da	tyu-da	mu-pi	mö-ḍḍa	mä-bi
	mo-du	tyu-dhi	mu-tu	mö-la	mä-tü
	mo-yu	tyu-khi	mu-yu	mö-yu	mä-yu
	mo-ya	tyu-khya	mu-ya	mö-no	mä-yo

Demonstratives can be used as direct deictics, a function that is usually restricted to direct speech in narratives (e.g. *moya* in (32)). Mostly they are discourse deictics. In the following

---

18 Also *tyiko, tyo(ko)*, but not **tyi; tyoda*, but not **tyida*.

example only the preceding text secures the interpretation of *mä khabo* and *mäyu* (cf. also Thulung *möla* in (42b)).

(45)   KHALING

mana **mä** khabo **mä-yu** läsü-su-lo   mä u-cö   mä-yu-ŋ
and   that beam that-loLOC withdraw-d-TEMP that her-child that-loLOC-EMPH
khlö-tä-na mis-tä.
crush-PT-SEQ die-PT

'And when the two of them let go of the beam down there, her child was crushed to death right down there.' (2.81)

6.2. Narrative style

The texts in this volume are all traditional narrations and therefore they might be expected to exhibit a certain formal style. This is, as far as I can tell, not the case. If the same episodes are chanted by a shaman in a ritual performance, the language is quite different (cf. Gaenszle 2002).

Formal, especially ritual speech is characterized by a feature which to a certain degree also exists in everyday language, namely parallelism. Parallelism shows itself in the present texts mainly in three ways: tail-head linkage, parallel events, and parallel words. In tail-head linkage the last verb or verb phrase is repeated at the beginning of the next sentence. This repetition can be applied sentence after sentence.

(46)   CAMLING

... hors-yi-ko   raicha.
   throw-3P-NML REP
horsyi-pana tyoda-ŋo ta-ci-ko   raicha nâ siri-wa   chupd-yi-ko raicha.
[repet.]-TEMP there-EMPH come-d-NML   REP   and basket-INST cover-3P-NML REP
siriwa chupdyi-hemaka. "..." ruŋmapa sen-yi-ko raicha.
[repet.]   -after   QUOTE   ask-3P-NML REP
senyi-pana ... kic-dyukha pa-puisa-ci.
[repet.] -TEMP their-distress INV-begin-d
kic-dyukha papuisaci-hemaka ...
[repet.]-   -after

'... he threw [some herbs].
'After throwing them, they [the sisters/birds] came and he covered them with a basket.
After covering them with a basket, he asked: "[Why do you do this?]".
After he asked, their problems started.
After their problems started ...' (Ebert 2000:44-45)

Events are often constructed in a parallel fashion. Khocilipa, the orphan-hero, throws the things he collected one after the other in the face of the cannibal who pursues him. This is told in a somewhat monotonous fashion through constant repetitions (Camling Ha2.63-70; Jh2.59-77 in Ebert 2000). In the same story, a stone gets into Khocilipa's fishing net, and he throws it back three times. Later the hero sends out animals to find his sisters; one after the other goes and is killed until finally the rooster succeeds (Camling Ha2.91-95; Lal296-99 in Ebert 2000; Thulung 81-85). Cf. this episode in the Bantawa version:

(47)   BANTAWA
          sit khara ... ser-khaisa-cu[19]   'louse went ...   they killed it'
          kippa khara ... i-sera-khaisa   'flea went ...   they killed it '
          ikta sekba khara . ..i-sera-khaisa   'a bedbug went ...   they killed it'
          lupmi khara ... i-sera-khaisa   'needle went ...   they killed it'
          ikta walapma khara ...   'a rooster went ...' (2.109-119)

Parallel words such as Camling *cama-duŋma* 'food and drink' are part of everyday language. But there are a number of parallel constructions in the narratives that are either ritual language or special narrative forms. Such parallel words can refer to places, like Camling *Tharuhõ-Bajuhõ* for the Tarai (Lal4.6f), *Niyama-Takuma* for low and fertile land (Jh1.27, Nir1.27), *Nakihõ-Dilihõ* for the underwater world (Nir1.233); they can refer to referents that play a special role in the mythology, such as Camling *Surlumi-Dolopa* 'shaman' (Nir.1.260), *kokma-pirima* 'grandmother('s spirit)', *bokhapopi-larewa* 'termite hill' .[20]

Some look like echo-compounds: *saruwa-kuruwa* 'bones' or *silum-halum* (< Nepali) 'funeral'; but the function is not the same as for echo compounds in other South Asian languages.[21] The first element usually carries the meaning; the second is added for the sound alone. Sometimes no meaning could be assigned to any part, the compound being used as a kind of proper name.

---

[19] For *-cu* vs. *i-* with dual actors cf. section 2.3.
[20] Parallel constructions in ritual language have been given a closer analysis in Gaenszle (2002).
[21] *saruwa-kuruwa* does not mean 'bones and such things'.

References

Allen, Nicholas J. 1975. *Sketch of Thulung grammar.* Ithaca: Cornell University.

Allen, Nicholas J. 1976. *Studies in the myths and oral traditions of the Thulung Rai of East Nepal.* Unpubl. Ph.D. dissertation, University of Oxford.

Driem, George van. 1993. *A grammar of Dumi.* Berlin: Mouton De Gruyter.

Ebert, Karen H. 1993. "Kiranti subordination in the South Asian areal context."In: *Studies in clause linkage.* K. H. Ebert (ed). Zürich: ASAS-Verlag. 83-110.

Ebert, Karen H. 1994. *The structure of Kiranti languages.* Zürich: ASAS-Verlag.

Ebert, Karen H. 1997. *Camling.* München: Lincom.

Ebert, Karen H. 1999. "The UP-DOWN dimension in Rai grammar and mythology."In: *Himalayan space: cultural horizons and practices.* B. Bickel & M. Gaenszle (eds). Zürich: Völkerkundemuseum. 107-134.

Ebert, Karen H. 2000. *Camling Texts and Glossary.* München: Lincom.

Ebert, Karen H. 2003a. "Kiranti languages: An Overview."In *The Sino-Tibetan Language.* G. Thurgood & R. LaPolla (eds.) Surrey: Curzon Press. 505-517.

Gaenszle, Martin. 1999. "Travelling up - travelling down: the vertcal dimension in Mewhang Rai ritual journeys." In: *Himalayan space: cultural horizons and practices,* B. Bickel & M. Gaenszle (eds). Zürich: Völkerkundemuseum. 135-163.

Gaenszle, Martin. 2002. *Ancestral Voices. Oral Ritual Texts and Their Social Contexts among the Mewahang Rai of East Nepal.* Münster: LIT-Verlag.

Glover, Warren W. 1974. *Sememic and grammatical structure of Gurung (Nepal).* Oklahoma: SIL.

Gvozdanovic, Jadranka. 1985. *Language system and its change.* Mouton de Gruyter. Berlin.

Rai, Novel K. 1985. *A descriptive study of Bantawa.* Unpubl. Ph.D. dissertation, Poona.

Toba, Sueyoshi. 1983. *Khaling texts.* Tokyo: Yak 7.

Toba, Sueyoshi. 1984. *Khaling.* Tokyo: ILCAA.

Winter, Werner. 1991-1992. "Diversity in Rai languages: an inspection of verb stems in selected idioms."*Lingua Posnaniensis* XXXIV: 141-56.

Winter, Werner. 2003. *A Bantawa Dictionary.* Berlin: Mouton de Gruyter.

Appendix: person-number markers

Camling, NW-dialect

A \ P	1s	1de	1pe	1di	1pi	2s	2d	2p	3s	3ns	itr.
1s						-na	-naci	-nani	-uŋa	-uŋ(cuŋ)a	-uŋa
1de									-cka		-cka
1pe									-umka	-um(cum)ka	-i(m)ka
1di									−ci		-ci
1pi									-um	-um(cum)	-i
2s	ta- -uŋa	ta- -cka	ta- -i(m)ka						ta- -u	ta- -u(cyu)	ta-
2d									ta- -ci		ta- -ci
2p									ta- -um	ta- -um(cum)	ta- -i
3s	pa- -uŋa	pa- -cka	pa- -i(m)ka	pa- -ci	pa- -i	ta-	ta- -ci	ta- -i	-u	-u(cyu)	-
3d									pa- -ci		-ci
3p									pa-	pa- u(cyu)	mi-

SE-dialect: 1st person patient scenarios

	1s	1de	1pe	1di	1pi
2s	kha-ta-				
2d	kha-ta- -ci				
2p	kha-ta- -i				
3s	kha-				
3d	kha- -ci				
3p	kha-mi-				

Bantawa (N.K.Rai)

A	P 1s	1de	1pe	1di	1pi	2s	2d	2p	3s	3ns	itr
1s						-na	-naci	-nanin	-uŋ	-uŋ-(ciŋ)	-ŋa
1de						-naca		im- -in	-ca		-a
1pe						im-	im- -ci		-umka	-um(cum)ka	-ika
1di									-cu		-ci
1pi									-um	-um(cɨm)	-in
2s	tɨ- -ŋa tɨ-	-ca	tɨ- -inka						tɨ- -u	tɨ- -u(ci)	tɨ-
2d	tɨ- -ŋaciŋ								tɨ- -cu		tɨ- -ci
2p	tɨ- -ŋaniŋ	tɨ- -nici							tɨ- -um	tɨ- -um(cɨm)	tɨ- -i
3s	-ŋa	-ca	(i-) -inka	-ci	(i-) -in	tɨ-	tɨ- -ci	tɨ- -in	-u	-u(ci)	-
3d	im- ŋa	im- -ca	ɨm- -inka	ɨm- -ci	ɨm- -in	ɨm-	ɨm- -ci	ɨm- -in	(ɨ-) -cu		-ci
3p									ɨ-	ɨm- -u(ci)	ɨm-

Thulung

A	1s	1de	1pe	1di	1pi	2s	2d	2p	3s	3d	3p	itr.
1s						-ni	-nici	-ni	-(p)u	-(p)uci	-(p)umi	-ŋu
1de						-naci		-nicimi	-cuku			-cuku
1pe						-nami	-nacimi	-nimi	-ku			-ki
1di									-ci			-ci
1pi									-i			-i
2s	-ŋi								-na			-na
2d	-ŋici								-ci			-ci
2p	-ŋimi	-ciki	-kimi						-ni			-ni
3s	-ŋi			-saci	-sa	-na	-naci	-nimi	-ü			-
3d	-ŋici								-ci			-ci
3p	-ŋimi			-sami		-nami	-nacimi		-mi			-mi

Khaling

A	1s	1de	1pe	1di	1pi	2s	2d	2p	3s	3d	3p	itr
1s						-nä	-su	-nu	-u	-su	-nu	-ŋa
1de						i-	i- -i	i- ni	-u			-cu
1pe									-ka			-ka
1di									-i			-ci
1pi									-ki			-ki
2s	i- -ŋa	i--ŋu	i--ka						i- -ü	i- -su	i- -nu	i-
2d	i- -ŋasu								i--i			i--ci
2p	i- -ŋanu								i--ni			i--ni
3s	i- -ŋa	i- -ŋu	i- -ka	i--i	i--ki	i-	i--i	i--ni	-ü	-su	-nu	-
3d	i- -ŋasu								-su			-ci
3p	i- -ŋanu								-nu			-nu

Mewahang

A	P											
	1s	1de	1pe	1di	1pi	2s	2d	2p	3s	3d	3p	itr
1s									-uŋ		-ukci	-ak/-aŋ
1de						-na	-naci	-ni		-cuga		-ciga
1pe										-upka		-ikka
1di										-cu		-ci
1pi										-um		-in
2s	-aŋ								-u		-uci	-na
2d	-akci									-cu		-ci
2p	-aŋni	-ciga	-ikka							-num		-ni
3s	-aŋ					--			-u			--
3d	-akci			-ci	-in		-ci	-ni		-cu		-ci
3p	-aŋmi					-mi					-uci	-mi

MYTHOLOGICAL TEXTS

Sources of the texts

Most of the texts are published here for the first time.

Camling myths were recorded by Karen H. Ebert during fieldwork trips to Nepal between 1984 and 1991. The version of the Camling Khocilipa myth (text 2) has been previously published, together with two other versions, in (Ebert 2000).

Mewahang mythology has been studied by Martin Gaenszle (cf. Gaenszle 2002). The narrations are published here for the first time, and they constitute practically the first documentation of the Mewahang language.

Texts from the other three languages are from unpublished dissertations or from other sources that are not easily accessible.

The Bantawa text is taken from Novel Kishore Rai's dissertation (Poona 1984), were it is presented with a word-by-word translation.

The original version of the Thulung Jaw-Khliw cycle is documented in the appendix to Nicholas Allen's unpublished dissertation (1976: 328-331). The territorial dispute is from the same source (348-250). The English translations are spread in various parts of chapters 3 and 4. The story of Baginanda, the flying shaman, appeared in Allen's Thulung grammar (1975: 140-148), which has been out of print for a long time.

The Khaling version of the orphan myth is from Toba (1983: 33-42), where it is presented together with an English translation. Sentences 69-82 are taken from the text "About housebuilding" (p. 85-88).

Thanks to the informants and to the colleagues who let us use their material!

References
Allen, Nicholas J. 1975. *Sketch of Thulung grammar.* Ithaca: Cornell University.
Allen, Nicholas J. 1976. *Studies in the myths and oral traditions of the Thulung Rai of East Nepal.* Unpubl. Ph.D. dissertation, University of Oxford.
Ebert, Karen H. 2000. *Camling Texts and Glossary.* München: Lincom.
Gaenszle, Martin. 2002. *Ancestral Voices. Oral Ritual Texts and Their Social Contexts among the Mewahang Rai of East Nepal.* Münster: LIT-Verlag.
Rai, Novel K. 1985. *A descriptive study of Bantawa.* Unpubl. Ph.D. dissertation, Poona.
Toba, Sueyoshi. 1983. *Khaling texts.* Tokyo: Yak 7.

Camling

1a. Paruhõ Naïma[1]

narrator: Jhanaman Rai, from Khamla (SE-Camling)
recording and analysis: K.H.Ebert

Kurima, the wind, makes Paruhõ and Naïma meet

1. **kainiuda dosona putt-i   ruŋma uko dim-wa   kaini-*lai*   kha-cãid-e.**
   we_pi here how   originate-1/2pS QUOTE this story-INST we_pi-DAT 1P-teach-IPFV

   How we originated here is taught to us through this story.

2. **uko mahowa-pahowa-ci pa-tata-ko   dim-ci kaŋa yen-ãi-ŋas-uŋ-ko   uda**
   this elder(f)-elder(m)-ns INV-bring-NML story-ns I   hear-1s-PERF-1s-NML here

   ruŋ-ma ruŋs-ãi.
   say-INF be.about-1s:IPFV

   The stories that the old women and men brought and that I have heard I am ready to tell here.

3. **le-ma-na   jhara pa-len-ãina-khõ   *pani* picha tat-ãi,   kuneu.**
   know-INF-TOP all   NEG-know-1s:NEG-COND even little bring-1s:IPFV INTJ

   Even though I do not know everything I will bring a little, okay? (As for knowing, I do not know everything, nevertheless ...)

4. **kainidosona putt-i   ruŋmapana mahowa-pahowa-ci mi-riŋa-ko.**
   we_pi how   originate-1/2p QUOTE   f:elder-m:elder-ns   3pS-say-NML

   How we originated the old women and men have told.

5. **uko Paruhõ *ra* Naïma-daka kaini putt-i-ko   *are*, putt-i-ko   *raicha*.**
   this Paruhõ and Naïma-ABL we_pi originate-1/2p-NML REP originate-1/2p-NML REP

   We originated from Paruhõ and Naïma, they say.

6. **tyudaka Paruhõ *ra*   Naïma dosona tim-mai-ma-ci ruŋmapana, Kurima-wa**
   then   Paruhõ and Naïma how   meet-CAUS-INF-ns QUOTE   Kurima-ERG

   kaŋa uko khaici-*lai* tim-mai-na-c-e   kou, ruŋmanâ riŋa-ko *raicha*.
   I   this you_d-DAT meet-CAUS-1>2-d-IPFV INTJ QUOTE   say-NML REP

   Now, Paruhõ and Naïma, how to make them meet? Kurima (the wind) said: "I will make you two meet."

Italics in the text indicate Nepali words or morphemes.
[1] *aï* [a]+[i]; otherwise Camling *ai* is [əj] ~ [ɒj]

7. **riŋa-hemo Paruhõ** *cahi* **khõ-ma isa-ko   khaisa-ko   hiŋa-ko.**
   say-after   Paruhõ   FOC look-INF be.bad-NML be.ugly-NML be-NML

   But Paruhõ was not nice to look at, he was ugly.

8. **tyudaka Kurima-*lai*   lod-yi-ko   *raicha*: Kurim-ou kaŋa oso-ko   khais-ãi.**
   then   Kurima-DAT tell-3P-NML REP   Kurima-APP I   like.this-NML bad-1s:IPFV

   So he said to the wind: "Kurima, I am so ugly.

9. **dosona thala Naïma kaŋa-tõda ta-e?**
   how   PART Naïma I-with   come-IPFV

   How will Naïma come with me?

10. **pa-t-ain-e   *hola*, kaŋa m-cai-ma   la-e-ko   hiŋ-ãi,   ruŋmapana,**
    NEG-come-NEG-IPFV MOD   I   her-disliking-INF VB-IPFV-NML be-1s:IPFV QUOTE

    Maybe she does not come, she won't like me," he said.

11. **Kurima riŋa-ko *raicha*: aina khana-tõda pa-t-aine-nakhõ   kaŋa-*lai***
    Kurima say-NML REP   INTJ you-with   NEG-come-NEG-IPFV-COND I-DAT

    i-*pattiko* a-labetuŋ woid-uŋa, lod-yi-ko   *raicha*.
    one-side   my-wing   break:APL-1s tell-3P-NML REP

    And Kurima answered: "Well, if she doesn't come with you, break one of my wings," he said to him.

12. *lo*   aso tyisona ta-khat-e nâ   kaŋa-*lai cahi* *kaliya*   ta-tir-e   nâ   Naïma
    INTJ now like.that 2-go-IPFV and I-DAT   FOC   negotiator 2-become-IPFV and Naïma

    kha-ta-khud-ãi-nakhõ i-*pattiko* kap-labetuŋ wot-ãi   kou, lod-yi-ko   *raicha*.
    1P-2-bring-NEG-COND   one-side your-wing break-1s:IPFV INTJ tell-3P-NML REP

    "Well, go then, but if you go as negotiator for me, and if you do not bring me Naïma, I shall break one of your wings," he said.

13. **lod-yi-hemo khata-ko *raicha*.**
    tell-3P-after go-NML   REP

    After that the wind went.

14. **khata kina Naïma-*lai* sen-yi-ko *raicha* Kurima-wa: Naïm-ou,   *lo* osona   ŋo**
    go   SEQ Naïma-DAT ask-3P-NML REP   Kurima-ERG Naïma-APP INTJ like.this EMPH

    Paruhõ-wa *cahi* khana-*lai* layo ta-maid-e.
    Paruhõ-ERG FOC   you-DAT   care 2-make-IPFV

    He went and asked Naïma, the wind: "Naïma, it is like this: Paruhõ cares for you.

15. *ani* khana tyo Paruhõ-tõda khai-ma tire, ruŋmanâ lod-yi-ko   *raicha*.
    then you   that Paruhõ-with go-INF must QUOTE   tell-3P-NML REP

    Now you must go with Paruhõ," he said to her.

16. **aina, khai-ma-na khat-ãi, kaŋa uda i-ruŋ khõ-maid-uŋ-nathala,**
INTJ go-INF-TOP go-1s:IPFV I here one-CL see-CAUS-1s-PARTPART

    lod-yi-ko *raicha* **Naïma-wa Kurima-***lai.***
tell-3P-NML REP Naïma-ERG Kurima-DAT

"I will go, but show him first to me," Naïma said to Kurima.

17. **Kurima khata kina:** *lo* **Paruh-ou, aso khana-***lai* **ta-khaŋ-e** *are* **Naïma-wa,**
Kurima go SEQ INTJ Paruhõ-APP now you-DAT 2-look-IPFV REP Naïma-ERG

    lod-yi nâ Paruhõ khata-ko *raicha* **khõ-si-kona, m-caima la-ko** *raicha* **Naïma.**
tell-3P and Paruhõ go-NML REP look-PURP-TEMP her-disliking VB-NML REP Naïma

The wind went: "Well, Paruhõ, Naïma says she will look at you first," he said, and when Paruhõ
went to be looked at, Naïma disliked him.

18. *lo* **oso-ko-tõda kaŋa-na pa-khai-n-ãi, riŋa-ko** *raicha.*
INTJ like.this-NML-with I-TOP NEG-go-NEG-1s:IPFV say-NML REP

"With such a guy I don't go," she said.

19. **riŋa-hemo khu-tõda-na pa-khat-aina.**
say-after he-with-TOP NEG-go-NEG

She spoke thus and did not go with him.

Paruhõ breaks Kurima's wing and causes a draught

20. **pakhatãi-hemo Kurima-mo kaŋa ruŋ-uŋ-ko ta-kõs-aina kap-labetuŋ wot-ãi,**
[repet.] -after Kurima-GEN I say-1s-NML 2-agree-NEG your-wing break-1s:IPFV

    ruŋa nâ m-labetuŋ wot-yi-ko *raicha.*
say and his-wing break-3P-NML REP

As she did not go, Paruhõ broke the Kurima's wing, saying: "As you did not accomplish what I said,
I will break your wing."

21. **Kurima-mo** *daine* **m-labetung wot-yi-kas-yi-ko** *raicha.*
Kurima-GEN right his-wing break-3P-V2:THROW-3P-NML REP

He broke the Kurima's right wing.

22. **wot-yi-kas-yi-hemo tyudaka Paruhõ-na /.../ jhara i-tuŋma-da cahi bokha-da**
[repet.]-after then Paruhõ-TOP all our$_{pi}$-village-LOC FOC earth-LOC

    cahi **wa hõsa-lo mu-ko** *raicha.*
FOC water dry-MAN make-NML REP

After that, Paruhõ made the water dry up everywhere, in our village, in the fields.

23. jhara*thãu* hõsa-lo   mu-hemo   waïma   mi-sya-ko *raicha*.
all   place   dry-MAN   make-after thirst   3pS-die-NML REP

When he made the whole place dry up, everybody suffered from thirst.

24. hõsa-lo   mu ki   i-ra suŋpuwa-mo*torka*-da   chorsa-da-ko
become.dry-MAN   do   SEQ one-CL tree-GEN   hole.in.tree-LOC urinate-V2:PUT-NML

***raicha*, Paruhõ chorsa-da-ko   *raicha*.**
REP   Paruhõ urinate-V2:PUT-NML REP

Then he urinated into a hollow tree, Paruhõ urinated.

25. tyudaka jhara hõsa-lo   mu ki   khu khata-ko *raicha* m-yuŋ-kha-di   ŋo.
then   all   dry-MAN   make SEQ he go-NML   REP   his-live-LocN-hiLOC EMPH

Now, having dried up everything, he went up to his living-place.

26. myuŋkhadi ŋo khata-nâ yuŋsa-ŋasa-ko   *raicha*.
[repet.]   -LINK sit-V2:STAY-NML REP

He went up to his living-place and stayed there.

Naïma sends out animals in search of water

27. mdõsi-na Naïma waïma   sya-ko *raicha*.
after-TOP Naïma   thirst   die-NML REP

After that Naïma became very thirsty.

28. waïma sya-hemo wa   lam-si   chuid-yi-ko *raicha*.
[repet.]   -after   water search-PURP send-3P-NML REP

She sent (the animals) to search for water.

29. kho-ni   *pani* pa-dhit-ãi-c-ãi   wa lam-sim   lam-sim   mu-pana pa-dhit-
where-ALL also   NEG-find-NEG-ns-NEG watersearch-ManN search-ManN do-TEMP NEG-find-

ãi-c-aina.
NEG-ns-NEG

Nowhere they found water, searching searching (they went), but did not find any.

30. daka: *lo* aso khat-ine   lam-si,   ruŋmanâ mi-lamta-ko *raicha*.
then   INTJ now go-2pIMPER search-PURP QUOTE   3pS-walk-NML REP

"Now, go to search," she said and they took the road.

31. wa lam-si   khawa,   chirkucipa, bhuwale, tyudakai-ra cikalemma
water search-PURP   woodpecker grasshopper owl   then   one-CL (bird)

ruŋmako wasa mi-khata-ko *raicha*.
called   bird   3pS-go-NML REP

In search for water went the woodpecker, the grasshopper, the owl and a bird called 'cikalemma'.

32. **mikhata-kona i-ra   khopra-da   hiŋa-ko wa-na   khawa-wa   diŋ-u-ko**
    [repet.]   -TEMP one-CL hole.in.tree-LOC be-NML water-TOP woodpecker-ERG drink-3P-NML

    raicha.
    REP

As they went, the woodpecker drank the water that was in the hole of a tree.

33. **khawawa diŋu-pana:** *lo*   **uko wa diŋ-u, mi-riŋa ki   tyiko-pa-mo**
    [repet.]   -TEMP INTJ this waterdrink-3P 3pS-say SEQ that-NML-GEN

    m-lem   pa-bhurda-ko   *raicha*.
    his-tongue INV-pull.out-NML REP

After he drank, they said "he drank," and pulled out his tongue.

34. **mlem pabhurda ki   kamalapa   pa-maida-ko   *raicha*.**
    [repet.]   SEQ upside.down INV-make-NML REP

They pulled it out and put it back the wrong way round.

35. **kamalappa pamaida tyudaka*arko thaũ* mi-khata-kona tyuda *pani* hiŋa-ko**
    [repet.]   then   other place 3pS-go-TEMP there also be-NML

    wa-na   chirkucipa diŋ-u-ko   *raicha*.
    water-TOP grasshopper drink-3P-NML REP

After that, when they came to another place, grasshopper drank the water that was there.

36. **tyudaka m-*philu*-da nel.*theŋgra* ŋo   pa-poda-ko *raicha*.**
    then   his-foot-LOC nail   EMPH INV-put-NML REP

So they drove long nails through his legs.

37. **tyudaka lam-sa   lam-sa   mi-khata-panacikalemma ruŋmako wasa-wa:**
    then   search-SIM search-SIM 3pS-go-TEMP cikalemma   called bird-ERG

    tyuda hiŋ-e! tyuda hiŋ-e! lod-yi-ŋas-yi-ci-ko   *raicha* ki, tyiko-ci-*lai*
    there be-IPFV there be-IPFV tell-3P-V2:STAY-3P-ns-NML REP   SEQ that-ns-DAT

    khõ-maid-yi-ci-ko tyuko wa-na   khu-wa tyiko diŋ-u-ko   *raicha*.
    see-CAUS-3P-ns-NML that water-TOP she-ERG that   drink-3P-NML REP

As searching searching they went, the cikalemma bird kept telling them: "Here is some, here is some," and she (Naïma) drank.the water which he showed them

Naïma gets pregnant from drinking Paruhõ's urine and gives birth to Tiger, Bear, Man and Dog.

38. diŋu-pana   Paruhõ chorsa-da-ko   Naïma-mo m-khori khur-yu-ko *raicha.*
[repet.]-TEMP Paruhõ urinate-V2:PUT-NML Naïma-GEN her-belly carry-3P-NML REP

After drinking Paruhõ's urine, Naïma became pregnant.

39. mkhori khuryu-hemo-daka hiŋ-sim hiŋ-sim ŋala-pa m-cha-ci   tir-ma   *bela*
[repet.]   -after-ABL   sit-MAN sit-MAN do-TEMP her-child-ns become-INF time

tira-ko   *raicha*.
become-NML REP

After becoming pregnant, while she was waiting, waiting, the time for childbirth came.

40. tyudaka m-cha-ci   tira   po, aso de   ŋal-ma.
then   her-child-ns become PART now what do-INF

Now that the children were born, what to do?

41. aso Kurim-ou, khana mna oso   ta-ruŋ-hoda-ko, khata   Paruhõ-*lai*
now Kurima-APP you   FOC like.this 2-say-AMB-NML   go(:IMPER) Paruhõ-DAT

sãi-si   khata-kha,   lod-yi-hema chuid-yi-ko *raicha*.
ask-PURP go-PART   tell-3P-after   send-3P-NML REP

"Now, Kurima, it was you who kept talking like this; go! go to ask Paruhõ!" she said and sent him.

42. chuidyi-kona khata-kona Paruhõ-*lai*   lod-yi-ko   *raicha*.
[repet.] -TEMP   go-TEMP   Paruhõ-DAT   tell-3P-NML REP

He went and spoke to Paruhõ.

43. de   de   wat-yi-ŋas-yi-ci   thala, Kurim-ou! lod-yi-pana,
what what give.birth-3P-PERF-3P-ns PART Kurima-APP   tell-3P-TEMP

"What is it then that she has given birth to, Kurima?" he asked,

44. capca, hõcha, borpa, syoki[2] wat-yi-ŋas-yi-ci,   jhara *carota* hiŋ-e,
tiger   man   bear   dog   give.birth-3P-PERF-3P-ns all   four   be-IPFV

lod-yi-ko *raicha*-pana,
tell-3P-NML REP-TEMP

"Tiger, Man, Bear and Dog she bore, they are four together," (Kurima) said.

45. *lo*   aso tyiso-nakhõ aŋa ŋo   a-cha-ci   *raicha*-khõ hõcha-*lai* layo-
INTJ now like.that-COND my   EMPH my-child-ns MIR-if   man-DAT   care-

---

[2] These are ritual names; in everyday Camling it is *cabha* 'tiger', *mina* 'man', *mosa* 'bear', *khlipa* 'dog'. *hõ-cha* - king/chief-child.

tyoŋai-da pak-u-nyo-nâ   ŋas-yi-nyo.
basket-LOC put-3P-OPT:3P-LINK keep-3P-OPT:3P

"Now if it is like that, if they turned out to be my children, she must put Manchild in a caring-basket and keep him there.

46. *aru-ci-lai   cahi /.../ labo-sippa-ci lam-u-nyo-nâ   tyuda im-maid-yi-ci-nyo,*
other-ns-DAT FOC   leaf-?-ns   search-3P-OPT:3P-LINK there sleep-CAUS-3P-ns-OPT:3P

lod-yi-ko *raicha.*
tell-3P-NML REP

As for the others, she should collect leaves and put them to sleep there," he said.

47. tyudaka Kurima ya   ki   tyoso lod-yi-ko *raicha.*
then   Kurima come.down SEQ   like.that tell-3P-NML REP

Then Kurima came down and spoke thus:

48. *lo   hõcha-lai* **osona im-maid-yi** *are* **layo-tyoŋai-da pak-u-nâ ŋas-yi**
INTJ man-DAT   like.this sleep-CAUS-3P REP care-basket-LOC put-3P LINK keep-3P

are, **lod-yi-ko** *raicha.*
REP   tell-3P-NML REP

"Well, he says to put Manchild in a caring-basket and keep him there.

49. *aru-ci-lai   cahi* **labo-sippa-da-ni im-maid-yi-c-yo.**
other-ns-DAT FOC leaf-?-LOC-ALL   sleep-CAUS-3P-ns-3P:IPFV

As for the others, put them to sleep on leaves."

The four brothers go hunting

50. daka tyiko-ci mi-pora-saŋa,   miporasaŋa-hemodakakholi-da-ni
then that-ns   3pS-grow-V2:COME:UP [repet.]   -after then jungle-LOC-ALL

aso cama lam-si   mi-khata-ko *raicha.*
now food search-PURP 3pS-go-NML REP

Then they grew up, and after that they went into the forest in search for food.

51. camalamsi mikhata-kona m-ma-wa   aso cama-*kuro*-ci *khaja*   pod-yi-
[repet.]   -TEMP his-mother-ERG now food-thing-ns snack   put:APPL-3P-

chuŋs-yi-ci-ko, delo *pani* **capca-wa** dõsi hiŋa ki   **c-yo-pak-u-ko**
V2:SEND-3P-ns-NML always also   tiger-ERG back be   SEQ   eat-3P-V2:PUT-3P-NML

raicha, **kic-nicho-ci-*lai*   cahi saka.**
REP   their-y.sibling-ns-DAT FOC hunger

Whatever food the mother put into the bag for them, Tiger always stayed behind and ate up
everything, the younger brothers remained hungry.

52. **namduŋ ta-e-ko** *raicha,* **kic-[3]nicho-ci** **saka** **kic-***dajai* *cahi*
    evening come-IPFV-NML REP their-y.sibling-ns be.hungry their-e.brother FOC

    khasa-nâ **ta-ko.**
    be.sated-LINK come-NML

    Evening came, and his younger brothers were hungry, but the elder brother (Tiger) came with
    a full stomach.

53. **m-ma-wa** **lod-yi-ko** *raicha*: **ei** **capca,** **kap-tõya** **chek-ou,**
    his-mother-ERG tell-3P-NML REP INTJ tiger your-wits guard-APP

    hõcha-wa m-tõya-da **ta-dhas-e,** **lod-yi-ko** *raicha.*
    man-ERG his-wits-LOC 2-make.fall-IPFV tell-3P-NML REP

    His mother said: "Ei, Tiger, watch out! Manchild will outwit you," she said,

54. **kaŋa depa-mo tyiko hõcha-***lai-***na kaŋa** **set-ãi** **bo,** **lod-yi-ko** *raicha.*
    I what-GEN that man-DAT-TOP I kill-1s:IPFV PART tell-3P-NML REP

    "Not me, I'll kill that Manchild."

55. **ta-cap-un-yo** **lod-yi-ko** *raicha.*
    2-can-NEG-3P:IPFV tell-3P-NML REP

    "You cannot," (Naïma) said.

56. **tyudaka** *pheri* **m-selam** *pani* **mi-khata-ko** *raicha.*
    then again REL-next.day also 3pS-go-NML REP

    The next day they went again.

57. **mikhata-pana m-bulma la-ko** *raicha* **m-nicho** **hõcha** *cahi* **mbulma lako** *raicha.*
    [repet.] -TEMP his-anger VB-NML REP his-y.sibling man FOC [repet.]

    As they went, the younger brother became angry, Man became angry.

58. *lo* **ale-na** **khaici** **m-bhusi** **syo-***nani* **kaŋa dõsi hiŋ-ãi,** **lod-yi-ko**
    INTJ today-TOP you_d his-in.front proceed-2pIMPER I behind be-1s:IPFV tell-3P-NML

    raicha **hõcha.**
    REP man

    "Now, today you two go ahead, I will stay behind," he said.

59. **daka** **mi-khata-ko** *raicha* **aru-ci** **capca borpa syoki-ci mi-khata-ko** *raicha*
    then 3pS-go-NML REP other-ns tiger bear dog-ns 3pS-go-NML REP

---

[3] The plural possessive prefix is used also if there are several participants in the relationship, i.e. the
"possessor" can be singular.

kholi-da-ni.
jungle-LOC-ALL

Then they went, the others, tiger, bear and dog, they went into the forest.

60. **kholi-da-ni   oso-ko   cama-ko lam-si   mi-khata-kona hõcha-wa m-tei**
jungle-LOC-ALL like.this-NML food-NML search-PURP 3pS-go-TEMP   man-ERG   his-clothes

lais-yi   ki   i-ra   suŋpuwa-*lai* waid-yi-ko   *raicha* ki   mina   oso   mu   ki
take.off-3P SEQ one-CL tree-DAT   put.on:APL-3P-NML REP   SEQ man   like   make SEQ

suŋpuwa-da waŋa-ŋasa-ko   *raicha*.
tree-LOC   enter-V2:STAY-NML REP

As they went into the forest to search for food, Man took off his clothes and put them on a tree to make it look like a man, and he climbed up the tree.

61. **daka huilo-ka   ta-pana   oso   khaŋ-u-pana *khaja*-ci *pani* c-yo-pak-u**
then below-ABL   come-TEMP like.this look-3P-TEMP snack-ns also   eat-3P-V2:PUT-3P

nâ dhalo yuŋsa-ŋasa-ko   *raicha*.
and above   wait-V2:STAY-NML REP

Then when he (Tiger) came from below and looked around, Man had eaten up the snacks and was waiting above.

62. **dhalo-ka hui-ni   *takba*   mu-ŋas-yi-ko   *raicha* ban-wa.**
above-ABL down-ALL aim:LW do:3P-V2:STAY-3P-NML REP   arrow-INST

From above, he was aiming down with his bow and arrow.

63. **tyudaka ta   kina   m-bulma-wa: uda khana ta-hiŋ-e, ruŋmanâ tyiko**
then   come SEQ his-anger-INST here you   2-be-IPFV QUOTE   that

suŋpuwa-*lai*   wapd-yi-nâ   khatrak-khutruk mu-ko   *raicha*.
tree-DAT   scratch-3P-LINK (sound)   do:3P-NML REP

Tiger came and in his rage he scratched the tree 'khatrak-khutruk', saying "Here you are!"

64. **m-tei   jhara cet-yi-kas-yi-ko   *raicha*.**
his-clothes all   tear-3P-V2.THROW-3P-NML REP

He tore all his clothes to pieces.

65. **dhalo bo   ri-e-ko   *raicha*.**
above   PART laugh-IPFV-NML REP

(Man sitting) in the top was laughing.

66. **tyuda ta-hiŋ-e ruŋa nâ   waŋ-uŋsa-pa,   dhalo-ka õ   ap-u-dhas-yi   ki**
there   2-be-IPFV say and   enter-PROG-TEMP above-ABL EMPH shoot-3P-V2:DOWN-3P SEQ

set-yi-ko   *raicha*.
kill-3P-NML   REP

Tiger said "There you are!" and as he was climbing up, he (Man) shot him from above and killed him.

67. setyiko   tyudakami-khata-ko *raicha* khim-da-pana   m-ma-wa   sen-yi-ko
[repet.]   then   3pS-go-NML   REP   house-LOC-TEMP his-mother-ERG ask-3P-NML

raicha: aina, ale   khoi thala kai-*dajai*?   ruŋmapana kai-hõ-pa   ruŋmapa.
REP   INTJ   today where PART your_p-brother QUOTE   your_p-chief-m QUOTE

When he was killed and they went home, his mother asked: "Where is your elder brother today?" she asked "your chief?"

68. walali.totika   khu suisuiya cayaluŋ-bayaluŋ mu-sa ta-e,   ruŋmanâ
young.man   he (sound) fuss-ECHO   do-SIM come-IPFV QUOTE

lod-yi-ko   *raicha* hõcha-wa m-ma-*lai*.
tell-3P-NML REP   man-ERG his-mother-DAT

"The young man comes whistling and joking," Man told his mother.

Tiger is revived by Naïma and kills her

69. lod-yi-pana aina *lo* khana ale   kap-tõya-wa ta-dhas-yi, ruŋmanâ
tell-3P-TEMP INTJ INTJ you   today your-wits-INST 2-fell-3P   QUOTE

Naïma, *pheri* i-ra   luŋto *ani* i-cha bodiya khaid-yi ki   khata-ko *raicha*.
Naïma   again one-CL stone then one-CL straw take-3P SEQ go-NML   REP

Then Naïma said: "Well, today you probably outwitted him," and she took a stone and a bundle of straw and went.

70. *ani* khaid-yi-ko *raicha*-pana jhara-pa nhai-sa   pa-khaida-ko *raicha*-pana
then   take-3P-NML REP-TEMP   all-NML follow-SIM INV-take-NML REP-TEMP

sya-ŋasa-ko.
die-V2:STAY-NML

While she took (those things), when they all took up things and followed, (Tiger) was dead.

71. tyudaka tyiko m-nicho-wa   ap-u-ko   m-khouwa-da tyiko *lohoro*
then   that his-y.sibling-ERG shoot-3P-NML his-wound-LOC that stone(for grinding)

ŋas-yi ki mi mu-pana oso   haid-yi-pana leta-ko   *raicha*.
put-3P SEQ fire do-TEMP like.this fan-3P-TEMP revive-NML REP

She put the round stone (for grinding pepper) on the wound shot by his younger brother, made a fire, and when fanning (the burning grass over him). he became alive.

72. *lo* imsuŋ.duŋ-ko *raicha*, ruŋ-sa khupsa-ko *raicha*.
INTJ fall.asleep:1s-NML MIR   say-SIM get.up-NML REP

He got up saying "I must have fallen asleep."

73. **aina ta-imsa.da-ko-na,   hõcha-wa m-tõya-da   ta-dhasa-ko,** *lo* **syo**
INTJ 2-fall.asleep-NML-TOP man-ERG his-wits-LOC 2-make.fall-NML INTJ proceed

khim-da, lod-yi-ko *raicha*.
house-LOC tell-3P-NML REP

"You think you fell asleep, no, Man outwitted you. Move on home!" (the mother) said.

74. **aso hõcha-wa m-tõya-da kha-dhasa aso kaŋa khim-da pa-khai-n-ãi,**
now man-ERG his-wits-LOC 1P-make.fall now I house-LOC NEG-go-NEG-1s:IPFV

aso kaŋa m-nicho tir-uŋa khu aŋa a-*dajai* tira, lod-yi ki
now I his-y.sibling become-1s he my my-e.brother become tell-3P SEQ

pa-kõs-ãi-ko *raicha*, chaida-ko *raicha* /.../
NEG-agree-NEG-NML REP refuse-NML REP

"Man tricked me, I will not go home. Now I have become the small one, he became my big brother," he said and did not agree, he refused.

75. **chaida-hema** *lo* **a-ma kap-*ghicro*-da-na kuŋ bo hiŋ-e.**
refuse-after INTJ my-mother your-throat-LOC-TOP louse PART be-IPFV

Then he said: "Mother, there is a louse at your throat."

76. **kumd-uŋ-kha** *nani*! **lod-yi-pana kumd-yi-hema m-*naŋgra*-wa m-lamo**
pick.off-1s-PART child tell-3P-TEMP pick.off-3P-after his-claw-INST her-throat

wapd-yi-set-yi-ko *raicha*.
scratch-3P-V2:KILL-3P-NML REP

"Pick it off, child!" she said, and after taking it off, he scratched her throat with his claws and killed her.

77. **tyudaka capca kholi-di waŋ-khata,borpa** *ra* **syoki yõhoda-ci.**
then tiger jungle-hiLOC enter-V2:GO bear and dog roam-d

Then Tiger went up into the forest; Bear and Dog roamed about.

78. *ani* **hõcha-wa chaid-yi** *raicha* **ki khata ki sen-yi-ko: aina, mama de**
then man-ERG know-3P REP SEQ go SEQ ask-3P-NML INTJ mother(adress)

de tira-ko: ruŋa-kona capca-wa set-yi, ruŋanâ dum pa-maida-ko *raicha*
what become-NML say-TEMP tiger-ERG kill-3P QUOTE speech INV-make-NML REP

borpa *ra* **syoki-wa.**
bear and dog-ERG

Man understood, and he went and asked, "What became of Mother?" - "Tiger killed her," they told him, Bear and Dog.

Bear eats Naïma

79. **daka hõcha-wa   lod-yi-ko   *raicha*: *lo*   borpa, uko hyalo   khaid-yi nâ**
then man-ERG   tell-3P-NML   REP   INTJ bear   this over.there take-3P and

mama-*lai*   silum-holum   mu.
mother(address)-DAT   (burial)   do

Man said: "Bear, carry Mother away and make the *silum-holum*."

80. **silum-holum mu-si   khaid-yi kina m-ma-*lai*-na   c-yo-hod-yi-ko   bo   *raicha*,**
burial   do-PURP take-3P   SEQ his-mother-DAT-TOPeat-3P-AMB-3P-NML PARTREP

borpa-wa-na.
bear-ERG-TOP

He carried her to make the silum-holum, and he moved about eating his mother, Bear did.

81. **ta-dir-aina? — dir-uŋs-ãi,   m-*philu* dat-e-ŋas-e.**
2-finish-NEG   finish-PROG-1s:IPFV her-foot   visible-IPFV-V2:STAY-IPFV

"Have you not finished?" (Man asked). — "I am finishing, her foot is still visible."

82. ***pheri*   ta-dir-aina? — aina m-chu   dat-uŋse.**
again   2-finish-NEG   no   her-hand visible-PROG

Again: "Have you not finished?"— "No, her hand is still visible."

83. **khoko khoko   ca-ma-khai-ma   mi-dir-u-ŋas-yi-ko,   tyiko tyiko *cahi***
which   which   eat-INF-V2:GO-INF NEG-finish-3P-V2:STAY-3P-NMLthat   that   FOC

hiŋ-e   lod-yi-ko   *raicha*.
be-IPFVtell-3P-NML REP

Whatever part he had not finished eating, of that part he said "it is there."

84. **tyudaka   ta-dir-aina? — m-takhlo dat-uŋs-e,   m-takhlo ca-ma   ruŋsa-ko.**
then   2-finish-NEG   her-head visible-PROG-IPFV her-head   eat-INF be.about-NML

Then: "Have you not finished?" — "The head is still visible," he was about to eat her head.

85. ***ani*   ta-dir-yu? — dir-uŋa, *ani* bana-ko *raicha*.**
then   2-finish-3P   finish-1s   then come-NML REP

Then: "You finished?" — "I finished," so he came.

86. **mama-*lai*   ta-khipt-yi he bo ta-c-yo? —   khipt-uŋa.**
mother(address)-DAT   2-bury-3P   or PART2-eat-3P:IPFV   bury-1s

Now (Man asked:) "Did you bury Mother or did you eat her?" — "I buried her."

87. **rya-ce   thala.**
laugh-d:HORT PART

"Let's laugh then."

88. **rya-ci-kona borpa-mo-na m-kuŋ-da-na m-ma-mo m-muse bo**
laugh-d-TEMP bear-GEN-TOP his-tooth-LOC-TOP his-mother-GEN her-hair PART

hapta-ŋasa-ko *raicha.*
stick-V2:STAY-NML REP

When they laughed the mother 's hair was hanging in Bear's teeth.

89. *lo* **mama khana ta-c-yo, lod-yi-ko** *raicha.*
INTJ mother(address) you 2-eat-3P:IPFV tell-3P-NML REP

"You ate Mother," (Man) said.

90. **khana aso kholi-di waŋa, lod-yinâ phyabd-yi-chuŋs-yi-ko** *raicha* **borpa-lai.**
you now jungle-hiLOC enter tell-3P and slap-3P-V2:SEND-3P-NML REP bear-DAT

"Go into the forest now!" he said and slapped him, chasing Bear away.

91. **phyabd-yi ki khu** *pani* **kholi-di waŋ-khata-ko** *raicha.*
slap-3P SEQ he also jungle-hiLOC enter-V2:GO-NML REP

He hit him and he (Bear) also went up into the forest.

Dog stays with Man

92. **syoki-*lai pani* sei-ma ruŋs-yi-ko** *raicha.*
dog-DAT also kill-INF be.about-3P-NML REP

(Man) was ready to kill Dog.

93. **mi-sei-n-uŋ, dajai, kaŋa khamo kap-*philu*-da ims-ãi.**
NEG-kill-NEG-1s e.brother I your your-foot-LOC sleep-1s:IPFV

"Don't kill me, elder brother! I'll sleep at your feet.

94. **kaŋa khosaimakhamo kap-khim-da mi-ta-e-ko-ci-*lai* hya-ni hyani**
I night your your-house-LOC 3pS-come-IPFV-NML-ns-DAT across-ALL [repet.]

rhok-ãi-c-ãi, nâ m-nicho-*lai* cahi tat-yi.
chase-1s:IPFV-ns-[copy] and his-y.sibling-DAT FOC bring-3P

Those who come to your house at night, I will chase them away," he said, and (Man) took his younger brother home.

95. **syoki ruŋmako imo jhara** *bhanda kancha.*
dog QUOTE our$_{pi}$ all than youngest.son

Syoki, Dog, is said to be our youngest brother.

1b. imo i-dum - our tradition

narrator: Nirempa; a shaman from Khamla (SE-Camling)
recording and analysis: K.H.Ebert

Salapa and Simnima are created

1. **imo i-dum-na, bokhaphopi-larewa[1] ruŋmako[2]-na, wa-koya-ni kaini-*lai***
   our   our-story-TOP (rit.:termite-hill)   that.is-TOP   water-inside-EMPH   we_p-DAT

   kha-muna[3]-ko.
   1P-create-NML

   Our story of creation: termite-hill it is called, inside the water we were created.

2. **khamuna-pana imo Salapa-na bokhaphopi-larewa-da-ka tirsa-khata,**
   [repet.] -TEMP   our   Salapa-TOP   (rit.:termite-hill)-LOC-ABL   be.born-V2:GO

   bokhama-da-ka-ni roŋkhama tirsa-khata nâ
   earth-LOC-ABL-EMPH   white.ant   be.born-V2:GO and

   When we were created, our Salapa was born from a termite hill, and from the soil a white ant was born,

3. **tyudaka tyiko roŋkhama-da-ka misa laida ...**
   then   that   white.ant-LOC-ABL   flying.ant   emerge

   and out of the white ant came a flying ant...

4. **misa laida-daka *pheri* tyiko Salapa muna.**
   [repet.]   -after   again   that   Salapa   originate

   After the flying ant Salapa came into being.

5. **Salapa muna-pana tyiko bokhaphopi-larewa-da-ka-na Simnima m-nicho**
   [repet.]   -TEMP   that   (rit.:termite-hill)-LOC-ABL-TOP   Simnima   his-y.sibling

   bo tira, muna, tyiko Simnima ruŋmako khasima.
   PART   become   originate   that   Simnima   that.is   housefly

   After Salapa originated from the termite-hill, his younger sibling Simnima came into being; Simnima means 'housefly'.

6. **osoko muna-pana *pheri* tyiko m-chala-ŋo *raicha*, m-chala *ra***
   like.this   originate-TEMP   also   that   her-brother-EMPH   MIR   her-brother   and

---

1 In mythological narration such double-word constructions are typical. The second part (here *larewa*) doesn't mean anything (cf. *sikiwa-roloho* in 12, *Niyama-Tatuma* in 27).

2 *ruŋmako*: an imitation of Nepali *bhan-eko* (say-PCPL) 'named; it is'. The Nepali quote particle *bhan-era* (say-CONV) is rendered in Camling by some form of *ruŋ-*, the most neutral speech act verb. Sometimes a form of Nep. *bhan-* is borrowed; see 11. I leave these forms unanalyzed.

3 *mun-* 'create; originate' is used transitively and intransitively (cf. sent. 4f).

m-cheikuma *raicha*.
his-sister   MIR

It turned out that he was her brother and that she was his sister.

7. **khu-wa-na chaid-yu-ŋas-yo,   m-cheikuma-na pa-chaid-ãi.**
he-ERG-TOP know-3P-V2:STAY-3P:IPFV his-sister-TOP   NEG-know-NEG

He knew it, but his sister did not know.

8. **pachaidãi nâ   tyudakalyona: aso ale-ŋo   uko a-cheikuma, uko**
[repet.]   and then   now today-EMPH this my-sister   this

    Simnima-khida   hiŋ-ãi   kã-lyona is-e,   a-cheikuma.
    Simnima-together   be-1s:IPFV I-TOP   be.bad-IPFV my-sister

Later [he thought]: "Now it is bad that I stay together whith this Simnima, she is my sister.

9. **aso** *pheri* **kaŋa khat-ãi Wabuma-di,   riŋa nâ   Wabuma-di waŋ-khata.**
now again   I   go-1s:IPFV (ritual.place)-hiLOC say   and   Wabuma-hiLOC climb-V2:GO.

I will go up to Wabuma," he said, and he climbed up to Wabuma.

10. **tyu-khi   m-nicho   chit-yi-dyo   nâ   waŋ-khata, waŋkhata dha-ni.**
that-loLOC   his-y.sibling leave-3P-V2:PUT:3P   and   climb-V2:GO [repet.]   up-ALL

He left his younger sibling down there and went up.

11. **dha-ni waŋa-hema de tira   *bhane*?**
up-ALL climb-after what became   QUOTE

After he went up - what happened then?

Simnima sends animals as go-betweens

12. **huilo tyiko m-nicho   Simnima-na   sikiwa-roloho-ci-wa   pa-kaita.**
down that   his-y.sibling Simnima-TOP   (rit.:wild.animals)-ns-ERG   3ns>3-tend

Below the wild animals tended for his little sister Simnima.

13. **sikiwa-rolohociwa pakaita nâ   tyiko târuni tira,   bhaipa tira   *ni*.**
[repet.]   and that   maid become big   become EVI

She grew up to be a young woman, she became big.

14. **khu-mo m-tõ-da   saŋa   mtõda saŋa-hema huilo-ka chuid-yi-ci.**
s/he-GEN her-head-LOC come.up [repet.]   -after below-ABL send-3P-ns

When she was at a marriageable age, she sent [messengers] from below.

15. **huiloka chuidyici nâ: aso thau-di   uko Wabuma-di Salapa hiŋ-e, Rikoppa.**
[repet.]   and now place-hiLOC this Wabuma-hiLOC Salapa be-IPFV (name)

She sent them: "Up in a place, at Wabuma, lives Salapa Rikoppa.

16. aso s o   thala uko-*lai phakai* mui-si   khai-ma ta-cap-i-ne,   donipaya
    now who PART   this-DAT court   make-PURP go-INF   2-can-1/2pS-IPFV [kutumba]

    phakai mu-ma   so-pa-wa   ta-cap-u-m-ne?
    court   make-INF   who-NML-ERG 2-can-3P-1/2pA-IPFV

    Which of you can go to court him? Who of you can court the *kutumba*?

17. ta-cap-u-m-ne-ko-*lai*   *mohar*-mo *pati* woi-na-n-e,   ruŋma-pana,
    2-can-3P-1/2pA-IPFV-NML-DAT mohar-GEN piece? put.on-1>2-2p-IPFV QUOTE-TEMP

    To him who can I shall give a mohar [as reward]," she said.

18. tyiko totimi-wasa: cam-ma-na   kaŋa cap-ãi,   wa-kuya   yuŋ-ma
    that totimi-bird   can-INF-TOP I   can-1s:IPFV water-inside stay-INF

    pa-cap-n-ãi,   riŋa-pana,
    NEG-can-NEG-1s:IPFV say-TEMP

    The totimi-bird said: "I can, but I cannot stay under water."

19. cipuŋka-wa bo: kaŋa wa-kuya   waŋ-ãi,   kaŋa cap-ãi   uko Salapa-*lai*
    crab-ERG   PART I   water-inside enter-1s:IPFV I   can-1s:IPFV this Salapa-DAT

    lai-ma,   ruŋmanâ riŋa-pana,
    bring.out-INF QUOTE   say-TEMP

    The crab said: "I go into the water, I can bring out Salapa."

20. *lo*.thala, mi-riŋa nâ   Salapa-*lai* m-dei-si   m-khum-si   *phakai*
    alright   3pS-say and Salapa-DAT his-make.appear-PURP his-wake-PURP court

    mu-si   mi-khata.
    make-PURP 3pS-go

    "Alright," they said and they went in order to make Salapa appear, to wake him up, to make
    courtship.

21. mikhata   nâ   dhalo tare-wasa wa-kuya   wõ-ma pa-cap-ãi-ko, — wasa dei
    [repet.] and up   tare-bird   water-inside enter-INF NEG-can-NEG-NML bird never

    wa-kuya waŋa-kona — luŋto-dhõda yõs-ãica.
    water-in enter-PART   stone-on   rest-REFL

    They went, and up there the tare-bird (=totemi) could not go into the water, — birds never go
    under water, do they? — he rested on a stone.

22. luŋtodhõda yõsãica tyudaka cipumkawa waŋa wa-kuya-ni,
    [repet.]   then   crab   enter water-in-EMPH

    Then the crab went into the water

23. cipumkawa waŋa nâ tyiko cipumkawa chik-yu-ko *raicha*.
    [repet.]   and that crab   pinch-3P-NML REP

    The crab went into the water and pinched him.

24. *ekdam* **Salapa-*lai* chik-yu-pana:s o   thala uko?   de mu-si   ta-ta-i-ko,**
just   Salapa-DAT pinch-3P-TEMP who PART this   what do-PURP 2-come-1/2pS-NML

de ruŋ-si   ta-ta-i-ko?   ruŋmana
what say-PURP   2-come-1/2pS-NML QUOTE

As soon as it pinched Salapa he asked: "Who is this? What for have you come? What to say have
you come?"

25. **...*lo*   lai-ma   *paryo*, riŋa nâ   laida.**
okay emerge-INF must   say   and emerge

[He thought by himself:] "Well, I must come out," and he emerged.

26. *pakhada* **laida-pa: s o   thala uko? khainide   ruŋ-si   khona-ka ta-ta-i**
outside   emerge-TEMP who PART this   you_p   what say-PURP where-ABL 2-come-1/2pS

thala, ruŋmanâ lod-yi-ci-pana, tare-wasa pisa, tyuko totimi-wasa pisa:
PART   QUOTE   tell-3P-ns-TEMP tare-bird   speak that totimi-bird   speak

When he emerged and asked: "Who is this? What to say and where from have you come?"
the tare-bird, the totimi-bird, spoke:

27. *baba*, **kaŋa khaimo kai-nuŋ   kai-la-da   t-uŋ-ko... Niyama-i-Tatuma-i[4]**
INTJ I   your_p   your_p-name your_p-language come-1s-NML (rit.place)-loLOC

wa.timma.la-i-ka   uko Simnima pora.
water.meet.PLACE-loLOC-ABL this Simnima grow.up

"Baba, I have come in your name, in your language; down at Niyama-Tatuma, down at the place
where the waters meet, Simnima has grown up.

28. **pora-pana   khaimo kai-nuŋ   kai-la-da   kha-chuidanâ   kaika**
grow.up-TEMP your_p   your_p-name your_p-language-LOC 1P-send   and we_pe

saŋ-i-ka-ko,   ruŋmanâ
come.up-1/2pS-e-NML QUOTE

She sent us in your name, in your language, and we came up," he said.

29. **tyiko totimi wasa, cipuŋkawa, khidi   mi-khata nâ tyoso pa-loda-palyona**
that   totimi bird crab   marten 3pS-go and like.that INV-tell-TEMP

That Totimi bird, the crab and the marten went and told him like that.

Salapa gives orders to plant and sow

30. *lo*   **tyoso nakhõ m-chuŋu-choni, m-chuŋu.choni, *lo*   khata-ni.**
INTJ like.that if   REL-truth-[jingle] [repet.]   okay go-2p

"Okay, if it is really true, then go!

---

[4] *Niyama-Tatuma* (or: *-Tapkuma*) is a ritual name for the fertile lowlands (=Tarai).

31. **khatan nâ** *bhâdoure* **kepta-ni rukhuwapalheta-ni.**
[repet.] and [bushes] hew-2p stalk burn-2p

Go and hew down the bushes, burn the stalks.

32. **tyudaka wacori-wa** *ghaiya*-**ci sapaphero[5]-ci, jhara** *junelo*-**ci roda-ni,**
then digging.stick-INST wheat-ns millet-ns all (grain)-ns plant-2p

makai **rodani,** *ghaiya* **rodani.**
maize wheat

With the digging stick plant wheat, plant millet, plant maize and so on.

33. **tyudaka tyiko waruŋ(?) taro du-m-ne nâ waruŋ tims-e.**
then that next.season ? sow:3P-1/2pA-IPFV and next.season ripen-IPFV

You must sow now (?) and it will ripen in next season.

34. **tims-e-ko** *bela* **liso taida-ni khor taidani pasotaidani dharap taidani.**
ripen-IPFV-NML time glue bring-2p noose trap trap

At the time when it ripens bring glue and a noose, bring two types of traps.

35. **tyupa** *bela* **kaŋa iy-ãi, lod-yi-ci nâ chuid-yi-ci.**
that time I come.down-1s:IPFV tell-3P-ns and send-3P-ns

At that time I will come, he told them and sent them back.

36. **chuidyici-hema khu** *pheri* **waŋ-khata nâ wa-koya-ni wa-koya hiŋa.**
[repet.]-after he again enter-V2:GO and water-in-ALL water-in be

After that he went again into the water and lived in the water.

37. **tyudaka, namduŋ tyoso: oso oso ruŋa-chuŋsa-ko hiŋe hai! tyupa** *bela*
then evening like.that thus thus say-V2:SEND-NML be INTJ that time

iy-e, ruŋmanâ Simnima-*lai* pa-loda-pana...
come.down-IPFV QUOTE Simnima-DAT 3ns>3-tell-TEMP

Then in the evening they told Simnima that he had said so-and-so when he sent them back, that he would come at that [certain] time.

38. **wacori-wa** *makai* **pa-ronda, sapaphero paronda** *ghaiya* **paronda syolomaci**
digging.stick-INST maize 3ns>3-plant millet wheat (millet?)

paronda— imo i-la-da-ka syolomaci.
our our-language-LOC-ABL *syolomaci*

With the digging stick they planted maize, they planted millet, they planted wheat, they planted millet — *syolomaci* it is in our language.

39. **tyuko-ci paronda nâ timsa-laida duŋdapa.**
that-ns and ripen-V2:OUT autumn

---

5 Some of these grains are not cultivated any longer and could not be identified; *phero* is known as a type of millet.

They planted all this and it ripened in the autumn (after the monsoon).

40. **duŋdapa-na:** **aina osoko bo** **kaŋa** **lod-uŋ-chuŋs-uŋ-c-uŋ-ko,** **kaŋa aso**
autumn-TOP   well thus   PART I   tell-1s-V2:SEND-1s-ns-1s-NML   I   now

khai-ma *paryo,* **riŋa nâ** **Salapa-na laida.**
go-INF   must   say   and   Salapa-TOP emerge

In the autumn the thought: "Well, thus I said when I sent them, I must go now," and he emerged.

Salapa comes down to the earth as a boar

41. **laida**   **nâ**   **dhalo-ka dhas-ãica**   **nâ**   **rhõs-ãica** **nâ**   *pheri* **huilo-ka bokhaphopi**
[repet.]   and   above-ABL descend-REFL and   shake-REFL and   again   below-ABL termite.hill

khata-ko Salapa tyuda waŋ-khata.
go-NML   Salapa   there   climb-V2:GO

He emerged and descended from above and shook himself — he who had gone from the termite hill below, Salapa, he climbed down.

42. **dhalo-ka laida**   **nâ**   **iya-pa**   **rõbho tira.**
above-ABL emerge   and   come.down-TEMP boar   become

After emerging from above and coming down he turned into a boar.

43. **rõbho tira nâ**   **iya**   **nâ, tyo pa-taida-ŋasa-ko**   **dharap-da** *par*-ba   **la.**
[repet.]   and   come.down and   that 3ns>3-take-PERF-NML   trap-LOC   catch-LW   VB

As he came down, he was caught in the trap they had set up.

44. *parba* **la-hema, Simnima-***lai*: **osoko-osoko bo** *par*-ba   **laye-ŋase, pa-loda.**
[repet.]   -after   Simnima-DAT   such-such   PART catch-LW   VB-PERF   3ns>3-tell

After he was caught they told Simnima: "Such and such has got caught.

45. **osoko parba layeŋase paloda-pana khu-wa i-muthi**   *bâdiya,* **ira**   **syutimi,**
[repet.]   -TEMP s/he-ERG one-handfull   straw,   one   firebrand

i-*muthi*   **mudhimma, ira** *lohoro*   **baid-yu**   **ki**   **tyiko** *cot*   *par*-ba
one-handfull   ashes   one   round.stone take.along-3P SEQ   that   wound catch-LW

la-ko-da **ŋas-yu-pak-u** **ki,**
VB-NML-LOC keep-3P-V2:PUT-3P SEQ

When they told her, she took along a handfull of straw, a firebrand, a handfull of ashes and a round stone (for grinding pepper), and this she put in the wound of the captured one.

46. *lohoro* **ŋasyupaku** **mudhimma bhud-yi, tyuda syutimi-da-ka**   **mi**   **muidh-yi-**
[repet.]   ashes   pour-3P   then   firebrand-LOC-ABL   fire   blow-3P-

lais-yi	ki	tyiko	bâdiya-ni	hutip.hutip	maid-yi-pana	dhâp.dhâp	sorcha
V2:START-3PSEQ	that	straw-EMPH	(sound)	make:APPL-3P-TEMP	(sound)	man

muna.
originate

She poured the ashes, from the firebrand she blew a fire; then she blew hutiphutip! into the straw and dhapdhap! a man came into being.

[The following passage is mainly in Nepali:]
47.-48. He went through five or six reincarnations, so that he could marry his sister. Because of this we must avoid brother-sister marriage; we must only go to propose many generations away from our children, our sisters.

Naïma refuses Paruhõ

[As Nirempa's account is somewhat lengthy and in part almost identical with Jhanaman's version (see preceding text) I give the following parts only in translation:]

49. Then their child Naïma was born. 50. When Salapa and Simnima's child was born, she was crying, she was constantly crying. 51. Her mother went to fetch water, the father stroked her. 52. "Eee! my child, why do you cry? Don't cry! 53. Your mother Simnima is from one root, your father is a brother from the same root, don't cry!" he told the child. 54. When Simnima heard this, Naïma's mother heard this, she thought: "So we are brother and sister," and she went away. 55. She went away and Salapa Rikoppa went again to live up in his place. 56. The wild animals — in former times everything, even the stones spoke, even the birds spoke, even the earth spoke, the things lying around, everything spoke. —

57. Things being like that and the jungle animals looking after her, Naïma grew up, and when she was grown up, she thought: 58. "In later years my husband's family will not be satisfied. 59. They will not be satisfied, so I must learn to weave," she thought and learned to weave; she sowed cotton. 60. Then she span, she combed (the cotton), she carried out everything. 61. She made a thread and after making the thread - what was it? making the thread - she started to make a loom. 62. When she started the wind came, Kurumi - Kurumi in our language means 'wind' - the wind came from above and every day he overthrew the loom to this side and that side. 63. When he overthrew the loom, what did Naïma say? 64. "Eee! Why is somebody playing this joke on me? 65. In later years my husband's family will not be satisfied. 66. I am learning to weave and everything. 67. I am learning; my relatives will not be satisfied. 68. I am learning to make a loom, to weave, so don't play jokes on me!" Naïma said. 69. Every day the wind came and did like this.

70. Then one day he came and said: "Well, Naïma, if somebody proposes to you and courts you, would you go (with him)?" 71. "I'll go," she said. 72. "Up in the sky there lives my uncle Paru, my mother's brother, will you go with him? " 73. "I'll go," she said and they agreed like that. 74. "Allright then,when I will come at a certain day, a certain month, when we come to fetch you, have one mana rice and curry prepared; have one mana rice and black lentils prepared and keep it; we will come to fetch you, okay?" he said to her and left. 75."Alright," she said, "go".

76. He went up to Paruhõ, and when he went up to Paruhõ, what did he say? 77. "My uncle, I have spoken to a girl for you. 78. In suchand-such place down there lives Naïma-Cinima; speaking so-and-so I have courted her. 79. Now we must go to fetch her," the wind said to Paru, the nephew to his mother-brother. 80. "What is this wind saying?" (Paruho) thought. 81. "She is good-looking. I have twisted legs, my face is flat, full of saliva, snot and black dirt. 82. Does the beautiful Naïma agree to go with such a person?" he asked. 83. "Yes, she agrees, she agrees. 84. On such and such day I have told her (we will come). 85. If she does not agree, then break my left wing," Kurumi promised.

86. Then in the next season they went to fetch Naïma with elephants and music and a big parade. 87. When they came down she had actually cooked rice from one mana and prepared curry from one mana. 88. Then they came gududud! up at Barhungdãdã. 89. "Whom have they come to fetch so nicely?" Naïma thought, "it would be nice if they also came to fetch me like this." 90. Then later they arrived, the bridegroom's party remained over there. 91. Then Kurumi came and (asked) Naïma: "Naïma, did you get ready the rice and the curry?" 92. "It is ready." 93. Everything was pretty and shining; whichever she looked at was beautiful. 94. "Now, which one is the bridegroom?" she asked. 95. "Over there, he is wearing a head-dressing and rests in a hammock," wind said. 96. In all that big crowd she kept looking, looking. 97. Then she saw him! His face was flat and full of saliva and pus, his legs were twisted! 98. So Naïma said to Kurumi: "Oh, Kurumi, I see his legs are twisted, I see his face is flatnosed, I am upset! 99. Rice and curry, your food and drinks that I have prepared, eat and drink! 100. Follow your way and go," she said and went, carrying her basket; Naïma went into the forest.

101. "Well, Kurumi, I have told you, haven't I? Now I will break your left wing", (Paru) said and crack! he broke his left wing. 102. After that he carried together the rice and the curry and fed his party. 103. Then he made a thunderstorm, hail and heavy rainfalls flooded the place. 104. He urinated in three places in a hole in the tree. 105. After he went, the water, the big rivers as well as the small brooks, dried up; no water came; only sun and draught.

Naïma sends out animals in search of water

106. Naïma was almost dying without water. 107. "I am dying, so animals of the jungle, go and look for water!" she called them all. 108. "Okay," they said and all the jungle animals of different kinds put on their clothes. 109. The one called 'syolotumma' (cicada), which makes noise in the month of kartik, made a skirt and a headcloth. 110. Then the other birds and small animals also made clothes of different colours. 111. The grasshopper heard (the news) only when it was time to go. 112. Hastely he sewed a waistcoat; that one is jumping like this phuntai! today.

113. Now they went searching searching for water, but the rivers were dried up, the brooks were dried up, there was only sun and no water. 114. The cicada found one of the three places where Paru had urinated; he found a little humidity. 115. He licked a little water. 116. "Eee! he did like this," said the cipurke-bird, who saw it. 117. He saw it and they put nails into it (the cicada). 118. Then the khlawa-bird drank at one of the other places. 119. "The khlawa found something and licked it," so they pulled out khlawa's tongue and twisted it around. 120. Then the cipurke-bird found another place. 121. "Here is some, here is some," he said [nodding in the typical way of the cipurke], and he brought Naïma a little of this humidity.

Naïma gets pregnant from drinking Paruhõ's urine and gives birth to Tiger, Bear, Man and Dog

122. After they made her drink, Naïma became pregnant, her body became double. 123. After that she waited for the next season and her children were born, four brothers. 124. First Tiger was born, then Man, then Bear, then Dog was born - *syoki* means 'dog'. 125. Now Tiger and Bear were always biting their mother 126. And to make it worse, manchild was constantly crying *cya!cya!* 127. Dog, the youngest, was just lying around. 128. "This is unbearable," Naïma said to Kurumi, "Kurumi, Paruhõ's children, such-and-such, were born. 129. Go and ask what I shall do," she said and sent him.

130. He went (and reported): "My uncle, your children, four brothers, were born: Tiger, Man, Bear, and Dog. 131. Now they are biting their mother and she is half dead. What to do with them?" 132. "Naïma did not agree to go with me, they are not mine." 133. "But she says they are your's." 134. "Mine?" 135. "She says they are your's, uncle." 136. "Well then, go and tell her that Tiger, Bear and Dog must go into the mountains and bring *wasep* plants. 137. She should dry them in the sun. 138. Then let her give them milk, and after they have drunk, let her put them to sleep on the *wasep* blades. 140. Let her spread a cloth in the basket for manchild. 141. Let her warm him, wash him, rub him with oil, warm him. 142. After he drinks milk, let her put him to sleep."

The four brothers go hunting

143. When they were growing up, Tiger, Bear and Man went hunting, the Dog watched the house. 144. The mother was doing this and that, moving here and there and preparing food, rice and curry. 145. The mother used to put food for them and Tiger, when Bear and Man had gone away and come back, had eaten everything. 146. He used to send Bear and Man into the forest in order to hunt. 147. They brought wild boar, deer, ghoral; one or two they killed. 148. Tiger usually ate all the food, they were starving. 149. Now, Paru had given Man bow and arrow. 150. Man has been created as a brain-animal. 151. He became angry and said: "Mother Naïma, you have put food for us three, my brother Tiger has eaten everything. 152. We two, Bear and I, are starving. 153. Nevertheless, we two had to carry the killed animals home. 154. Talk to him; if he does not do what you tell him, and if he again treats us like this, I, Man, will use my brain to destroy him," he said to his mother. 155. "My child, don't do it, I will scold your elder brother, don't do it," she said to him. 156. "Okay, if he does not go on behaving like that, I have no objections." 157. Then one day the mother scolded (Tiger): "You act like this, my child, so Man will destroy you with his wits." 158. "I shall be destroyed?" he said, "If I scratch that Man with my nails, if I bite him, I'll make three pieces of him." 159. After that he went on acting in the same way.

160. One day Man was fed up, he sent Tiger and Bear (to chase the game). 161. "My brother," Man said (to Tiger), "today you go out there, go out there and chase them. 162. I will then kill them here. 163. I will stay here today," he said. 164. "My younger brother tells me what to do?" (Tiger) thought, and he went full of anger. 165. Then in the jungle he chased the animals. 166. (In the meantime) Man left his place and ate all the rice and curry. 167. He hung his clothes to the stump of a tree. 168. He prepared bow and arrow and climbed up in the tree and waited there. 169. When (Tiger) came, there was nothing killed, there was no food, there was nothing; Man also was not there. 170. In his anger he bit the tree. 171. Then he became tired and stretched out on his back and looked up. 172. When he looked up: "Hallo Man, will you come down or shall I come up?" 173. "Come up, brother!"

and while he was climbing up pyaccai! (Man) shot him. 174. He shot him and killed him. 175. Then he killed a chital and made Bear carry it home.

176. The mother suspected something and she asked him: "Where is your elder brother, my child?" 177. "Mother, he comes loitering on the way, he is some good-for-nothing. 178. Let's prepare and cook (this animal)," he said. 179. "No, let's talk first!" 180. "Prepare this meat, let us eat, afterwards let us talk." 181. They made their mother prepare it quickly. 182. Then she gave to the children. 183. She had no appetite, she pretended to eat from her pot. 184. Then what happened? 185. "Now we must talk," she said.

186. "Well, tomorrow let us two go over there and look," she said to them. 187. She took ash, a round stone etc, as told before, and went to revive the dead Tiger. 188. After making him alive he said: "Mother, I have been in a deep sleep, you woke me up, isn't it?" 189. "As I have told you, your younger brother Man, the clever one, outwitted you and killed you, I have made you alive," she told him. 190. "Well if it is like this, then I will not go home from today on." 191. "You go, you and Bear go!" 192. "I will be the jungle watcher from today. 193. From today, even though Man is my younger brother I will not look in his face. 194. I will be the jungle watcher, the king of the jungle; he will be the king of the village. 195. From today I will not look at him," he said.

Tiger kills Naïma and Bear eats her

196. The mother asked him again and again to come home. 197. A thought arose in the Tiger's heart: "I will kill her," he thought, and he said: "Ee, mother, there is a louse at your necklace." 198. "Take it off me then, child," she said and swattai! he broke her neck. 199. As Tiger killed his mother, a lot of blood came out. 200. From this the hitya-bird originated, that bird says hit!, it is red and yellow, yellow the female. 201. They were created in her blood and if we find them, we should kill them; but we never see them. 202. Now that the mother was dead, (Tiger) said to Bear: "Make the burial for our mother. 203. Then come up and go to the house, I will go into the jungle." 204. "Alright," Bear said and took his mother, and further down the hill he started to eat her. 205. Tiger suspected something (and asked): "Did you finish?" 206. "Her head is still showing." 207. "You finished?" 208. "Her leg is still showing." 209. "You finished?" 210. "Her head is still showing," he said. 211. "You finished?" 212. "I finished." 213. "Alright, come up then," he said, "you go over to the house now and I will go down into the jungle. 214. But let's laugh once both," (Tiger) said. 215. "Alright, brother." 216. "Will you laugh or shall I laugh?" 217. "You laugh, elder brother!" 218. "Hehe," he (Tiger) made and showed his teeth "Now you!" 219. "Hehe," he (Bear) made and the hair from the mother he had eaten was still in his mouth. 220. — Even today we can see the mother's hair in the bear's mouth! —

221. Then he (Tiger) said: "I told you to bury our mother, did you hear that I said "eat her!?" and he slapped him in the face, and by slapping he made his cheeks flat and threw the unconscious bear into the bamboo-wood. 222. After he had gone the bear became again conscious. 223. Today he lives in this bamboo-wood. 224. Now Man and Dog remained in the house. 225. "Well, Dog, Tiger killed our mother; we also got rid of Bear, now I will kill you," he said to the Dog. 226. "Please, elder brother, do not kill me! Do not kill me, elder brother! 227. I will sleep at your feet, I will eat your left overs. 228. I will announce to you if somebody comes," he said, and Man could not kill Dog. 229. Dog grew up, and no matter if it is the king or the jackal who comes, he will bark. 230. "Dog, you watch the house, I will go now to look for a girl to marry," Man said to his younger brother. 231. "Alright, elder brother," he said.

Hõcha and Nakima

232. *ekdam*   **Niyama-Tapkuma khata-ko** *raicha,* **cheikumakhõ-sa khõ-sa khata**
rigth.away (place)   go-NML   REP   sister   look-SIM look-SIM go

wa.timma-i
water.meeting.place-loLOC

Right away [Man] went to Niyama-Tapkuma, he went down to the water-meeting-place,
lookingfor a girl to marry.

233. wa-koyã-ko Nakima, Nakihõ-Dilihõ[6]-ci-mo kic-cha   kic-cheikuma *samundra* ...
water-in-NML Nakima   (snake.king)-ns-GEN   their-child their-sister   ocean

In the water there lived Nakima, child of the snake kings, in the ocean ...

234. *sun-***mo   ŋo   m-tõ, m-bulim** *sun-***mo,** *sikhip kor-***ba   maid-yo**
gold-GEN EMPH her-hair, her-body gold-GEN comb   comb-LW make-3P:IPFV

Her hair was of gold, her body was of gold, she used to comb it.

235. u-khya-ka   hõcha-wa oso chu wapdh-yo   tyiko Nakima-mo m-cha *pani*
this-levLOC-ABL Man-ERG like hand wave-3P:IPFV that Nakima-GEN her-child also

**hyalo-ka chu wapdh-yo-ko   ** *raicha.*
far-ABL   hand wave-3P:IPFV-NML REP

Whenever he waved his hand, that Nakima-child also waved her hand.

236. Nakima, khamo kap-nuŋ kap-lada   ŋo   t-uŋ-ko.
Nakima   your   your-name your-language-LOC EMPH come-1s-NML

"Nakima, I have come in your name in your language [i.e. to propose].

237. kaŋa doso mu-sa ban-ãi   nâ wa-kuya waŋ-khat-ãi?"
I   how   do-SIM come-1s:IPFV and water-in enter-V2:GO-1s:IPFV

How can I come, how can I go into the water?

238. mchuŋo.mchoni khana hõcha kaŋa-*lai   **aŋa a-nuŋ   a-la-da**
truly.truly   you   Man you-DAT my   my-name my-language-LOC

ta-ta-ko   nakhõ, a-ŋaya-da khaŋ-u nâ bana nâ ta-ban-e-chud-e.
2-come-NML if   my-face-LOClook-3P and come and 2-come-IPFV-V2:REACH-IPFV

If you Man really want to propose to me, look at my face and come, you will arrive.

239. m-ŋaya-da khaŋ-u nâ khata.
her-face-LOC look-3P and go

He looked at her face and went.

240. chuda-hemo: aŋa a-*gaũ-***di-ni   khata-c-e,** *bhando raicha* **hõcha-wa.**
reach-after   my my-village-hiLOC-ALL go-d-HORT said   REP   Man-ERG

---

6 *Naki-hõ-Dili-hõ* (snake-king-?-king): the underwater kingdom of the snakes.

After he arrived Manchild said: "Let's go up to my village."

241. **aina aŋa a-*gaũ*-i   khata-c-e, *bhando* raicha Nakima-wa.**
no   my   my-village-loLOC go-d-HORT said   REP   Nakima-ERG

"No, let's go down to my village," said Nakima.

242. **aina kaŋa wa-kuyã doso ŋal-e   nâ wa-kuyã ŋo   si-ãi.**
no   I   water-in how do-IPFV and water-in EMPH die-1sIPFV

"How can I live under water? Under water I will die.

243. **khamo kap-chala-ci-wa   kha-mi-caidh-e, de   ŋal-ãi?"**
your your-brother-ns-ERG 1P-3pS-beat-IPFV   what do-1s:IPFV

Your brothers will beat me, what shall I do?"

244. **aina, ta-caidha-ne.**
no   2-beat-NEG:IPFV

"No, they will not beat you.

245. **dhalo dilapa osoko ŋo   hiŋ-e, jhara huilo *pani*.**
above earth like EMPH be-IPFV all   below also

Like there is on earth all is also down there."

246. **huilo *pani* osoko hiŋ-e?**
below also like be-IPFV

"Below is the same?"

247. **en-eu   thala! lod-yi nâ doli-*paisa* lais-yu   ki thaŋ! ap-u   nâ**
listen-APP PART   tell-3P and doli-money take.out-3P SEQ (sound) throw-3P and

huilo-ka bodko-da   rwaiya! tira.
below-ABL bronze.pot-LOC (sound) become

"Listen now!" she told him and she took out a dolipaisa and threw it and it sounded from below from a bronze pot.

248. **khamo de de hiŋ-e? ruŋapa,**
your what what be-IPFV QUOTE

"What have you got?" she asked,

249. **aŋa-na dei   *pani* paina, ira wachinari.bebenari onom   hiŋ-e.**
mine   whatever also is.not   one (wishhing stone)   as.much be-IPFV

"I have nothing, only as much as a wishing stone."

250. ***lo*   tyoso nakhõ, *sun*-mo *darwar* hiŋ-e   a-chala-ci-mo.**
INTJ thus if   gold-GEN palace be-IPFV my-brother-ns-GEN

"Well, if it is so, my brothers have a golden palace.

251.tyiko *sun*-**mo**   *darwar*-**mosikuwa-da** *hatma*-**lo**   **lham   ma-c-e**   **nâ**
that   gold-GEN   palace-GEN   court-LOC   embrace-MAN catch   do-d-HORT   and

phuida-c-e.
jump-d-HORT

Let's embrace in the court of the golden palace, let's jump.

252.kaŋahui   khim-koyã-i   waŋ-khat-ãi.
I   down   house-in-loLOC   enter-V2:GO-1s:IPFV

I will go down into the house.

253.a-pa   a-chala   so   pa-ta-e   tyukoci-*lai***uko   wachinari.bebenari**
my-father   my-brother   who   3pS-come-IPFVthey-DAT   this   wishing.stone

ŋasa-ni *baba   bhanerajumla   hat*   **maid-an-eu!**   *bhanera***lod-yu-ko** *raicha.*
put-2p   ADDR   QUOTE   join   hand make IMPER:2p-APP   QUOTE   tell-3P-NML   REP

My father, my brother, whoever comes, put this wishing stone before them and join your hands," she told him.

254.lo   riŋa   nâ, phuida-waŋa-ci nâ *sun*-**mo** *darwar*-**da repa-paka-ci.**
okay say   and jump-V2:enter-d   and gold-GEN   palace-LOC   stand-V2:PUT-d

"Okay," he said and they jumped in and came to stand in the golden palace.

255.repapakaci-hema tyudakatyiko basuki *nag*   **cama-***lai* **laid-uŋsa-ko.**
[repet.]   -after   then   that   ?   snake   eat-DAT   emerge-PROG-NML

A huge snake was coming out to eat him.

256.m-dyo   hok-u-kas-yu   nâ: nani,   simma,   ukona hõcha *gandha* **bo**
his-mouth open-3P-V2:THROW-3P and   child:ADDR   daughter   this   man   ?   PART

ta,   ruŋ-sa *ghicro phulai*   **maid-yu nâ   lãid-uŋsa-ko.**
PART   say-SIM throat   hiss   make-3P   and come.out-PROG-NML

He opened his mouth and saying: child, I smell human flesh, he hissed his throat, coming out.

[257.-259. The following sentences are again mainly in Nepali: Man joined his hands and laid down the wishing stone. "You are tricky, Man," the snake said and kept the wishing stone (which is with the snakes till this day). Man and Nakima now lived together in the water.]

260.ira   Surlumi-Dolopa[7] tira,   sorcha tira.
one   (rit.: shaman)   became,   boy   became.

Surlumi-Dolopa was born, a boy was born.

261.tyudaka *dinai picchi***tyiko hõcha-wa** *phakai* **maid-yo: khat-ine   aso**
then   day   every   that   Man-ERG   ask   make-3P:IPFV   go-1p:HORT   now

---

7 *Dolopa rungmako khatowa, Surlumi rungmako mopa.* (Ms23) 'Dolopa means seer, Surlumi means shaman.' - According to the shaman of Nerpa, Dolopa and Surlumi, two types of shamans, where created when Naïma was pregnant. Surlumi put on a cock's feather and became shaman, Dolopa did not put on a cock's feather, he only wore the *mala* (necklace) and became a healer-shaman.

aŋa dilapa-di laid-ine,   lod-yo-ko   raicha .
my earth-hiLOC emerge-1p:HORT tell-3P:IPFV-NML REP

Every day Man urged her: "Let's go, let's go out and up to my earth."

262. khu *pani aunebhai-sakyo, abo*   tyo wachinari.bebenari khuci-wa pa-ŋasa.
     s/he also go agree -V2:PT but   that wishing.stone   they-ERG 3ns>3-keep

Finally she agreed to go, but the wishing stone, they [the snakes] kept it.

263. huilo khuci-mohubuma *raicha*, *pheri* tyiko hubuma sõ-ma   lam-yo-ko
     below they-GEN (lightning) REP   again that (lightning) bring.up-INF try-3P:IPFV-NML

     raicha Sikurimawa.
     REP   Sikurima-ERG

Below they also had a *hubuma* (lightning), Sikurima (Nakima) tried to bring up that *hubuma*.

[264.-268. They gave her everything as a dowry, animals, gold and silver, still she refused. The snake king's eldest son said: "So much we gave our sister, and still she does not go?!" Then he saw the *hubuma* and added it also to the dowry.]

269. Surlumi-Dolopa camukhi pa-ida,   dapkhewa pa-ida, syolãima pa-ida,
     (rit.: shaman)   cymbals 3ns>3-give bell   gourd

     bechu pa-ida.
     ginger

To Surlumi-Dolopa they gave cymbals, they gave a bell, they gave a gourd, they gave ginger.

270. tyudaka: uko aso dilapa-di ta-laid-e-pa,   *nati*,   khana uko
     then   this now earth-hiLOC 2-emerge-IPFV-TEMP grandson you   this

     khatõwa-yobokum khana Surlumi-Dolopa ta-tira-ko   *hunale.*
     seer-[jingle]   you (rit.: shaman) 2-become-NML will.be

"When you go up to the earth, grandson, you will be seer, you will be shaman."

271. dhalo *pheri* dilapa-di cyodum-cha-ci mi-tir-e-pa   uko dapkhewa *hallai*
     above again earth-hiLOC heir-child-ns 3pS-become-IPFV-TEMP this bell   (sound)

     ta-maid-yo,   uko camukhi ta-khrobd-yo, bechu ta-ris-yo,   uko wasim
     2-make-3P:IPFV this cymbals 2-beat-3P:IPFV ginger 2-predict-3P:IPFV this beer

     syolãima-da-ka   ta-ris-yo,   bortan ta-hel-yo,   khuku-khumbi-wa
     gourd-LOC-ABL   2-predict-3P:IPFV ?   2-shake-3P:IPFV (rit.:khukri)-INST

     yari   ta-ap-yo,[8]   ruŋmanâ pa-loda-chuŋsa nâ, khu *aune bhayo.*
     (rit.:ginger) 2-throw-3P:IPFV QUOTE   3ns>3-tell-V2:SEND and s/he went

---

8 The shaman cuts the ginger (rit.: *yari(bori)*), throws it and makes predictions from the way the cuts fall. Cf. from text Noc1.13: *yaribori mupa huini lupsapa uko kiyama riŋa, dhani lupsapa uko chiyama riŋa.* 'When he does the yaribori and it points down [i.e the cut points down] it means good, if it points up it means bad.'

When up on the earth there will be children, heirs, you will sound the bell, you will beat the cymbals, you will cut the ginger [and predict from it], you will predict with the beer from the gourd, you will shake the *bortan*, you will cut the ginger with the khukri and throw it," they told him and sent him away.

[272. in Nepali: There thus remained almost nothing down in the water; but the snakes returned the hubuma with a lightning.]

273. **uda dilapa** *tetikai* **uko** **Surlumi** *ra* **Dolopa maŋai mu-m-ne-ko.**
　　　 here earth   thus   this Surlumi and Dolopa (rite) do:3P-1p-IPFV-NML

Here on earth we shamans and seers perform the Mangai ritual.

274. **dha-ni khat-i-ne-pa** **khaba ŋo-ma maŋai,** *biha* **mu-m-ne-pa**
　　　 up-ALL go-1pi-IPFV-TEMP money beg-INF (rite) marriage do:3P-1p-IPFV-TEMP

maŋai mu-m-ne-ko.
(rite) do:3P-1p-IPFV-NML

When we go up (ritually) to beg for money, we perform the Mangai rite, when we marry, we perform the Mangai.

2. Tõwama, Khliyama, Khocilipa

narrator: Harka Bahadur Rai, Nerpa (NW-Camling)
recording and analysis: K.H.Ebert

Saphopte eats Khliyama

1. **Khocilipa-mo m-na-ci   haka-po   hiŋa-ci-ko *thyo*[1], tuŋma-ko**
   Khocilipa-GEN   his-e.sister-ns two-CL:HUM be-d-NML   was   eldest.daughter-FOC

   Tõwama *ra*   m-nicho   Khliyama.
   Tõwama   and   his/her-y.sibling Khliyama

   Khocilipa had two sisters, the elder Tõwama and the younger Khliyama.

2. **tyuko haka-po-mo kic-nicho   kic-chala   Khocilipa.**
   that   two-HUM-GEN their-y.sibling their-brother(of fem.) Khocilipa

   Khocilipa was their younger brother.

3. **tyudaka Tõwama *ra*   Khliyama Khocilipa-mo   ... kic-kuruŋpa**
   then   Tõwama   and   Khliyama Khocilipa -GEN   their-maternal.uncle

   kic-cuka   Saphopte *alik* isa-mina hiŋa *niko*.
   their-maternal.uncle Saphopte little bad-man   be   PART

   Now Tõwama and Khliyama's maternal uncle, Saphopte (the owl),[2] was a somewhat vicious
   person.

4. **nâ kic-na-ci-wa   kic-nicho-*lai*   kic-chalapa-*lai*, uko i-cuka-*lai***
   and their-elder.sister-ns-ERG their-y.sibling-DAT their-brother-DAT this our$_p$-mo.brother-DAT

   i-kuruŋpa-*lai*   mi-cit-y-ou!   pa-luda-ŋasa-ci-ko   *ni*.
   our$_p$-mat.uncle-DAT NEG-tease-3P-APP INV-tell-V2:KEEP-d-NML PART

   And the sisters kept telling their younger brother: "Do not annoy our maternal uncle!"

5. **i-lẽi-na   raichakupa-wa m-cuka-*lai*   cit-yi-lais-yi-ko   *raicha*.**
   one-day-TOP   orphan-ERG   his-mo.brother-DAT tease-3P-V2:INCH-3P-NML REP

   One day the orphan (i.e. Khocilipa) started to tease his uncle.

6. **Saphopte banauâ m-duŋse-da lhap-u nâ m-duŋse pramd-yu-khaid-yu-ko *raicha*.**
   Saphopte   come and his-throat-LOC catch-3P and his-throat claw-3P-V2:TAKE-3P-NML   REP

   Saphopte came, caught him by his throat and clawed his throat to pieces.

---

[1] The form is a calque of the Nepali perfect *-eko thyo*.
[2] The three siblings are also birds.

7. **tyudaka raichakupa set-yi-ko   *raicha*.**
   then   orphan   kill-3P-NML REP

   He killed the orphan.

8. **nâ m-na-ci-wa   kic-nicho-*lai*   pa-lam-hoda-ci-ko   *raicha*.**
   and his-e.sister-ns-ERG their-y.sibling-DAT INV-search-AMB-d-NML REP

   The sisters went around searching for their younger brother.

9. **pa-tyek-ãi-c-aina khoda*pani*.**
   INV-see-NEG-d-NEG where also

   They did not find him anywhere.

10. **tyudaka kic-kuruŋpa   Saphopte-*lai*-ŋo   pa-sena-ci-ko *raicha*.**
    then   their-mat.uncle Saphopte-DAT-EMPH INV-ask-d-NML REP

    So they asked their uncle Saphopte:

11. **a-cuk-ou,   a-chala,   ta-tek-u-m bo aina de ta-mu-m?**
    my-mo.brother-APP my-brother 2-see-3P-1/2pA PARTPARTwhat 2-do:3P-1/2pA

    pa-sena-ci-ko *raicha*.
    INV-ask-d-NML REP

    "Uncle, did you see him maybe? What did you do?" they asked.

12. **Saphopte-wa: hya   luŋto-dhuŋda hiŋ-e,   lud-yi-c-yi-ko *raicha*.**
    Saphopte-ERG across stone-on   be-IPFV tell-3P-ns-3P-NML REP

    Saphopte told them: "He is sitting over there on a rock."

13. **Tõwama *ra* Khliyama luŋto-dhuŋda pa-khaŋa-ci-palyo m-saruwa**
    Tõwama   and Khliyama stone-on   INV-look-d-TEMP   his-bone

    m-kuruwa[3] *matrei*hiŋa *ni*.
    ECHO   only be PART

    When Tõwama and Khliyama looked on the rock only his bones were left.

14. **tyudaka m-na-ci   Tõwama *ra* Khliyama-wa wabu-da wasim**
    then   his-e.sister-ns Tõwama and Khliyama-ERG gourd-LOC beer

    pa-paka-ci nâ ito saruwa pa-kupa-ci nâ pa-leta-ci-ko   *raicha*.
    INV-pour-d and onebone INV-pick.up-d and INV-reanimate-d-NML REP

    Then the sisters Tõwama and Khliyama poured beer into a gourd, picked up a bone and reanimated him, it is told.

15. **tyudakalyo kic-nicho   raichakupa-na: ims-uŋ-d-uŋ-ko   bo *raicha!***
    then   their-y.sibling orphan-TOP   sleep-1s-V2:PUT-1s-NML PARTMIR

---

3 Camling echo-compounds differ from the general South Asian pattern: a) the echo does not convey the meaning 'and such things', b) there is no fixed pattern for initial CV replacement.

ruŋ-sa   khrupsa-londa   *ni*.
say-SIM   wake-V2:UP   PART

Their little orphan brother woke up saying: "I must have fallen asleep!"

16. **khoda ta-imsa-da? i-kuruŋpa-wa   khana-*lai*-na ta-seta nâ   ta-ca-ko.**
where   2-sleep-V2:PUT our$_p$-mat.uncle-ERG you-DAT-TOP 2-kill   and 2-eat-NML

"Where did you fall asleep? Our uncle killed you and ate you.

17. **kocka bo   les-umca nâ   ta-leta-ko,   pa-luda-ci-ko *raicha*, nâ kic-nicho-*lai***
we$_{de}$ PART learn-REFL and   2-reanimate-NML   INV-tell-d-NML   REP   and their- y.sibling-DAT

khim-da   pa-tata-ci-ko   *raicha*.
house-LOC INV-bring-d-NML   REP

We found out and made you alive," they said, and then they took their brother home.

Khocilipa's 'death'

18. **khuci-*lai* ca-ma-mo kham-ma-mo [..]*dyukha*   hiŋa *niko*.**
they-DAT   eat-INF-GEN cover-INF-GEN   distress   be PART

Their food and clothing was in a miserable condition.

19. **tuŋma-da dha-pa khim hui-pa   khim chupu-da-ni uso   lam- sa   ca-sa**
village-LOC up-NML house down-NML house mortar-LOC-ALL like.this search- SIM eat-SIM

bui-sa   kic-na-ci-wa   pa-ida-ci-ko kic-nicho-*lai*.
sweep-SIM their-e.sister-ns-ERG INV-give-d-NML their.y.sibling-DAT

They went in the village from the upper houses to the lower houses in search for food, sweeping together whatever they found, and gave it to their younger brother.

20. **tyudakalyo tuŋma-da-ko   mina-ci: uko-ci khali pa-lam-e   nâ**
then   village-LOC-NML   person-ns this-ns   always INV-look.for-IPFV and

pa-ca-e;   ale-na   de-i   *pani* mi-chita-ny-ou! mi-riŋa-ko *raicha*.
INV-eat-IPFV today-TOP what-INDEF also   NEG-leave-2p-APP   3pS-say-NML REP

Then the villagers said: "These (girls) search and eat always; don't leave anything today."

21. **tyudaka i-po-wa-na: u⁴-*mana* chita-ny-ou! ruŋa uso   yen-yi nâ**
then   one-HUM-ERG-TOP one-mana leave-2p-APP   say this.like hear-3P and

u-*mana*   camacam chit-yi-ko   *raicha* chupukhuŋ-da
one-mana   rice   leave-3P-NML REP   mortar-LOC

One (woman) heard: "Leave one mana!" she left one mana rice in the mortar.

22. ***ani* tyudaka tyuko camacam pa-tata   nâ buchalu-da rõ pa-khrapsa-ko   *raicha*.**
then then   that   food   INV-bring and pot-LOC   rice INV-put.on.fire-NML REP

---

4 = *i-mana*. For free variation between *u* and *i* see Ebert (1997:10).

[The girls] took the rice and put it on the fire in a cooking pot.

23. rõ plui-ma puis-yu, tyudaka raichakupa-na m-*sikha*   la nâ daya
rice boil-INF begin-3P then   orphan-TOP   his-happiness VB and fireplace

hya-ni-ukhya-ni   *naci* mu-ma puis-yu-ko *raicha*. ...
across-ALL-over.here-ALL dance do-INF begin-3P-NML REP

The rice started to boil and the orphan in his joy started to dance around the fireplace.

24. huida-ko suŋ   khlak-u-palyo tyuko rõ-na   mobdh-yu-thod-yu-chuŋs-yu-ko
burn-NML firewood step.on-3P-TEMP that   rice-TOP spill-3P-kick-3P-V2:SEND-3P-NML

***raicha*, nâ rõ   dha-mobdha-kasa.[5]**
REP   and rice fall-spill-V2:THROW

When he stepped on a piece of burnt firewood, he kicked over the rice, and so the rice was spilled.

25. *naci*   ta-ma nâ rõ   ta-mobdh-yu, pa-luda-ci nâ kic-na-ci-wa
dance   2-do and rice 2-spill-3P   INV-tell-d and their-e.sister-ns-ERG

pa-rhaika-ci-ko *raicha*.
INV-scold-d-NML REP

"You danced and spilled the rice," his sisters said and scolded him.

26. tyudaka *pheri* ca-ma-ko lam-si   kic-na-ci   khata-ci, tyuko
then   again eat-INF-NML look.for-PURP their-e.sister-ns go-ns   that

khram-sim khram-sim khram-sim tira,   tyudaka ŋo imsa-da-ko   *raicha*.
cry-ManN   cry-ManN   cry-ManN   become then   sleep-V2:PUT-NML REP

Then the sisters went again in search of food, he was crying, crying, crying, then he fell asleep.

27. kic-na-ci   halo ta-ci-palyo kic-nicho-na   imsa-da-ko.
their-e.sister-ns later come-d-TEMP their-y.sibling-TOP sleep-V2:PUT-NML

When the sisters came back later, their brother was asleep.

28. imsadako-na i-nicho-na   i-chala-na   sya-khata-ko *raicha*,
[repet.]   -TOP our_p-y.sibling-TOP our_p-brother-TOP die-V2:GO-NML MIR

hyuŋsa-ci-ko *raicha*, nâ ŋosi   labo pa-tata-ci nâ
think-d-NML REP   and banana leaf INV-bring-d and

"Oh, our brother died", they thought, and they brought banana leaves;

29. aso i-nicho-*lai*   i-chalapa-*lai*   *silum-hâlum* maida-c-eu, ruŋa-ci nâ
now our_p-y.sibling-DAT our_p-brother-DAT funeral-ECHO make-d-APP say-d   and

ŋosi   labo-da pa-paka-ci nâ *silum-hâlum* mu-si   pa-khaida-ci.
banana leaf-LOC INV-put-d and funeral-ECHO do-PURP INV-take-d

---

[5] Concatenation of three verbs is rare in Camling; it signals a peak of the story.

"Now let's make *silum-halum* for our brother," they said and put him on the banana leaves and took him to make the funeral.

30. **silum-hâlum pa-ma-ci, tyuko ŋosi   labo karaŋ.kuruŋ! ruŋa   nâ ...**
funeral-ECHO INV-do-d   that   banana leaf (sound)   say   and

âc-chala-mo   m-saruwa wota-ŋo,   ruŋa-ci *ni*.
our_d-brother-GEN his-bone   break-EMPH say-d   PART

They made the *silum-halum*, the banana leaves went *karang-kurung!* and they said: "Our brother's bones broke."

31. **tyudaka m-romma-dhuŋdaito liblowa-mo *sano*m-cha liblowa-mo**
then   his-grave-on   one   knife-GEN   small its-child knife-GEN

m-romma-dhuŋda pa-ŋasa-da-ci.
his-grave-on   INV-keep-V2:PUT-d

On his grave they put down a small knife.

32. **tyudaŋo ŋosi-ca   *pani* pa-ŋasa-da-ci   nâ   m-na-ci   dha-khata-ci.**
there   banana-fruit   also INV-keep-V2:PUT-d and his-e.sister-ns descend-V2:GO-d

There they also put a banana, and the sisters descended.

The cannibal woman

33. **halonam-im-ma-da   khrupsa nâ m-romma-da-ka khrupsa-londa *ni*.**
later   his-sleep-INF-LOC get.up   and his-grave-LOC-ABL wake-V2:UP   PART

Later he awoke from his sleep and got up from his grave.

34. **tyudakalyo ŋosi   *ra* tyuko *sano*liblowa m-chu-wa   raŋ-u   nâ**
then   banana and that small knife   his-hand-INST take.in.hand-3P and

ŋosi   khrom-saca-sa mu *ni*.
banana bite-SIM   eat-SIM do:3P PART

Then he took the banana and the small knife in his hand and ate the banana.

35. **ŋosi khromsa casa mu-palyo, tyuda ŋosi-mo   m-leiya *pani* data   *ni*.**
[repet.]   -TEMP   there banana-GEN its-seed also appear PART

When eating the banana, the banana seed became apparent.

36. **tyudaka tyudaŋo luid-yi-pak-u   *ni*.**
then   there   stick.in.earth-3P-V2:PUT.IN-3P PART

He stuck it into the earth.

37. **ta-laid-e-khõ   laida! nakhõ uko a-liblo-wa   phophopcha**
2-come.out-IPFV-COND come.out if.not this my-knife-INST [pieces]

mai-n-e,   lud-yi*ni*;   tyuko ŋosi tyoda laida   *ni*.
make-1→2-IPFV tell-3P PART that   banana there come.out PART

"If you come out, come out! If not, I will cut you with my knife," he said; and the banana
came up.

38. **ta-por-e-khõ   pora! nakhõ uko a-liblo-wa-ŋo   phophopcha mai-n-e,**
2-grow-IPFV-COND grow if.not this my-knife-INST-EMPH [pieces]   make-1→2-IPFV

lud-yi-ko *raicha*; pora *ni*.
tell-3P-NML REP   grow PART

"If you grow, grow! If not, I will cut you with my knife," he said; it grew up.

39. **ta-tups-e-khõ   tupsa! lud-yi*ni*;   nakhõ uko a-liblo-wa-ŋo   phophopcha**
2-ripen-IPFV-COND ripen tell-3P PART if.not this my-knife-INST-EMPH [pieces]

mai-n-e,   lud-yi*ni*;   tupsa *ni*.
make-1→2-IPFV tell-3P PART ripen PART

"If you ripen, ripen! If not, I will cut you with my knife," he said, and it ripened.

40. **tyudakalyo tyuko ŋosi-mo   m-cuŋ-dhuŋdi-ŋo hiŋ-ma pusa*ni*,   ŋosi tupsa *ni*,**
then   that   banana-GEN its-top-on-EMPH   stay-INF go   PART banana ripen PART

ca-sa hiŋa-ŋasa *ni*.
eat-SIM be-V2:STAY PART

Then he [Khocilipa, the mythological bird] went to stay in the top of the banana tree ; the banana
tree bore fruit and he stayed there eating bananas.

41. **tyudakalyo ito Cakrodhomasuŋ   khop-sa ta   *ni*   tyoda.**
then   one Cakrodhoma firewood cut-SIM come PART there

Then Cakrodhoma [the cannibal] came along cutting firewood.

42. **tyuko ŋosi kaŋa-*lai* ito id-uŋ-na,   raichakup-ou! lud-yi*ni*.**
that   banana I-DAT one give-1s-PART orphan-APP tell-3P PART

"Give me one of those bananas, orphan," she said.

43. **kaŋa u-dhi   hiŋ-ãi,   khana huilo ta-hiŋ-e, dosona i-n-e   thala?**
I   this-hiLOC be-1s:IPFV you   below 2-be-IPFV how   give-1→2-IPFV PART

lud-yi *ni*.
tell-3P PART

"I sit here and you are down there, how shall I give it to you?" he asked.

44. **tyuko kap-tõ-da   ch-yu nâ khos-yi-dhas-yi-na,   lud-yi*ni*.**
that   your-hair-LOC tie-3P and hang-3P-V2:DOWN-3P-PART tell-3P PART

"Tie it to your hair and let it hang down," she said.

45. m-tõ-da   ch-yu nâ   id-yu-kolyo m-tõ-da-ka   raichakupa-*lai*-na
his-hair-LOC tie-3P and give-3P-TEMP his-hair-LOC-ABL orphan-DAT-TOP

Cakrodhoma-wa   bokha-da dhaps-yi-dhas-yi *ni*.
cannibal-ERG   earth-LOC pull-3P-V2:DOWN-3P PART

When he tied it to his hair and gave it to her, Cakrodhoma, the cannibal, pulled the orphan down by his hair.

46. tyudaka Cakrodhoma-wa   raichakupa-*lai* khur-yi nâ   m-khim-da tat-yi   *ni*.
then   Cakrodhoma -ERG orphan-DAT   carry-3P and her-house-LOC bring-3P PART

Then Cakrodhoma carried the orphan to her house.

47. Cakrodhoma-mo m-cha   mari Jhuŋma hiŋa-ko   *thyo* m-khim-da.
Cakrodhoma -GEN her-child   girl Jhungma be-NML   was her-house-LOC

In the house there was Cakrodhoma's daughter Jhungma.

48. Jhuŋm-ou!   uko raichakupa set-yi nâ   m-chu laptikho-da khos-uŋ-ŋaid-uŋ,
Jhungma-APP this orphan   kill-3P and his-hand door-LOC   hang-1s- V2:KEEP:APL-1s

m-hi   rosaluŋ-da ŋaid-uŋ-ŋaid-uŋ!
his-blood   trough-LOC keep:APL-1s-V2:KEEP:APL-1s

"Jhungma, kill this orphan, hang his hands at the door and keep his blood in the trough for me!

49. kaŋa a-chala-ci   bui-si   khat-ãi, ruŋa nâ   Cakrodhomam-chala-ci   bui-si
I   my-brother-ns call-PURP go-1s:IPFV say and Cakrodhoma   her-brother-ns call-PURP

khata *ni*.
go   PART

I will go to bring my brothers," the cannibal said and set off to fetch her brothers.

50. tyudakalyo tyuko Jhuŋma *ra*   raichakupa sor   sei ma-ci *ni*.
then   that Jh.   and orphan   louse   kill make-d PART

Jhungma and the orphan were killing lice.

51. bhaipa-ko m-tõ   hiŋa-ko *thyo* raichakupa-mo.
long-FOC   his-hair be-NML was   orphan-GEN

The orphan's hair was long.

52. raichakup-ou! uko bhaipa kap-tõ   dosonâ tira?   lud-yi *ni*.
orphan-A PP   this long   your-hair how   become tell-3P PART

"Orphan, how did your hair become so long?" she asked.

53. uko-na kebha *beli* pluidh-e-lo mu-ŋa, tyudakachupu-da
this-TOP much oil   boil-IPFV-MAN do-1s   then   mortar-LOC

a-takhlo [...] pak-uŋa, dhapala   tyuko pluidha-ko *beli* pak-uŋa nâ
my-head   put-1s   from.above that boil-NML oil   put-1s   and

dokhli-wa bhan-uŋ nâ *lamo* tira-ko, lud-yi*ni*.
pestle-INST stamp?-1s and long become-NML tell-3P PART

"I brought a lot of oil to the boil, then I put my head in a mortar and poured the boiling oil from upside and pounded with the pestle and it grew long," he said.

54. Jhuŋma-wa: *lo*.thala, kaŋa-*lai* tyisoŋo maid-uŋa, ruŋa *ni*, nâ
Jh.-ERG INTJ I-DAT like.that make-1s say PART and

**   *beli* khraps-yi *ni*, pluidh-e-lo mu *ni*.**
oil put.on.fire-3P PART boil-IPFV-MAN make:3P PART

Jhungma said: "Well then, do the same to me," and he put oil on the fire and made it boil.

55. tyudaka chupu-da Jhuŋma-*lai* kamalapa pak-u nâ dhapala *beli*-wa
then mortar-LOC Jh.-DAT upside.down put-3P and upside oil -INST

**   nad-yi nâ dokhli-wa dhip-u-set-yi *ni*.**
?-3P and pestle-INST beat-3P-V2:KILL-3P PART

Then he put Jhungma upside down in the mortar and from above he poured the oil and beat her to death with the pestle.

56. tyudaka m-chu laptikho-da khos-yu-ŋas-yi *ni*, m-hi rosaluŋ-da
then his-hand door-LOC hang-3P-V2:KEEP-3P PART his-blood trough-LOC

**   pak-u-ŋas-yi *ni*.**
put-3P-V2:KEEP-3P PART

Then he hung her hands at the door and put her blood in the trough.

57. halo Cakrodhomata *ni*; Jhuŋm-ou! lud-yi-palyo huuu! ruŋa *ni*.
later Cakrodhoma come PART Jhungma-APP tell-3P-TEMP INTJ say PART

Later when Cakrodhoma came and called "Junghma!" he answered "huuu!".

58. Jhuŋma-mo m-tei jhara raichakupa-wa khaps-yi-ŋas-yi-ko *thyo ni*.
Jhungma-GEN her-clothes all orphan-ERG cover-3P-PERF-3P-NML was PART

The orphan had put on Jhungma's clothes.

59. tyudakana tyuko Jhuŋma-mo m-sa cyo-ko-pa Cakrodhoma-*lai*-na
then that Jhungma-GEN her-flesh eat:3P-NML-TEMP Cakrodhoma- DAT-TOP

**   set-yi-lais-yi-ko raicha, nâ imsa-da *ni*.**
get.drunk-3P-V2:INCH-3P-NML REP and sleep-V2:PUT PART

When Cakrodhoma ate Jhungma's meat, she really started getting high, and then she fell asleep.

60. tyudaka raichakupa-wa owa tat-yi nâ m-micuk-da bod-yi-pod-yi *ni*.
then orphan-ERG glue bring-3P and her-eye-LOC smear:APL-3P-V2:PUT:APL-3P PART

The orphan brought glue and smeared it on her eyes.

61. tyudakalyo khõwamata nâ Jhuŋma ca-pa! Jhuŋma capa! lud-yi*ni*.
then roof come and Jhungma eat-AP [repet.] tell-3P PART

Then he climbed up on the roof and shouted: "Jhungma-eater! Jhungma-eater!"

62. **uko raichakupa-wa-na ale Jhuŋma bo ca-ma pa-id-uŋ-*ko* *raicha,* hyuŋsa *ni.***
    this orphan-ERG-TOP   todayJh.   PARTeat-INF 3>1-give-1s-NML MIR   think   PART

"The orphan gave me Jhungma to eat today!" she realized.

Creation of the landscape

63. **m-micuk tu-sa   tu-sa   khrupsa-palyo raichakule-wa mudhima, bukhleiya,**
    her-eye   rub-SIM rub-SIM wake.up-TEMP orphan-ERG   ash   potsherd

    wa-dima   asim-ŋo   *tayar* mu-ŋas-yi-ko   *thyo ni.*
    chicken-egg earlier-EMPH ready make:3P-PERF-3P-NML was PART

When she woke up, rubbing her eyes, the orphan had prepared ashes, a potsherd and an egg.

64. **Cakrodhoma-wa   raichakupa-*lai* nhai-ma   puis-yi *ni*; nhai-sa   khaid-yu**
    Cakrodhoma -ERG orphan-DAT   pursue-INF begin-3P PARTpursue-SIM go.after-3P

    khaid-yu khaid-yu.
    [repet.]

Cakrodhoma started to pursue the orphan, she went after him, pursuing him.

65. **tyudakalyo dhei-ma puis-yi-palyo mudhima-wa ap-u-chuŋs-yi   *ni.***
    then   reach-INF begin-3P-TEMP ashes-INST aim-3P-V2:SEND-3P PART

When she nearly reached him, he threw the ashes at her.

66. **tyudakalyo tyuko mudhima-na mompa tira   nâ tyuda Cakrodhoma ...**
    then   that ashes-TOP   cloud become andthere Cakrodhoma

    pa-tyok-aina *ni*,   hya-ni-ukhya-ni   tira   *ni.*
    NEG-see-NEG PART   across-ALL-over.here-ALL become PART

The ashes became a cloud, so Cakrodhoma could not see, she erred here and there.

67. ***pheri* mam-mam-sim-sim[6] ŋal-sa nhai-sa-ŋo   pusa *ni*,   *pheri* dhei-ma**
    again   grope-grope-ManN-ManNact-SIM pursue-SIM-EMPH go   PART   again   reach-INF

    riŋa-palyo   *pheri* bukhleiya-wa ap-u-chuŋs-yi   *ni* raichakupa-wa
    be.about-TEMP again   potsherd-INST aim-3P-V2:SEND-3P PARTorphan-ERG

Then, groping-groping, she followed him, and when again she nearly reached him, he threw the potsherd, the orphan did.

68. **tyuko bukhleiya khleta nâna   bhaipa rokuŋ tira   *ni.***
    that   potsherd   break and.then tall   rock become PART

As the potshed broke, it became a huge rock.

---

6 The suffix *-sim* derives manner nominals; one would expect *mam-sim mam-sim.*

69. rokuŋ-da *pani* **pram-pram-sim-sim ŋal-sa nhaid-yi (nâ..)** *ni,* *pheri* **dhei-ma**
rock-LOC also crawl-crawl-ManN-ManN act-SIM pursue-3P PART again reach-INF

puis-yi-palyo wa-dima-wa ap-u-chuŋs-yi *ni.*
begin-3P-TEMP chicken-egg-INST aim-3P-V2:SEND-3P PART

On the rock, crawling-crawling, she pursued him, and when again she nearly reached him, he threw the egg.

70. tyuko wa-dima-na khleta nâ.na *thulo* **wahui tira** *ni.*
that chicken-egg-TOP break and big river become PART

The egg broke and it became a huge river.

71. tyudakalyo hyaparhe uparhe tira-ci nâ
then across.side this.side become-d and

Now they found themselves on opposite sides.

72. raichakup-ou! dosonâ ta-londa khana? lud-yi *ni.*
orphan-APP how 2-come.out you tell-3P PART

"Orphan, how did you get out?" she asked.

73. raichakupa-wa: kaŋa-na moboruci-wa-ma-chu a-philu khord-uŋa nâ
orphan-ERG I-TOP rope-INST-EMPH my-hand my-foot tie-1s and

waŋ-uŋ-ko *thyo,* **lond-uŋa, lud-yi** *ni.*
enter-1s-NML was come.out-1s tell-3P PART

The orphan said: "I tied my hands and feet with a rope and entered. Thus I came out."

74. tyudakalyo Cakrodhoma*pani* **moboruci-wa m-chu m-philu khord-yi nâ**
then Cakrodhoma also rope-INST her-hand her-foot tie-3P and

waŋa-pana wahui-wa undh-yi-khaid-yi *ni.*
enter-TEMP river-ERG float-3P-V2:TAKE-3P PART

Then Cakrodhoma also tied her hands and feet with a rope, and when she entered, she was swept away by the river.

Khocilipa fishes a stone

75. tyudaka tyuko raichakupa wasa ŋasa tai-sa hya-ni-ukhya-ni ŋala nâ
then that orphan bird fish bring-SIM across-ALL-over.here-ALL move and

hiŋa *ni.*
live PART

The orphan moved around, catching bird and fish, and he lived there.

76. cãyu raŋ-u nâ wahui khata *ni,* **am-sa saŋa** *ni.*
net take.in.hand-3P and river go PART shoot-SIM come.up PART

He took a net and went to the river, he came up throwing [the net].

77. **demno   cãyuap-yo   temno   ira   khaine-ko   luŋto   cãyu-da**
how.much net   aim-3P:IPFV that.much one beautiful-NML stone   net-LOC

par-**ba   la-e   ni.**
catch-LW VB-IPFV PART

But whenever he threw it, he caught a beautiful stone in his net.

78. **khaŋ-e   ni,   luŋto   lais-yo   nâ   hors-yo-kas-yo   ni.**
look-IPFV PART   stone   take.out-3P:IPFV and throw-3P:IPFV-V2:THROW-3P:IPFV PART

He would look, take the stone out and throw it away.

79. **tyudaka** *pheri* **cãyu   ap-yo   ni,   pheri   tyuko   luŋto-ŋo   par-ba   la-e   ni,**
then   again   net   aim-3P:IPFV PART again   that   stone-EMPH catch-LW VB-IPFV PART

lais-yo-kas-yo   ni.
take.out-3P:IPFV-V2:THROW-3P:IPFV PART

Whenever he threw the net again, he caught that same stone, he took it out and threw it away.

80. *pheri* **ap-yo   ni   tyuko   luŋto-ŋo   par-ba   la-e   ni.**
again   aim-3P:IPFV PART that   stone-EMPH catch-LW   VB-IPFV PART

He threw again and caught the same stone.

81. **dhya   tira   nâ   tyuko   luŋto   m-*goji*-da pak-u nâ tat-yi   ni,   nâ**
wondering become   and   that   stone   his-bag-LOC put-3P and bring-3P   PART and

m-khim-da   ŋas-yi   ni,   pinne-dhuŋda   ŋas-yi   ni.
his-house-LOC keep-3P PART shelf-on   keep-3P PART

He wondered and put the stone in his bag and took it; he kept it in the house, he kept it on
the shelf.

82. **hya-ni-ukhya-ni   yõho-si   raichakupa khata-palyo tyuko luŋto**
across-ALL-over.here-ALL walk.around-PURP orphan   go-TEMP   that   stone

dha   nâ   haka-*phesa*   tira   ni.
fall   and   two-piece   become   PART

When the orphan left, the stone fell down and split into two pieces.

83. **tyudaka** **lyo ira   yaya-ma   marichalonda   ni.**
then   one child-f   girl   come.out PART

A young girl came out.

84. **tyudaka   khim   jhara   byu-ma   puis-yi ni,   rõ-khai   mu-ma   puis-yi ni,**
then   house   all   sweep-INF begin-3P PART   rice-curry make-INF begin-3P PART

jhara *kuro* **mu   nâ   pheri   luŋto   tira   nâ   hiŋa-ŋasa   ni.**
all   things make   and   again   stone   become   and   be-V2:STAY PART

She started to sweep the house, she started to cook rice and curry, she did everything and became a
stone again and remained there.

85. **raichakupa ta** *ni*; **yuŋ-kha bika-ŋasa-ko, rõ muita-ŋasa-ko** *thyoni.*
orphan   come   PART   sit-PLACE sweep-PERF-NML rice get.done-PERF-NML was PART

The orphan came back; the court was swept, the food was ready.

86. **m-selam   tyosoŋo tira** *ni* **m-suspalei [...]**
3sPOSS-next.day like.that become PART 3sPOSS-day.after.next

The next day the same happened and the next day again.

87. **i-lẽi-na   kho-ma** *paryo,* **riŋa nâ tyodaŋo khus-u-ŋas-unca** *ni* **palyo**
one-day-TOP see-INF must   say and there   hide-[u]-V2:STAY-REFL PART TEMP

tyuko luŋto-ŋo   bhoka-dadha *ni,* **khleta** *ni.*
that   stone-EMPH earth-LOC fall   PART split   PART

One day he thought: "I must watch," and when he had hidden there, the stone fell to the ground, it broke.

88. **tyudaka ira yaya-ma londa** *ni.*
then   one child-f come.out PART

A girl came out.

89. **londa bittikai! hepd-yu-lat-yi** *ni* **raichakupa-wa.**
[repet.] IDEO   embrace-3P-V2:HOLD-3P PART orphan-ERG

The orphan embraced her tightly.

90. **kaŋa-*lai* mi-lham-n-uŋ! milhamnuŋ! ase-ŋo   ta-hors-uŋ-ko,**
I-DAT   NEG-catch-NEG-1s   yesterday-EMPH 2-throw-1s-NML

achummalei-ŋo   ta-hors-uŋ-ko; denata-lhap-ãi? lud-yi *ni,*
day.before.last-EMPH 2-throw-1s-NML why 2-catch-1s:IPFV tell-3P PART

raichakupa-wa **pa-chit-aina** *ni.*
orphan-ERG   NEG-leave-NEG PART

"Don't catch me! Don't catch me! Yesterday you threw me away, the other day you threw me away. Why do you catch me now?" she said, but the orphan did not let her go.

Khocilipa sends out animals to find his sisters

91. **tyisoŋo ... khomari   pani ŋal-ma tire, hyuŋsa nâ kic-na   Tõwama** *ra*
thus   (marriage rite) also do-INF must think and their-e.sister Tõwama and

Khliyama-*lai* bui-si   kupama pa-chuida.
Khliyama-DAT bring-PURP flea   INV-send

Then he thought that he had to perform *khomari,* and they sent the flea to fetch the sisters Tõwama and Khliyama.

92. Tõwama Khliyama-ci-wa pa-bila-seta.
Tõwama   Khliyama-ns-ERG   INV-squeeze-V2:KILL

Tõwama and Khliyama squeezed it to death.

93. sobhama pa-chuida tyoko pa-bila-seta.
bedbug   INV-send   that   INV-squeeze-V2:KILL

They sent the bedbug and it was squeezed.

94. tyudaka dhya   tira   nâ wapa chuid-yu raichakupa-wa.
then   wondering become androoster send-3P orphan-ERG

Then he was wondering what to do and he sent the rooster, the orphan did.

95. wapa khata Tõwama *ra* Khliyama-*lai* bui-si   wapa-lyo kokoreko!
rooster go   Tõwama   andKhliyama-DAT bring-PURP rooster-TOP (sound)

raichakule! ruŋ-sa khata *ni*.
orphan   say-SIM go   PART

The rooster went to fetch Tõwama and Khliyama, he went crowing "kokoreko! the orphan!"

96. tyoso-pa bo   Tõwama *ra* Khliyama raichakupa-na oc-nicho   âc-chala
thus-NML PARTTõwama andKhliyama orphan-TOP   our_d-y.sibling our_d-brother

bo   thala; *lo* uko wapa-*lai* nhai-sa   nhai-sa   khaida-c-e,
PART PART INTJ this rooster-DAT pursue-SIM pursue-SIM go.after-d-IPFV

ruŋa-ci nâ tyuko wapa-*lai* nhai-sa   nhai-sa   nhai-sa   khata-ci *ni*.
say-d   and that   rooster-DAT pursue-SIM pursue-SIM pursue-SIM go-d   PART

Tõwama and Khliyama thought: "This orphan may be our brother, let's go and follow this rooster," and they went, always following the rooster.

Reconciliation

97. khataci-palyo raichakupa-mo timmari basari ruŋrisaka dum mu   raicha.
[repet.] -TEMP   orphan-GEN   (ritual language)   report make:3P REP

They went and the orphan's *rungrisaka* (the long-life-ceremony) was performed.

98. nâ *lo*.thala, kaici *pani* oso rosaluŋ ma-c-e, ruŋa-ci nâ ito ito
and INTJ   we_di also so (gift)   do-d-IPFV say-d   and oneone

kic-so   pa-dhela-ci nâ kic-chala-*lai* pa-ida-ci *ni*.
their-feather INV-pull.out-d andtheir-brother-DAT INV-give-d PART

"Now let's also make *rosalung*," they said and one by one they pulled out their feathers and gave them to their brother (as a marriage gift).

99. tyudaka m-selama   *pheri* kic-na-ci   kic-khim kic-khim-da khai-ma
then   REL-next.day   again their-e.sister-ns their-house their-house-LOC go-INF

pa-tira-ci-palyo khu-wa *pani* **laŋai-thyoŋai sasi**[7]**-ŋo khurbu**
INV-become-d-TEMP he-ERG also   (basket)   (rit.) -EMPH

jharapod-yi-chuŋs-yi   *ni*.
all   put.in:APL-3P-V2:SEND-3P PART

The next day when the sisters had to go again each to her house, he put the *khurbusasi* into a basket and sent them off.

100. nâ Tõwama ra Khliyama ase-na-ni   huilo Halesi *Mahadeu thaũ*
and Tõwama and Khliyama before-TOP-EMPH below Halesi   Mahadeu place

u-dhi-pala   Towa.cuŋ[8] **rokuŋ-dhuŋda hiŋa *niko*.**
this-hiLOC-side (place name) rock-on   live PART

Before Tõwama and Khliyama lived down in Halesi, at a place (now called) Mahadeu, up here this side, on a rock called *towacung*.

101. tyudakaŋo m-na   Tõwama hui-ni Ninama-ni   waŋa *niko*,
then   her-e.sister Tõwama down-ALL (place name)-ALL climb PART

m-nicho   Khliyama dha-ni Salapa-ni   waŋa *niko*.
her-y.sibling Khliyama up-ALL (place name)-ALL climb PART

Then the elder sister Tõwama went down to the low lands (to Ninama), the younger sister Khliyama went up to the high lands (to Salapa).

---

[7] *khurbu-sasi*: dowry for sisters.
[8] The sisters are said to have lived at *towacung ~ tuwacup* in Halesi, where they invented the technique of weaving.

3. Escaping from Khowalung

narrator: Nirempa, a shaman from Khamla (SE-Camling)
recording and analysis: K.H.Ebert

1. **bhusi mi-saŋa-ko   huilo-ka Niyama-Tapkuma[1]-i-ka.**
   before 3pS-come.up-NML down-ABL (rit.place)-[jingle]-loLOC-ABL

   In the beginning they [the Kiranti brothers] came up from Niyama-Tapkuma.

2. **tyudaka dõsi saŋa-ko   Dõsiri,   m-bhusi   saŋa-ko   Bhusiri.**
   thereafter behind come.up-NML "Late.comer" REL-before come.up-NML "First.comer".

   Dosiri (the Thulung?) came up later, before him came Bhusiri (the Camling?).[2]

3. **Bhusiri-ci nochuŋ mi-tir-e-pa   wapa   sei-ma *pardaina*.**
   Bhusiri-ns shaman 3pS-become-IPFV-TEMP chicken kill-INF must:not

   When the Bhusiri become shaman, they must not kill chicken.

4. **Dõsiri-ci bijuwa nochuŋ mi-tir-e-pa   wapa   pa-set-e   nâ**
   Dõsiri-ns shaman shaman 3pS-become-IPFV-TEMP chicken 3ns>3-kill-IPFV and

   kyarkaŋcõ-di   bhog   pa-id-e   *ni*,   dhani Wabuma[3]-di mi-khat-e-pa.
   (rit.:ladder)-hiLOC sacrifice 3ns>3-give-IPFV PART up   (place)-hiLOC 3pS-go-IPFV

   When the Dosiri become shaman, they do kill chicken and sacrifice them up on the ritual ladder when they go up to Wabuma.

5. **huilo-ka-na de — Khowaluŋ[4]-i, Bhusiri-ci Khowa-la-i-ka   mi-laida-khata-**
   down-ABL-TOP what (rit.place)-loLOC Bhusiri-ns Khowa-MED-loLOC-ABL 3pS-get.out-V2:GO-

   palyona, dõsi saŋa-ko   de lod-yu:
   TEMP   behind come.up-NML what tell-3P:

   From below down at Khowalung — when Bhusiri ascended from the Khowa side below, the one who came up later, what did he say:

6. **aina, khana doso ŋala-lo ta-laida a-woini-ou! lod-yu-pana,**
   INTJ you how do-MAN 2-get.out my-friend-APP tell-3P-when

   "What did you do to get out, my friend?" he asked.

---

[1] *Niyama:* the fertile lowlands, origin of the female ancestors.
[2] There is considerable confusion as to the order in which the Rai subgroups escaped from Khowalung (cf. Allen 1976:144-151). Note that in the next text the Thulung ancestor is called *B(h)usiri.*
[3] *Wabuma*: seat of the male ancestor gods in the high mountains.
[4] *Khowa-lung*: lit. wound-stone, the place where a rock blocked the ascent of the ancestors.

7. **kaŋa   ira   a-cheikuma   hiŋa-ko,   tyukom sip-uŋ-set-uŋ   ki   uda   bhog   id-uŋ   ki**
   I   one   my-sister   exist-NML, that-NML cut-1s-V2:KILL-1s   SEQ   here sacrifice give-1s SEQ

   laid-uŋ-ko,   ruŋmanâ   lod-yu   dõsi   ka-sõ-lai;
   get.out-1s-NML   QUOTE   tell-3P   behind AP-come.up-DAT

   "I had a sister, I cut her up and offered her here, thus I got out," he told the one who came later.

8. *tara* **khu-lyona   tyosoŋo laida-khata-ko.**
   but   he-TOP   like.this get.out-V2:GO-NML

   But he had got out just like this.[5]

9. **tyuko   dõsi   ka-sõ-mo-na   ira   m-cheikuma *raicha*-pana, tyuko**
   that   behind AP-come.up-GEN-TOP   one   his-sister   REP-TEMP   that

   m-cheikuma   set-yi-nyo   ruŋmanâ   tyoso   lod-yu-ko *raicha*.
   his-sister   kill-3P-OPT:3P QUOTE   like.this tell-3P-NML REP

   As the Latecomer had a sister, (the other one) thought: let him kill his sister.

10. **set-yi-ko *hunale* dõsi   saŋekopa   tyuko bhog   id-yo   nâ   saŋ-e.**
    kill-3P-NML because   behind come.up.NML that   sacrifice give-3P:IPFV and come.up-IPFV

    Because he killed her, the Latecomer does this sacrifice when he (ritually) comes up.

11. **bhusi-kotyoso-ŋo   laida-khata   nâ   khuci-wa pa-set-yi-nyo   *ni*, tyo   dhol-*lai***
    first-NML   like.this   get.up-V2:GO and they-ERG NEG-kill-3P-OPT:3P PART that drum-DAT

    hipa   pa-id-yi-nyo   *ni*.
    blood   NEG-give-3P-OPT:3P PART

    The first one got out like this, and he should not kill, he should not give blood to the drum.

12. **tyoso   tira-ko.**
    like.this become-NML

    This is how it began.

---

[5] The one who got out first is said to have offered a bird.

4. The quarreling ancestors: Wachappa Busiri

narrator: Lal Bahadur Rai, from Bamrang (NW-Camling)
recording and analysis: K.H.Ebert

1. **ase[1]   kai hõ-cha   kho-pa-la   mun-i-e-ko   ruŋmapana,**
   olden.times we$_{pi}$ king-child where-NML-SIDE originate-1/2pS-IPFV-NML QUOTE

   Where we Camling (we King's children) originated in olden times [you want to know?] —

2. **mbhusi[2]-na Salapa *ra* Naïma hiŋa-ci *niko*.**
   first-TOP   Salapa   and Naïma be-d   PART

   First there were Salapa and Naïma.

3. **Naïma-mo m-cha   Phromo-ma hiŋa *niko*, Phromo-mo m-cha   kaini.**
   Naïma-GEN her-child Phromo-fem. be PART Phromo-GEN her-child we$_{pi}$

   Naïma's child was Phromo(ma), Phromo's children are we.

4. **ase   Phromo-mo m-cha   so ruŋmapa Suŋpana *ni*.**
   olden.times Phromo-GEN her-child who QUOTE   Sungpana PART

   Who was Phromo's child in olden times? — It was Sungpana.

5. **Suŋpana-mo m-cha   Wachappa Busiri mi-hiŋa *niko*.**
   Sungpana-GEN her-child Wachappa Busiri 3pS-be   PART

   Sungpana's children were Wachappa and Busiri [i.e. the Camling and Thulung ancestors].

6. **khoda mi-tira   *niko* Tharuhõ-Bajuhõ[3]-da *ni*.**
   where 3pS-become PART   (rit.:Tarai)-LOC   PART

   Where they were born? — Down in the Tarai.

7. **jhara Tharuhõ-Bajuhõ-*dekhi* mi-ras-umca *ni*   mi-pharaka *ni*.**
   all   (rit.:Tarai)-from   3pS-divide-REFL PART 3pS-separate PART

   They all [the Kiranti brothers] divided and separated in the Tarai.

8. **nâ, Salapa Naïma-wa doso-mu-sa kai hõ-cha   muni[4] *niko* ruŋmapa,**
   INTJ Salapa Naïma-ERG how-do-SIM we$_{pi}$ chief-child create PART QUOTE

   Well, how Salapa and Naïma created us Camling?

---

[1] *ase* 'yesterday, in olden times'.
[2] *mbhusi* (also *mbusi*) is a relational form with the 3rd person possessive prefix *m-*. I gloss it here as one word.
[3] *Tharu-hõ-Baju-hõ* (Tharu-king + jingle) is a ritual name for the Tarai.
[4] *mun-* 'originate; create; come/bring into being' is used as intransitive and transitive verb. The past intrans. is normally *muna*.

9. oko haikhama*paila* **muni,   haikhama-daruŋkhama bo muni-ko** *raichani.*
this earth   first   originate   earth-LOC   termite   PARToriginate-NML REP   PART

First the earth originated, and on the earth a termite originated.

10. *ani* **ruŋkhama-wa bokhaphopi muni,   bokhaphopi-dekhi kai Roduŋ[5]-hõ-cha**
the   termite-ERG   termite. hill   originate   termite.hill-from   we$_{pi}$ Rodung-king-child

muni   niko.
originate   PART

The termite made a termite hill, and from the termite hill we Camling originated.

11. **tyoso mu-sa   jhara.maiya** *car-bhai*   **mi-hiŋa** *niko*: **Tharu, Khambu, Limbu,**
thus   do-SIM   all.together   four-brother   3pS-be   PART   Tharu   Khambu   Limbu

kai oko Camliŋ Wachappa *cahi* **m-*santan-ni*   m-cyodum-ci.**
we$_{pi}$ this Camling Wachappa   FOC   his-descendant-EMPH his-descendant-ns

There were four brothers alltogether: Tharu, Khambu, Limbu, and we the Camling, Wachappa's heirs, his descendants.

12. **ase   Tharuhõ-Bajuhõ-*dekhi* saŋ-i   niko.**
olden.times   (rit.:Tarai)-from   come up-1/2pS PART

In olden times we came up from Tharuhõ-Bajuhõ, from the Tarai.

13. **nâ Tharuhõ-Bajuhõ-da-ka pu-sa   wailuŋ   tom-sa saŋ-i   niko.**
and   (rit.:Tarai)-LOC-ABL   walk-SIM obstacle   see-SIM come.up-1/2pS PART

We came up from Tharuhõ-Bajuhõ, walking and encountering obstacles.

14. **nâ   ase   uko Diktel-ko Yapsuŋma-da   ta-i   niko.**
and   olden.times   this Diktel-NML Yapsungma-LOC   come-pS   PART

Finally we reached Diktel Yapsungma .

15. **nâ   oda-ko   cari**[6] **sol-sa   buto sol-sa   imo Wachappa i-chappa**
and   here-ATTR *cari*   clear-SIM   shrub clear-SIM   our Wachappa   our$_{pi}$-grandfather

hiŋa *niko.*
live PART

Here our Wachappa, our ancestor, cleared a place and settled down.

16. **nâ   khu-wa oda hiŋa nâ   ruŋrisaka mu   buwariwari mu.**
and   he-ERG here live and   (ritual)   make   (ritual)   make.

He lived here and performed the *rungrisaka* and *buwariwari*.

---

[5] *Roduŋ* = Camling.
[6] *cari*: a place where the ancestors settled and where to worship; also a name for a little round stone dug up in the *cari*. Cf. from a different account: 'In the cari place we ask for the cari. If it comes out, our cari will be good, if the cari does not come out, our cari will not produce food.'(Noc4.14-15).

17. **nâ jhara kai phak-i   *niko*.**
    and all   we_{pi} separate-1/2pS PART

    [Before] we all separated.

18. **uko-na Diktel-ko Yapsuŋma-da   ta-ci-palona, Busiri[7]-wa *paila* ta-ko**
    this-TOP Diktel-NML Yapsungma-LOC come-d-TEMP Busiri-ERG first   come-NML

    hiŋa *niko*.
    be   PART

    When the two [ancestors] came to Diktel Yapsungma, Busiri came first.

19. ***anta* Busiri-wa *pani* bo   oda khaŋ-u-ko *raicha,***
    then Busiri-ERG   also PART here look-3P-NML REP

    Busiri looked for a place here, too.

20. **khu *pani* cari buto sol-yi nâ hiŋa-ko.**
    he   also *cari* shrub clear-3P and live-NML

    He also cleared a place and settled down.

21. **Wachappa-na mdosi bo   ta-ko   *raicha,* Busirimbhusi ta-ko   *raicha.***
    Wachappa-TOP later PART come-NML REP   Busiri first   come-NML REP

    Wachappa came later, Busiri came first, it is told.

22. **khu *pani* oda cari sol-ma-*lai* m-sikha la-ko *raicha***
    he   also here *cari* clear-INF-DAT his-liking feel-NML REP

    He (Wachappa) also wanted to clear a *cari* place here.

23. **Wachappa-wa khaŋ-u-palona Busiribo ta-ko   *raicha,***
    Wachappa-ERG look-3P-TEMP Busiri PART come-NML REP

    When Wachappa looked (for a place), Busiri had already arrived,

24. ***ani* oko Busiri-*lai* aso tur-ma   do   ŋal-ma thala, ruŋa nâ**
    then this Busiri-DAT now chase-INF what do-INF PART say and

    and he thought: "What can I do to chase away this Busiri?

25. **aso cari sol-ãi,   ruŋa nâ cari sol-yi buto sol-yi-ko   *raicha* ruŋapa**
    now *cari* clear-1s:IPFV say and *cari* clear-3P shrub clear-3P-NML REP QUOTE

    I will clear a *cari*," he thought, and he cleared a place for settling, he cleared the shrub.

26. **râho   *pani* tat-yi-ko *raicha.***
    wild.boar also bring-3P-NML REP

    He also brough a wild boar.

---

[7] *Busiri* is the first-comer (*mbhusi* 'first'; cf. 21).

27. râho-mo   m-khli   tat-yi   nâ   kebha mu   nâ   ŋas-yi-ko *raicha*.
    wild.boar-GEN his-feces bring-3P and lot   make and keep-3P-NML REP

He brough the boar's feces and made a big heap.

28. hemaka Busiri-*neri*   pusa-ko   *raicha*.
    after   Busiri-near   walk-NML   REP

After that we walked off to Busiri's.

29. pusa nâ: hõ-b-ou,   dosoko khana oda ta-hiŋa-ko thala.
    go   and chief-brother-APP how   you   here 2-live-NML PART

"Brother, how come you live here?

30. kaŋa-lyona huilo khim *pani* m-uŋ-ko   hiŋ-e, râho   *pani* kot-uŋ-ko
    I-TOP   below house also make-1s-NML be-IPFV wild.boar also domesticate-1s-NML

    hiŋ-e.
    be-IPFV

It is me who has built a house below, I have also domesticated the boar.

31. lo, oda-na is-e,   oko-na aŋa bo.
    INTJ here-TOP bad-IPFV   this-TOP mine PART

Well, here it is bad for you, this is mine!

32. khana khoda ta-pus-e-ko   pusa! lud-yi-ko *raicha*.
    you   where 2-walk-IPFV-NML walk   tell-3P-NML REP

Go wherever you want to go!" he told him.

33. ludyi-pana Busiri lud-yi-ko *raicha:* delo, kaŋa bo   mbhusi t-uŋ-ko.
    [repet.]-TEMP Busiri tell-3P-NML REP   never I   PART first   come-1s-NML

Busiri answered: "Never; I came first.

34. aŋa a-khim   khaŋ-u-n-eu; cari sol-uŋ-ko   hiŋ-e, cari lhap-uŋ-ko hiŋ-e,
    my   my-house look-3P-2p-APP *cari* clear-1s-NML be-IPFV *cari* catch-1s-NML be-IPFV

    ruŋa-ko *raicha*.
    say-NML REP

Look at my house; I have cleared a *cari*, I have caught a *cari*," he said.

35. Wachappa: kaŋa bo   mbhusi t-uŋ-ko.
    Wachappa   I   PART first   come-1s-NML

Wachappa insisted: "I came first.

36. *lo*, aŋa kho-si   pusa, a-khim   khaŋ-u *lo*.thala.
    well mine look-PURP walk my-house look-3P INTJ

Well, let's walk to look at mine; look at my house.

37. **Busiri-*lai* dhas-yi-ko** *raicha.*
    Busiri-DAT bring.down-3P-NML REP

    He took Busiri down.

38. **dhas-yinâ khaŋ-u-ko** *raicha.*
    [repet.] and look-3P-NML REP

    He looked.

39. **râho-mo m-khli** *pani* **khõ-maid-yi-ko** *raicha.*
    wild.boar-GEN his-feces also see-CAUS-3P-NML REP

    He [Wachappa] showed him also the boar's feces.

40. **Busiri-mo m-kuŋ** **pa-lyok-aina-ko** *raicha.*
    Busiri-GEN his-tooth/heart NEG-arrange-NEG-NML REP

    Busiri did not agree.

41. **aina kaŋa-õ mbhusi t-uŋ-ko, ruŋa-pa**
    no I-EMPH first come-1s-NML say-TEMP

    "No, it is me who came first," he insisted.

42. **lo, tyoso nakhoaso kaici deno khya-c-e.**
    INTJ like.that if now we$_d$ why quarrel-d-IPFV

    "If it is so, why do we quarrel.

43. **mi-khya-c-e!**
    NEG-quarrel-d-HORT

    Let's not quarrel!

44. **ninama *ra* haikhama-*lai* sena-c-e thala aso so mbhusi ta-ci-ko** *raicha;*
    sky and earth-DAT ask-d-HORT PART now who first come-d-NML REP

    ninama *ra* haikhama-*lai* sena-c-e, ruŋa-pa,
    sky and earth-DAT ask-d-HORT say-NML

    Let's ask the sky and the earth as to who came first; let's ask the sky and the earth."

45. ***lou*.thala, riŋa nâ Busiri** *pani* **kosa-ko** *raicha.*
    INTJ say and Busiri also agree-NML REP

    "Okay," he said, Busiri agreed.

46. **hemaka Wachappa-na kholi-da pusanâ ito halace wasa-mo m-cha**
    after Wachappa-TOP jungle-LOC walk and one woodcutterbird-GEN his-child

    tat-yi-ko *raicha.*
    bring-3P-NML REP

    After that Wachappa walked into the jungle and brought a young woodcutter .

47. **haikhama-da** *khopi* **mu** **nâ** **tyodaŋo** **pak-u nâ** **ŋas-yi-ko** *raicha.*
earth-LOC   hole   make   and   there   put-3P and   keep-3P-NML   REP

He made a hole in the ground and put and kept it it in there.

48. **gope-rukhma-mo borcha** **maid-umca-ko** *raicha* **nâ** **tyodaŋo** **wa**
gope-bamboo-GEN pillar   make-REFL-NML   REP   and   there   water

pak-u-ko *raicha.*
put.in-3P-NML REP

He made a bamboo pillar and there he put water.

49. **wa paku nâ** **ŋas-yi-hemaka** **Busiri-***lai* **lud-yi-ko** *raicha:* **hõ-b-ou**
[repet.]   and   keep-3P-after   Busiri-DAT   tell-3P-NML   REP   chief-brother-APP

khana ninama-*lai pani* **howa maid-yu** **haikhama-***lai pani* **howa lud-yi**
you   sky-DAT   also prayer make:APPL-3P   earth-DAT   also   prayer tell-3P

thala, lud-yi-ko *raicha.*
PART   tell-3P-NML   REP

After he put water into it, he said to Busiri: "Brother, make a prayer to the sky and make also a prayer to the earth," he told him.

50. *ani* **Busiri khrupsa nâ** **ninama-***lai* **howa lud-yi haikhama-***lai* **howa lud-yi-palona**
then Busiri stand   and   sky-DAT   prayer tell-3P earth-DAT   prayer tell-3P-TEMP

ninama-*dekhi***-na wa** **phrurbuma tayar-tayar** **mu-ko** *raicha.*
sky-from-TOP   water ?   ready-ready   make:3P-NML REP

So Busiri got up and when he said a prayer to the sky and said a prayer to the earth, the water that [Wachappa] had made ready before came down from the sky..

51. *anta* **Wachappa-wa: aina hõ-ou,** **aso kha-mo-na tyonno-õ** **kuneu;**
then Wachappa-ERG   INTJ chief-APP   now you-GEN-TOP this much-EMPH PART

kaŋa ruŋ-ãi, **ruŋa nâ** **haikhama ninama-***lai* **howa lud-yi-ko** *raicha.*
I   speak-1s:IPFV say   and   earth   sky-DAT   prayer tell-3P-NML REP

Wachappa said: Well, brother, this much was your part: now I shall speak," and he prayed to the earth and to the sky.

52. **howa lud-yi-palona wasa-mo m-cha-***neri* **phunda-ko** *raicha.*
prayer tell-3P-TEMP   bird-GEN   his-child-near jump-NML   REP

When he prayed, he jumped near the little bird.

53. **tyoko bela wasa-mo m-cha** **cyacya! ruŋa nâ** **prata** *ni.*
that   time bird-GEN   his-child   (sound) say   and   cry   PART

Just then the little bird squieked *cyacya!*

54. **ta-en-yu hõ-ou?** **ruŋa-pa**
2-hear-3P chief-APP say-TEMP

"Do you hear, brother?" he asked.

55. **ninama   howa lud-yi-palona tyoko ase   pak-u-ŋas-yi-ko   wa-borcha**
sky   prayer tell-3P-TEMP   that   before put.in-3P-V2:KEEP-3P-NML water-pillar

hallai **maid-yu-palona: ta-khaŋ-o   hõ-ou!**
shake make:APPL-3P -TEMP 2-look-3P:IPFV chief-APP

When he prayed to the sky, and when he shook that water-pillar had prepared before, he said: "Do you see, brother?"

56. **ho, khaŋ-uŋa, riŋa nâ   Busiri.**
yes see-1s:PT   say and Busiri

"Yes, I saw it," said Busiri.

57. **oda amka Wachappa i-chappa   cari lhap-u *ni*   hiŋa *niko*.**
here our_pe Wachappa our-grandfather *cari* catch-3P PART live PART

So our Wachappa, our ancestor, occupied a *cari* here and lived here.

Camling woman at the hearth

5. Ajagut, the flying shaman

narrator: Dipama[1], from Nerpa (NW-Camling)
recording and analysis: K.H.Ebert

song: **puhaŋma sa-õ,   puhaŋ ruŋ-ou; nyauma   sa-õ,   nyau   riŋ-ou.**[2]
(bird)   meat-EMPH, (sound) say-APP (cat)   meat-EMPH (sound) say-APP

Puhangma, say puhang! nyauma, say nyau!

1.   **tyuko Ajagut mopa-*lai* *lo*   sei-ma tire, mi-riŋa nâ   hyalo *car lambar***
that   Ajagut   shaman-DAT INTJ kill-INF must 3pS-say and   across four number

pa-puda.
INV-take

"We must kill that shaman Ajagut,"they said and took along people fromward no. 4 (Bhojpur).

2.   **palona *dholetale*-ci-*lai:lo*,   ale-na   kai-na i-sei-si-po   mi-pusa-ko**
then   drummer-ns-DAT INTJ today-TOP we$_{pi}$-TOP our$_{pi}$-kill-PURP-PART 3pS-set.out-NML

thala pa-pud-i-ŋas-i-e-ko,   ruŋa nâ   Cakhewa-da buta-da *dhol*
PART   INV-take-1p-V2:STAY-1p-IPFV-NML say   and   (place)-LOC   bush-LOC drum

***kas-era*[3] **thema**[4] ***ni*   khaibo.**
tied-CONV perform PART lot

So he [Ajagut] said to his drummers: "Today they set out in order to kill us, they will be taking us," and he tied his drum to a bush in Cakhewa (east of Diktel) and performed there.

3.   **salaruŋma-õ, nyauma-õ, nyau riŋou, puhaŋma-õ, puhaŋ riŋou! ruŋa nâ   tyuda**
[song]   say   and   there

mi[5]**-thema   *ni*   khaibo.**
3p(HON)-perform PART lot

"Sala speak! nyauma, say *nyau!* puhang bird, say *puhang!*" he sang and he performed there.

4.   **tyudakana mi-pusa *ni*   sei-si   pa-puda-ko khim-da.**
then   3pS-go   PART kill-PURP INV-take-NML house-LOC

Then they (the people fromBhojpur) went into the house where they took him in order to kill him (Ajagut).

5.   **tyudaka khaibo sa-lum-ci   khaibo ca-ma duŋ-ma: ale   uko mopa-*lai***
thereafter lot   meat-piece -ns lot   eat-INF drink-INF today this shaman-DAT

[1] *Dipama*: the mother of Dipa; cf. Nirempa, the narrator of Text 1a and 3.
[2] The animals are called by ritual names: *nyauma* 'cat'; *puhaŋma* 'hornbill'?
[3] The shaman's drum is tied to a tree and beaten by two drummers.
[4] *thema*: performance with dancing of a shaman.
[5] *mi-*: honorific plural. As a honorific marker, the normally intransitive prefix is also used in 3s>3; cf. *mi-chaidyu* in 6 (cf. 3ns>3 *pa-chaida*). The honorific plural is not applied consistently in this text.

sei-ma tire, mi-ruŋa nâ pa-ma *ni*.
kill-INF must 3pS-say and INV-do PART

Then they prepared a big piece of meat, a lot of food and drink, saying: "Today we must kill this shaman."

6. **tyuko Ajagut nochuŋ[6]mopa-wa *aghi* mi-chaid-yu   *ni*,   m-kokma-wa**
that Ajagut priest shaman-ERG earlier 3p(HON)-learn-3P PART his-grandmother-ERG

aghi   **m-chui-wa dum   pa-maida *ni*.**
earlier her-spirit-INST speech 3INV-make PART

The shaman Ajagut knew it before, his grandmother had spoken earlier through her spirit.

7. **tyudakalona m-karcharipa-ci-*lai*:   oko kaŋa-*lai* sa pa-id-uŋ   *niko***
thereafter his-shaman's.helper -ns-DAT this I-DAT meat INV-give-1s PART

khaini-wa puda-ni *ra* ŋasa-ŋasa-ni, khai-mo kaŋa c-ãi.
you_p-ERG take-2p and keep-V2:KEEP-2p you_p-GEN I eat-1s:IPFV

Then he said to his helpers: "This meat they gave to me, take it and keep it; I'll eat yours.

8. **aŋa *cahi* khainiwa pudani *ra* ŋasaŋasaneu! lud-yu-c-yu nâ *arai* maid-yu-c-yu.**
mine FOC [repet.] tell-3P-ns-3P and order make-3P-ns-3P

Take mine and keep it," he ordered them.

9. **henâ karcharipa-ci-wa mi-pud-i-c-yu nâ tyuko nyauma-mo sa puhaŋma-mosa**
so helper-ns-ERG 3p-take-3P-ns-3P and that cat-GEN meat (bird)-GEN meat

/.../ *aghi* pa-puda nâ pa-khusa-kasa *ni* ca-ma-lyo pa-ma *ni*. /.../
earlier INV-put and INV-hide-V2:THROW PART eat-INF-TOP INV-do PART

So the helpers took it, the cat meat and hornbill meat, which they had hidden earlie, and they pretended to eat.

10. **tyudakana khaibo *bhatyar* khaibo pa-ma   nâ rõ-sa   mi-id-yu-c-yu *ni*.**
thereafter lot meal lot INV-make and divide-SIM 3p-give-3P-ns-3P PART

Then they (the Bojpur people) prepared a huge meal and dealt it out.

11. **tyudaka lai pa-maida, pa-seta[7]-ko *ni*. /.../**
thereafter exit INV-do INV-kill-NML PART

Then they made him come out, they tried to kill him.

12. **khaibo thema *ni* *phurti* tyuko mopa thema *ni*, m-kokma-ci**
lot perform PART vividly that shaman [repet] his-grandmother-ns

m-chui-ci howa lod-yu-c-yu *ni*   khaibo.
her-spirit-ns prayer tell-3P-ns-3P PART lot

---

[6] *nochuŋ :* any kind of shaman, traditional priest or healer; *mopa*: shaman in the narrow sense. Both can be applied to the same person.
[7] *si-* 'die, suffer' and *set-* 'kill' are not telic without a second verb that functions as a telicizer.

He danced, he performed skilfully, that shaman, and he said prayer to his grandmother's spirits.

13. tyudakalona haloma mi-thema mithema nâ: tyuko nyauma-sa *ra*   puhaŋma-
thereafter   later   3p-perform [repet]   and   that   (cat)-meat   and   (bird)-

sa-*lai*   kã howa lod-ãi   hai! ruŋa.
meat-DAT   I   prayer tell-1s:NPT INTJ say

He danced and danced and he said: "I shall make a prayer to this *nyauma* and to *puhangma*."

14. tyudakalona: nyauma sa-õ nyau riŋou, puhaŋma sa-õ puhaŋ riŋou! oko
thereafter   [repet. of song]   this

nasupi-nahemi-wa kaŋa-*laisijiro* pa-mun-ãi   kou! ruŋa nâ risiya ma   *ni*.
jealous -[jingle]-ERG I-DAT   finish? INV-make-1s-IPFV INTJ say and chant make PART

Then he sang: "Cat, say *nyau!* bird, say *puhang!* These jealous people are going to finish me off," he spoke and chanted.

15. tyuko puhaŋma sa-na   bhyat-bhyat ŋal-sa pera nâ   pera-khata *ni*.
that   (bird)   meat-TOP (sound)   do-SIM fly and fly-V2:GO   PART

The bird(-meat) *byat-byat !* flew up and away.

16. puhaŋma, nyauma sa   ruŋmako berma sa, *thaũ*-da *ni* phu-hod-e   *ni* *jagai*
(bird)   (cat)   meat means   cat   meat place-LOC PART jump-AMB-IPFV PART alive

maid-yu nâ
make-3P and

He made the *puhangma* and the *nyauma* meat — that means cat-meat — alive by jumping up and down.

17. tyudaka *dhol* *jammai* chadeko *dhol*-ci pa-phruŋsanâ   tyudakana tyuko
thereafter drum   all   tied   drum-ns INV-loosen and thereafter   that

mui-*lai*   tyukh-ya-ko   nochuŋ-*lai* mopa-*lai*   mi-lamta *ni*.
so.and.so-DAT there-levLOC-NML priest-DAT shaman-DAT 3p-walk PART

Then they untied the drum that was tied, the drums, and he walked over to the so-and-so, to the shaman(from Bhojpur).

18. tyudakana si-ma   riŋa *ni;* m-somo   *matrai* hiŋa *niko;* tyuko *ni*
thereafter   die-INF almost PART his-heartbeat only   be PART that   PART

ban-wa   ap-u-ko.
arrow-INST shoot-3P-NML

He (that shaman from Bhojpur) nearly died; only his heartbeat was there; he (Ajagut) shot him with the arrow.

19. tyudakalona khuci mi-saŋa   *ni* Cakhewa-da-ŋo, ase-õ   ale *jasto*
thereafter   they 3p-come.up PART (place) -LOC-EMPH yesterday-EMPH today like.that

mi-thema-ko   tyudaŋo mi-ta.
3p-perform-NML there   3p-come

Then they (the Bhojpur people) came up to Cakhewa, where they had performed earlier, there they came.

20. tyudakana tyudaŋo *baba* ruŋ-sa khaibo *raksi,* bhati, dhare.bose
    thereafter there (sorry) say-SIM lot liquor rice.beer male.pig

    pa-seta nâ koi tyuko nochuŋ-*lai* cheka mai-si mi-saŋa *ni baba* ruŋ-sa.
    INV-kill and some that priest-DAT stop make-PURP 3p-come PART(sorry) say-SIM

    Saying "baba! forgive us," they brought raksi, rice beer and killed a male pig, some came up to stop the priest (Ajagut), saying "forgive us".

21. tyadakana paisa *ni* khaibo nâ tyuda *pheri* thema *ni.*
    then money PART lot and there again perform PART

    They brought a lot of money and he performed there again.

22. tyudaka kaŋa-lai-a-sei-si ta-buid-um-ko khai-mo-*lai* tyosona *jal*
    thereafter I-DAT my-kill-PURP 2-call-2pA-PART your-GEN-DAT thus jealousy

    nasupi-wa kaŋa-*lai*a-sei-si ta-buid-um-ko *raicha.*
    jealous-ERG I-DAT my-kill-PURP 2-call-pA-NML MIR

    "You have come to kill me, with much intrigue and jealousy you have come to kill me.

23. khai-mo-*lai pani tesai* mu-m-ne, ruŋa *ni,* tyuko nochuŋ khya *ni.*
    youₚ-GEN-DAT also like.that do-1pA-IPFV say PART that priest quarrel PART

    We will do the same to you now," he said, the shaman was angry.

24. tyudaka *baba* mi-ruŋa nâ *paisa,* hopto, *raksi,* bhati mi-ŋaid-i-ci *ni.*
    thereafter (sorry) 3p-say and money pork liquor rice.beer 3p-leave-3P-ns PART

    Then saying "baba" they left money, pork, raksi, rice beer.

25. tyudaka karcharipa-ci *pani: lou.*thala *baba* mi-riŋa, m-*philu*m-*philu*-da
    thereafter helper-ns also alright (sorry) 3p-say his-foot his-foot-LOC

    syam pa-maida *ni* uda uda m-philulam-sa.
    (bow) INV-make PART here here his-foot search-SIM

    Then the shaman's helpers said: "Alright now, forgivenness", and they (the people from Bojpur) bowed to his (Ajagut's) feet - searching his feet.

26. tyudaka: *lou.*thala mi-riŋa nâ tyudaŋo*dhol* chad-*era* tyudaŋo mi-thema nâ
    thereafter INTJ 3p-say and there drum tie-CONV there 3p-perform and

    Then they said: "alright" and having tied the drum they danced there.

27. tyudaka: *lo,* pusa-ni khai-nochuŋ doso tira, ruŋa *ni* khu-mo*ban*
    thereafter INTJ go-2p yourₚ-priest what become say PART he-GEN arrow

    lais-yu nâ bana.
    take.out-3P and come

    "Go now, see what became of your priest," he took out his magic arrow and returned.

Bantawa

2. Taŋwama, Khiyama, Hecchakuppa

narrator/recording: N.K.Rai
analysis: K.H.Ebert

The three siblings suffer from hunger

1. **Taŋwama Khiyama-ci-wo unco-nicha Hecchakuppa yaŋa[1] nimaŋ.**
    Tangwama Khiyama-ns-GEN their-y.sibling Hecchakuppa was REP

    Tangwama and Khiyama had a younger brother Heccakuppa.

2. **unco-papa Patisiŋga unco-mama Diluŋduŋma yaŋa nimaŋ.**
    their-father Patisüngga their-mother Dilungdungma was REP

    Their father was Patisüngga, their mother Dilungdungma.

3. **unco-papa Patisiŋga dha-t[2]-nin unco-mama Diluŋduŋma yu-t-nin khara-ci**
    their-father Patisüngga up-(t)-ALL their-mother Dilungdungma down-(t)-ALL went-d

    nimaŋ.
    REP

    Their father Patisüngga went up (North), their mother Dilungdungma went down (South).

4. **unco-cheiwa   Hecchakuppa moci-ʔa kenta-ŋa-c-u nimaŋ.**
    their-brother(of fem.) Hecchakuppa they-ERG raised-IPFV-d-3P REP

    The two of them raised their brother Hecchakuppa.

5. **moci-ʔa unco-cheiwa Hecchakuppa aŋmawa pi-yaŋ-sa kenta-ŋa-c-u nimaŋ.**
    they-ERG their-brother Hecchakuppa pine.resin give-IPFV-SIM raised-IPFV-d-3P REP

    Those two raised their brother Hecchakuppa by giving him pine resin.

6. **moci-wo unco-*makanchi* chaŋ yaŋa nimaŋ.**
    they -GEN their-stepmother also was REP

    There was also their stepmother.

7. **mosa-ʔa Hecchakuppa: di ti-ca-yaŋ? yiŋ-sa sen-u-yakt-u-ŋ-u   nimaŋ.**
    s/he-ERG Hecchakuppa what 2-eat-IPFV say-SIM asked-3P-CONTV-3P-IPFV-3P REP

    She kept asking Hecchakuppa: "What do you eat?"

---

[1] -*a* is a past marker. In order to make the glosses more readable (the past marker is often repeated two or three times in a verb form), I have not separated it, but glossed with an English past form. Many verb forms are not tense marked in Bantawa(see p. 23-24).
[2] *t* is inserted before certain case suffixes; cf. sent. 35 ff.

8. **am-na-ci-ʔa   di ti-pi-ci-ŋ-ci? yiŋ-sa sen-u-yakt-u-ŋ-u   nimaŋ.**
your-e.sister-ns -ERG   what 2-give-d-IPFV-d say-SIM asked-3P-CONTV-3P-IPFV-3P REP

What do your sisters give you?" she kept asking.

9. **dichaŋ khaŋ man-mi-de!   yiŋma kiya³ Hecchakuppa i-na-ci-ʔa**
anything see   NEG-do-AUX:IMPER QUOTE SEQ   Hecchakuppa   his-e.sister-ns -ERG

lowa-yakta-c-u   nimaŋ.
told-CONTV-d-3P   REP

"Don't reveal anything!" his sisters kept telling Hecchakuppa.

10. **ik-len-lo   Hecchakuppa-ʔa: iŋka aŋmawa iŋ-na-ci-ʔa   i-m⁴-pi-ŋaŋa,**
one-day-TOP Hecchakuppa-ERG   I   pine.resin my-e.sister-ns -ERG INV-3p-give-1s:IPFV

yiŋma khaŋ-mett-u nimaŋ.
QUOTE see-CAUS-3P   REP

One day, Hecchakuppa revealed: "My sisters give me pine resin."

11. **khunkiyalo mo i-makanchi-ʔa   mo aŋmawa-da-lo   maŋsuwa**
and.then   that his-stepmother-ERG thatpine.resin-LOC-TOP soot

pakt-u-pi   nimaŋ.
put-3P-V2:GIVE:3P REP

So his stepmother put soot into the pine resin.

12. **khunkiyalo   moko aŋmawa-lo ca-ma man-nu nimaŋ.**
and.then   that pine.resin-TOP eat-INF NEG-good REP

So that pine resin did not taste good.

13. **han Hecchakuppa-wo   cama.cam dichaŋ matniŋa nimaŋ.**
now Hecchakuppa-GEN   food   anything was.not REP

Now Hecchakuppa had nothing to eat.

14. **moci-wo ikta unco-cheŋgara yaŋa nimaŋ.**
they-GEN one their-goat   was   REP

They had a goat.

15. **mosa-ʔa di dor-u-m-ko   khusko ŋa pi-ŋ-u-ci-wo   nimaŋ.**
s/he-ERG what ask-3P-1/2pA-NML such   EMPH give:3P-IPFV-3P-ns-NML REP

It would give whatever one [we] asked.

16. **munkiyalo unco-makanchi-lo tuk-ma niŋ mia-ncin nimaŋ.**
and.then   their-stepmother-TOP sick-INF name made-REFL REP

Then their stepmother pretended to be sick.

---

³ The sequential seems unmotivated here.
⁴ For the prefixes *i-* and *m-* cf. the introduction to Rai languages, §2.3.

17. depma   depma   maŋpa-ci-ʔa dici   i-metta, chaŋ man-nu   nimaŋ.
    how.much how.much shaman-ns -ERG treatment INV-made also NEG-well REP

No matter how much treatment the shamans gave her, she still didn't get well.

18. misari   ŋa   moko-lo   sikha   mia-yakta-ŋa   nimaŋ.
    like.that EMPH that/she-TOP pretence made-CONTV-IPFV REP

Thus she continued to pretend.

19. unco-*makanchi*-ʔa: moko Hecchakuppa-wo   cheŋgara set kiya mosa-ʔa
    their-stepmother-ERG that Hecchakuppa-GEN goat   kill SEQ s/he-INST

    dici   met *bhane matrei* nu-ŋa,   yiŋa nimaŋ.
    treatment do QUOTE only   well-1s said REP

Their stepmother said: "Only if the goat of Hecchakuppa is killed and medical treatment is done with it, will I get well."

20. khunkiya moci-ʔa   mo cheŋgara i-sera   nimaŋ.
    and.then they-ERG that goat   INV-killed REP

Then they killed the goat.

21. mo sera   kiya mosa-ʔa   dici   i-metta nimaŋ.
    that killed SEQ s/he-INST treatment INV-made REP

Having killed it they made a treatment with it.

22. moko cheiwa   chekuma   unco-cheŋgara i-sera   kiya im-khawa
    that brother(ego f.) sister(ego m.) their-goat   INV-killed SEQ 3pS-wept

    nimaŋ.
    REP

The brother and the sisters killed their goat, and they wept.

23. moko sera-kiyalo   mo unco-*makanchi*-lo   nuwa-lonta-wo   isa
    that killed-TEMP   that their-stepmother-TOP got.well-V2:INCH-NML like

    cia-lott-a   nimaŋ.
    acted-V2:INCH   REP

When it was killed their stepmother acted as if she started to get better.

24. hanlo unco-camawo matniŋa nimaŋ kiya camawo lam-si   khara-ci nimaŋ,
    now   their-food was.not REP   SEQ food   seek-PURP went-d   REP

    unco-nicha   khim-da   chira-da-c-u.
    their-y.sibling   house-LOC left-V2:PUT-d-3P

Now, there wasn't anything to eat and they went to look for food, they left their little brother at home.

25. kiya munhidalo moko siŋsa-ʔa imsa.ca⁵-khara nimaŋ.
    and right.then that/he hunger-INST fell.asleep-V2:WENT REP

And right away he fell asleep because of hunger.

26. moko-lo sakuyumwa-ʔa khatt-u nimaŋ.
    that/he-TOP starvation-INST take-3P REP

He became unconcious with hunger.

The sisters bury Hecchakuppa and separate

27. moci ta-ci kiya unco-nicha khaŋa-c-u nimaŋ-hidalo: sia-khara rəchə,
    they came-d SEQ their-y.sibling saw-d-3P REP-TEMP died-V2:WENT MIR

yiŋma kiya i⁶-khumta-c-u nimaŋ.
QUOTE SEQ INV-buried-d-3P REP

When the two came and saw their younger brother they [thought that] he died, and they buried him.

28. i-ʔepma-da ikta wabuk yukta-da-c-u nimaŋ.
    his-grave-LOC one calabash keep:APPL-V2:PUT-d-3P REP

On his grave they kept a calabash for him.

29. ikta ban chaŋ yukta-da-c-u nimaŋ.
    one knife also keep:APPL-V2:PUT-d-3P REP

They also left a knife.

30. ikta ŋaksi-taŋ chaŋ litta-da-c-u nimaŋ.
    one banana-plant also planted-V2:PUT-d-3P REP

They also planted a banana-tree.

31. moci *ghəseuta*-ci-ʔa bhukta-da-c-u nimaŋ.
    they twig-ns -INST buried-V2:PUT-d-3P REP

They covered him with twigs.

32. munkiya moko tima-c-u nopta-c-u nimaŋ-hidalo moko wabuk kera nimaŋ.
    and.then that pressed-d-3P stamped-d-3P REP-TEMP that calabash broke REP

When they pressed and stamped it, the calabash broke.

33. moko wabuk kera-wo-lo: anco-cheiwa-wo i-taŋ-yiwa kera-bhowa, yiŋma
    that calabash broke-NML-TOP our_d-brother-GEN his-head-bone broke-V2:TEL QUOTE

---

⁵ *imsaca* < *ims-* 'sleep' + *ca* 'enjoy, eat' is lexicalized; three verb-compounds are practically nonexistent.
⁶ The inverse marker *i-* is optional in 3d>3; cf. *khaŋacu* 'they (d) saw him' in the same sentence and the verb forms (all with a dual actor) in the following sentences. The dual suffix disambiguates the inverse prefix.

mina-ci   niman;   moko *ghəseuta*-ci   ora-hida: anco-nicha-wo   yiwatin-ci
thought-d   REP   that   twig-ns   broke-TEMP   our_d-y.sibling-GEN   bones-ns

ora,   yinma yina-ci   niman.
broke   QUOTE said-d   REP

When that calabash broke, they thought: "Our brother's head-bone broke;" when the twigs broke, they thought: "Our younger sibling's bones broke."

34. *lu*   hanlo anco-nicha   chan   khumta-da-c-u   inkaci   chan   anco-papa-mama-ci-
INTJ   now   our_d-y.sibling   also   buried-V2:PUT-d-3P we_de   also   our_d-father-mother-ns -

wo-da   khat-ci-ne,   yinma yina-ci   niman.
GEN-LOC   go-d-OPT   QUOTE said-d   REP

"Well, now as we buried our younger sibling, let's go to where our father and mother live," they said.

35. Tanwama-ʔa: inka papa   Patisinga-du-t-nin   khat-na,   khana mama
Tangwama-ERG   I   father   Patisüngga-hiLOC-(t)-ALL go-1s   you   mother

Dilundunma-yu-t-nin   khara,   yinma i-nicha   Khiyama-lo niman.
Dilungdungma-loLOC-(t)-ALL   go:IMPER   QUOTE her-y.sibling Khiyama-TOP REP

"I go up to father Patisüngga, you go down to mother Dilungdungma!" said Tangwama to her younger sibling Khiyama.

36. Khiyama-ʔa: maʔ? maʔan!   inka papa-du-t-nin   khat-na-ne,   nana,
Khiyama-ERG   no   it.is.not   I   father-hiLOC-(t)-ALL go-1s-OPT   e.sister:ADDR

khana-nin   mama-yu-t-nin   khara-ne,   yinma   yina niman.
you-p   mother-loLOC-(t)-ALL go-OPT   QUOTE   said REP

Khiyama said: "No, I will go up to father, elder sister, may you go down to mother's place," she said.

37. moloko   khana mo-du-t-nin   ti-khat-hida   am-kopa   Samphokdiwa
if   you   that-hiLOC-(t)-ALL   2-go-TEMP   your-grandfather   Samphokdiwa

ti-nett-u   kiya mosa-ʔa   ti-ca-khat,   yinma Tanwama-ʔa   Khiyama-lo niman.
2-tease-3P   SEQ s/he-ERG   2s-eat-V2:TAKE   QUOTE Tangwama-ERG   Khiyama-TOP REP

If you go up there, you will tease your grandfather Samphokdiwa and he will eat you," Khiyama was told by Tangwama.

38. inka-ʔa   i-net-n-i-n [7]   yinma kiya Khiyama papa   Patisinga-du-t-nin   khara.
I-ERG   (NEG)-tease-NEG-3P-1s QUOTE SEQ   Khiyama   father   Patisüngga-hiLOC-(t)-ALL went

"I won't tease him," she said and Khiyama went up to father Patisüngga.

39. Tanwama   mama Dilundunma-yu-t-nin   khara niman.
Tangwama   mother Dilungdungma-loLOC-(t)-ALL went   REP

Tangwama went down to her mother Dilungdungma.

---

[7] *i*- in 1>3 negative forms (cf. *i-sin-nin* in 42); ni + u + n > nin; cf. ci + u + n > cin (84).

Samphokdiwa kills Khiyama

40. han Taŋwama   lasa-ta-hidalo   i-nicha   Khiyama-lo man-ta   nimaŋ.
now Tangwama   reached-V2:CAME-TEMP her-y.sibling Khiyama-TOP NEG-came REP

Now, when Tangwama came back [to the place where they separated], her younger sibling
Khiyama did not come.

41. khunkiya   Taŋwama   i-nicha   lam-si   dha-t-nin   khara nimaŋ.
and.then   Tangwama   her-y.sibling seek-PURP above-(t)-ALL   went   REP

So Tangwama went up in order to look for her younger sibling.

42. unco-kopa   Samphokdiwa   sen-u nimaŋ-hidalo   mosa-ʔa   i-sin-n-i-ŋ,
their-grandfather Samphokdiwa   ask-3P REP-TEMP   s/he-ERG   (NEG)-know-NEG-3P-1s

yiŋa-yakta nimaŋ.
said-CONTV REP

When she asked their grandfather Samphokdiwa, he kept saying: "I don't know!"

43. kopa-wo,   khaŋ-mett-aŋ-ne   iŋ-nicha   kha-t-nin   khara, lo-hida
grandfather-APP see-CAUS-1sP-OPT my-y.sibling where-(t)-ALL went   tell:3P-TEMP

chaŋ mosa-ʔa   khaŋ-man-met-do   nimaŋ.
also s/he-ERG   see-NEG-CAUS-AUX:3P REP

She said to him again and again: "Grandfather, please show me where my younger sibling went,"
but he still didn't show her.

44. haninmaklo mosa-ʔa: iŋka netta-ŋ-yuŋsa-ŋ   kiya co-ŋ-khatt-u-ŋ,   yiŋa nimaŋ.
little.later s/he-ERG I   teased-1s-HAB-1s   SEQ   eat:3P-1s-V2:TAKE-3P-1s said REP

A little later he said: "She used to tease me and so I ate her."

45. khunkiya   mo-lo: moko i-yiwatiŋ khada ti-bhukta-da-num[8]   he di
and.then   that/she-TOP that   her-bones where 2-buried-V2:PLACE-2p>3 or   what

ti-mia-num, yiŋma sen-u nimaŋ.
2-did-2p>3   QUOTE ask-3P REP

Then she asked: "Where did you bury her bones or what did you do?"

46. Samphokdiwa-ʔa: mo-ya   i-yiwatiŋ-ci bhukt-u-ŋ-do-ŋ-ko   yaʔa-ŋ [9]
Samphokdiwa-ERG   that-levLOC her-bones-ns bury-3P-1s-V2:PUT:3P-1s-NML be-1s

yiŋma kiya khaŋ-mett-u nimaŋ.
QUOTE SEQ see-CAUS-3P REP

Samphokdiwa said: "Over there I have buried her bones," and he showed her.

---

[8] Honorific plural: Tangwama addresses her grandfather.
[9] -ko (NML) + 'be' is probably an imitation of the Nepali perfect (-eko + 'be'); cf. also the past perfect
forms in sentences 56 and 97.

47. **Taŋwama-ʔa moko Khiyama-wo yɨwatɨŋ-ci tar-u kiya bak-ci-khuŋ-da**
Tangwama-ERG that Khiyama-GEN bones-ns take-3P SEQ pig-ns -trough-LOC

tams-u-do nimaŋ.
gather-3P-V2:PUT:3P REP

Tangwama took Khiyama's bones and gathered them in a pig trough.

48. **mo-da-ŋka-lo moko bak-ci-khuŋ-da-lo ayɨ ayɨ maŋkolen maŋkolen**
that-LOC-ABL-TOP that pig-ns -trough-LOC-TOP this.day this.day next.day next.day

li-yaŋ-sa lo haŋ-cha li-yaŋ-sa khara-ŋa nimaŋ.
become-IPFV-SIM PART king-child become-IPFV-SIM went-IPFV REP

From there in that pig trough gradually gradually a person appeared.

49. **Taŋwama-lo dak mɨa-yakta-ŋa nimaŋ.**
Tangwama-TOP loom did-CONTV-IPFV REP

Tangwama used to weave.

50. **ɨk-len-talo moko bak-ci-khuŋ-da-ŋka lonta kiya dak mɨa-lotta-ŋa nimaŋ.**
one-day-TEMP that pig-ns -trough-ABL came.out SEQ loom did-V2:INCH-IPFV REP

One day, [Khiyama] came out from that pig trough and started weaving.

51. **moko khawo-lo dak-mɨ-kaba? yɨŋma Taŋwama-ʔa kha nimaŋ-talo Khiyama-ʔa:**
that which-TOP loom-do-AP QUOTE Tangwama-ERG PART REP-TEMP Khiyama- ERG

iŋka-wo ney nana, yiŋmalo kiya yɨŋa nimaŋ.
I-NML EMPH e.sister QUOTE SEQ say REP

"Who is she, the weaver?" Tangwama asked, and Khiyama said: "It's me, elder sister!"

52. **Taŋwama-ʔa khana-lo isa .isa tɨ-cɨa tɨ-lisa? yiŋmalo nimaŋ.**
Tangwama-ERG you-TOP like.like 2-did 2-became QUOTE REP

Tangwama asked: "You, what did you do, what did you become?"

53. **iŋka-lo o *bela* imsa-ŋ kiya puwa-ŋ-lonta-ŋ-ko isa lu-ŋaŋa, yɨŋa nimaŋ.**
I-TOP this time slept-1s SEQ stood-1s-V2:UP-1s-NML like feel-IPFV:1s said REP

"I feel like one who has slept and woken up," she said.

54. **munkiyalo moci dak mɨ-yaŋ-sa yuŋa-ŋa-ci nimaŋ.**
and.then they loom do-IPFV-SIM sit-IPFV-d REP

And then they stayed there weaving.

55. **moko unco-cheiwa Hecchakuppa-lo mun *bela* puwa-lonta nimaŋ kiya**
that their-brother Hecchakuppa-TOP then time stood-V2:UP REP SEQ

ɨ-na-ci butt-u-lott-u-ci nimaŋ.
his-e.sister-ns call-3P-V2:INCH-3P-ns REP

At that time their brother Hecchakuppa woke up and started to call his sisters.

56. **i-na-ci-ʔa**   **ikta kuna-da**   **esa-da-ci**   **ikta kuna-da**   **cheisa-da-ci**
his-e.sister-ns -ERG one corner-LOC shit-V2:PUT-d one corner-LOC urinated-V2:PUT-d

      ikta kuna-da   **thukta-da-c-u** **ikta kuna-da**   **nabu chinta-da-c-u-wo**
one corner-LOC spit-V2:PUT-d-3P one corner-LOC nose strained-V2:PUT-d-3P-NML

      yaŋa nimaŋ.
was REP

His sisters had shat in one corner, urinated in one corner, spat in one corner and cleared their nose in one corner.

57. **enana!**   **yiŋ-yaŋ-sa**   **butt-u-ci nimaŋ-ta,**   **moko khi-cheppa-ci ye həw!**
oh e.sister say-IPFV-SIM call-3P-ns REP-TEMP that feces-urine-ns PART hello

      yiŋ-yaŋ-sa   **yiŋa-yaŋa nimaŋ.**
say-IPFV-SIM say-IPFV REP

Whenever he called them: "Hey, elder sister!" the stool, urine, etc. would say "hello".

58. **munkiyalo mo Hecchakuppa-ʔa**   **mo ban-ʔa**   **moko ŋaksi-taŋ: ti-pon ti-pon**
then that Hecchakuppa-ERG that knife-INST that banana-plant 2-grow 2-grow

      khaŋ-na, ti-si   **ti-si**   **ca-na, mi-yaŋ-sa hakt-u-yakt-u**   **nimaŋ.**
look-1s>2 2-bear.fruit 2-bear.fruit eat-1s>2 do-IPFV-SIM measure-3P-CONTV-3P REP

Then Hecchakuppa kept fidgeting with his knife at the banana plant: "You grow, you grow, I look after you; you bear fruit, you bear fruit, I'll eat you."

59. **munkiyalo moko ŋaksi-taŋ-lo**   **poya-lonta**   **kiya che siya-lonta**   **nimaŋ.**
and.then that banana-plant-TOP grew-V2:OUT SEQ also bore.fruit-V2:OUT REP

Then that banana plant began to grow and to bear fruit.

60. **Hecchakuppa-lo mo ŋaksi-taŋ-da**   **waŋa**   **kiya mo ŋaksi la-ca-yaŋ-sa**
Hecchakuppa-TOP that banana-plant-LOC climbed SEQ that banana plucked-V2:ATE-IPFV-SIM

      yuŋa-ŋa nimaŋ.
stayed-IPFV REP

Hecchakuppa climbed the banana plant and remained there, plucking and eating bananas.

Heccakuppa and the cannibal woman

61. **ik-len-talo Cakrondhima ta**   **kiya: Hecchakupp-o! iŋka chaŋ ŋaksi**
one-day-TEMP Cakrondhima came SEQ Hecchakuppa-APP I also banana

      pi-aŋ-ne, yiŋmalo nimaŋ.
give-1sP-OPT QUOTE REP

One day Cakrondhima (a forest demon) came and said: "Hey, Hecchakuppa, give me also a banana."

62. **Hecchakuppa-ʔa ŋaksi**   **wett-u-chokt-u**   **nimaŋ-talo oko usko**   **wa-khi**
Hecchakuppa-ERG banana throw-3P-V2:THROW-3P REP-TEMP this like.this chicken-shit

wa-khɨ   bak-khɨ   lakta-wo   ca-nɨŋ,   yɨŋma kiya man-co-do   nimaŋ.
chicken-shit pig-shit   stained-NML eat-NEG:1s QUOTE SEQ NEG-eat:3P-AUX:3P REP

When Hecchakuppa threw a banana at her she said: "This which is stained with chicken and pig shit I don't eat," and she didn't eat it.

63. am-laŋ-ʔa   bɨpt-u   kiya pɨ-aŋ-ne,   yɨŋmalo   nimaŋ.
    your-foot-INST   hold-3P   SEQ give-1sP-OPT QUOTE   REP

"Hold it with your foot and then give it to me," she said.

64. khunkiya   mosa-ʔa   ɨ-laŋ-ʔa   bɨpt-u   kiya pɨ   nimaŋ.
    and.then   s/he-ERG   his-foot-INST hold-3P   SEQ give:3P REP

So he held one with his foot and gave it to her.

65. khunkiya   chaŋ: am-laŋ-ʔa   bɨpt-u-wo   ca-nɨŋ;   am-tuppi-ʔa
    and.then   also   your-foot-INST   hold-3P-NML   eat-NEG:1s your-pigtail-INST

    chɨms-u   kiya pɨ-aŋ-ne,   yɨŋma nimaŋ.
    tie-3P   SEQ give-1s-OPT   QUOTE REP

Then she said: "I don't eat that one, which you held with your foot; tie it with your pigtail and give it to me!"

66. ɨ-tuppi-ʔa   chɨms-u   kiya pɨ   nimaŋ-talo mosa-ʔa   sar-u-dhant-u   nimaŋ.
    his-pigtail-INST tie-3P   SEQ give:3P REP-TEMP   s/he-INST pull-3P-V2:DOWN:3P   REP

When he tied it with his pigtail and gave it to her, she pulled him down.

67. munkiya   Cakrondhima-ʔa   moko khatt-u kiya ɨ-khim-da   khara nimaŋ.
    and.then Cakrondhima-ERG that take-3P SEQ her-house-LOC   went REP

Then Cakrondhima took him and went to her house.

68. ɨ-khim-da   ɨ-cha   ərəi mɨ nimaŋ.
    her-house-LOC   her-child   order do REP

In her house she gave order to her child:

69. o   Hecchakuppa ɨ-taŋ-da-wo   sit sett-u;   munhida   moko im.ca.
    this   Hecchakuppa his-head-LOC-NML   louse kill:APPL-3P thereafter that/he fall.asleep

"This Hecchakuppa, kill the lice of his head for him, after that he will fall asleep.

70. moko im.ca-wo   bela-da kɨdaŋ-ʔa   dhatt-u-ser-u   kiya ɨ-laŋ-chuk
    that fall.asleep-NML   time-LOC pestle-INST beat-3P-V2:KILL-3P   SEQ   his-foot-arm

    kɨŋs-u-do.
    hang-3P-V2:PUT:3P

When he is sleeping, beat him to death with a pestle and hang up his legs and arms.

71. ɨ-yam-sa   ŋitt-aŋ-pɨ-aŋ.
    his-body-flesh   fry:APPL-1sP-V2:GIVE-1sP

Fry his body flesh for me.

72. **i-hi** **bak-ci-khuŋ-da** **tams-u-do.**
his-blood pig-ns -trough-LOC gather-3P-V2:PUT:3P

Gather his blood in a pig vessel and keep it."

73. **munkiya Cakrondhima khara-lawa niman.**
and.then Cakrondhima went-V2:TEL REP

And then, Cakrondhima left.

74. **Hecchakuppa-ʔa mo yiŋ pakha-ya-ŋka en-u-yakt-u-ŋ-u niman.**
Hecchakuppa-ERG that word outside-levLOC-ABL hear-3P-CONTV-3P-IPFV-3P REP

Hecchakuppa kept listening to her words from outside.

75. **Hecchakuppa-wo sit Cakrondhima-wo i-cha-ʔa sett-u-ŋ-u niman-talo**
Hecchakuppa-GEN louse Cakrondhima-GEN her-child-ERG kill:for-3P-IPFV-3P REP-TEMP

moko Cakrondhima-wo cha y e imsa.ca-khara niman.
that Cakrondhima-GEN child FOC fell.asleep-V2:WENT REP

As Cakrondhima's child killed Hecchakuppa's lice, Cakrondhima's child fell asleep.

76. **Hecchakuppa-ʔa moko-lo kidaŋ-ʔa dhatt-u-ser-u niman.**
Hecchakuppa-ERG that-TOP pestle-INST beat-3P-V2:KILL-3P REP

Hecchakuppa beat her to death with the pestle.

77. **munkiya i-yam-sa ŋitt-u-pi niman.**
and.then her-body-meat fry:APPL-3P-V2:GIVE:3P REP

Then he fried her flesh for her [Cakrondhima].

78. **i-laŋ-chuk-ci kiŋs-u-do niman.**
her-foot-arm-ns hang-3P-V2:PUT:3P REP

He hung her legs and arms up.

79. **i-hi bak-ci-khuŋ-da tams-u-do niman.**
her-blood pig-ns -trough-LOC gather-3P-V2:PUT:3P REP

He kept her blood in a pig trough.

80. **hatna Cakrondhima ta kiya mo hi duŋ-u yam-sa-ci co kiya**
after.a.while Cakrondhima came SEQ that blood drink-3P body-flesh-d eat:3P SEQ

ser-u-wo *bela* i-laŋ-chuk-ci chaŋ co niman.
be.drunk-3P-NML time her-foot-arm-d also eat:3P REP

After a while Cakrondhima arrived and drank the blood, ate the pieces of meat, and when she was drunk, she even ate the legs and arms.

81. **moko Hecchakuppa-ʔa Cakrondhima-wo i-cha-wo tit-ci hums-u-dis-u**
that Hecchakuppa-ERG Cakrondhima-GEN her-child-GEN cloth-ns put.on-3P-V2:ENTER-3P

kiya khim-dhuri cok-du waŋa-khara nimaŋ.
SEQ house-roof top-hiLOC climbed-V2:WENT REP

Hecchakuppa put on the clothes of Cakrondhima's child and climbed on the top of the roof.

82. mo cok-du-ŋka mo-ko-lo: Wakalama Rotnambhekma! Wakalama Cakrondhima
that top-hiLOC-ABL that-NML-TOP (rit) cannibal(rit) (rit) Cakrondhima

Rotnambhebhe! yiŋ-yaŋ-sa para-ŋa nimaŋ.
cannibal(rit) say-IPFV-SIM shouted-IPFV REP

From the top he shouted: "Wakalama Rotnambhekma! Cannibal, Cakrondhima is a cannibal!"

83. hona oko cha khusa di yiŋ-yaŋ; khusa yiŋ-in-min-ko ye yiŋma
oh! this child like.that what say-IPFV like.that say-1/2pS/P-NEG-NML PART QUOTE

Cakrondhima-ʔa lo nimaŋ.
Cakrondhima -ERG tell:3P REP

Cakrondhima thought: "Oh, what is this child saying? - We do not speak like that," she told him.

84. iŋka iŋ-kiyaŋpa-ci chemt-u-ŋ-yaŋ-c-i-ŋ, yiŋma yiŋa-ŋa nimaŋ.
I my-maternal.uncle-ns attract-3P-1s-IPFV-ns-3P-1s QUOTE said-IPFV REP

"I am attracting my maternal uncles," he said.

85. khunkiya: Rakalama cha ka-ca-ma Cakrondhima Rotnambhebhe! yiŋma
and.then Rakalama child AP-eat-f Cakrondhima cannibal(rit) QUOTE

sumka *khepa* yiŋa nimaŋ.
three times said REP

So he shouted three times: "...Cakrondhima is a childeater, Cakrondhima is a cannibal!"

86. mo *bela* ye oko-lo iŋ-cha-lo maʔaŋ-ko ye *rəchə*, yiŋma kiya
that time FOC this-TOP my-child-TOP not.be-NML FOC MIR QUOTE SEQ

thil-u-lott-u nimaŋ.
chase-3P-V2:INCH-3P REP

At that time she realized that he was not her child, and she started to chase him.

87. Hecchakuppa thin-yaŋ-sa thin-yaŋ-sa khatt-u nimaŋ.
Hecchakuppa chase-IPFV-SIM chase-IPFV-SIM go.after-3P REP

She went after Hecchakuppa, chasing him all the way.

88. Hecchakuppa-ʔa layo-nin wa-din tem-yaŋ-sa tem-yaŋ-sa
Hecchakuppa-ERG fried.rice-COM chicken-egg throw-IPFV-SIM throw-IPFV-SIM

khatt-u-ŋ-u nimaŋ.
go.after-3P-IPFV-3P REP

Hecchakuppa followed her, throwing fried rice and chicken eggs.

89. moko layo-nin   wa-din   kup-ca-yaŋ-sa   yuŋa-ŋa-lo
that   fried.rice-COM chicken-egg pick.up-V2:EAT-IPFV-SIM remained-IPFV-TEMP

Cakrondhima mosa-ʔa *bəddhe* chir-u-do   nimaŋ.
Cakrondhima s/he-ERG more   leave-3P-V2:PUT:3P REP

As she stopped picking up the fried rice and the chicken eggs, he left Cakrondhima more behind.

90. ik-*china*-da   dhit-ma   hakt-u-ŋ-u-hida   *pheri* layo-nin
one-moment-LOC find-INF   be.about-3P-IPFV-3P-TEMP again fried.rice-COM

wa-din   wett-u-chokt-u   nimaŋ.
chicken-egg throw-3P-V2:THROW-3P REP

Whenever she was about to reach him, he again threw fried rice and chicken eggs at her.

91. moko kuw-u-co-ŋ-u-hida   *pheri* lipt-u-khatt-u   nimaŋ.
that   pick.up-3P-V2:EAT:3P-IPFV-3P-TEMP again cross-3P-V2:TAKE-3P REP

When she picked it up and ate it, he crossed over.

92. misa   mɨ-sa mɨ-sa Hecchakuppa-lo ikta toppaŋ honku-da ta.la
like.that do-SIM do-SIM Hecchakuppa-TOP one big   river-LOC arrived

nimaŋ   kiya *majhi*-ci-ʔa   moko honku *tərəy* metta-khatta nimaŋ.
REP   . SEQ fisherman-ns -ERG that river crossing made-V2:TOOK REP

Like this Hecchakuppa came to a large river; and fishermen took him across the river.

93. khaisari oko honku *tərəy* ti-mɨ-khatt-u   Hecchakupp-o   yɨŋma mo
how   this river crossing 2-do:3P-V2:TAKE-3P Hecchakuppa-APP QUOTE that

Cakrondhima sen-u nimaŋ.
Cakrondhima ask-3P REP

"Oh Hecchakuppa, how did you cross the river?" Cakrondhima asked him.

94. iŋka-lo *kəmila*-ci   lam-u-ŋ   kiya iŋ-keŋtaŋ-da   tew-u-ŋ-dis-u-ŋ,
I-TOP   ant-ns   sought-3P-1s SEQ my-buttocks-LOC throw-3P-1s-V2:ENTER-3P-1s

yɨŋma mosa-ʔa lo   nimaŋ.
QUOTE s/he-ERG tell:3P REP

"I collected ants and threw them into my buttocks," he told her.

95. mosa-ʔa chaŋ *kəmila* lam-u kiya i-keŋtaŋ-da   tew-u-dis-u   kiya
s/he-ERG also ant   seek-3P SEQ her-buttocks-LOC throw-3P-V2:ENTER-3P SEQ

honku-da phinta-disa-lo   honku-ʔa   khuy-u-khatt-u   nimaŋ.
river-LOC jumped-V2:ENTERED-TOP river-INST carry-3P-V2:TAKE-3P REP

She also collected ants and put them into her buttocks, and when she jumped into the river, the river carried her away.

96. honku-ʔa khuy-u-khatt-u   kiya yuni lonta-hidalo   Hecchakuppa-wo
river-INST carry-3P-V2:TAKE-3P SEQ below came.out-TEMP Hecchakuppa-GEN

i-kɨyaŋpa-ci-ʔa   **i-dhira-khatta**   **nimaŋ.**
his-maternal.uncle-ns -ERG INV-found-V2:TOOK REP

When the river carried her away and she came out downstream, Hecchakuppa's maternal uncles found her.

97. **Hecchakuppa chaŋ mo-yu** **ŋa** **ta.la-wo** **yaŋa** **nimaŋ.**
Hecchakuppa also that-loLOC EMPH arrived-NML was REP

Hecchakuppa had also arrived down there.

98. **moci-ʔa** **moko** **Cakrondhima** **i-sena** **nimaŋ:** **khana bak-khɨ wa-khɨ**   **sat-sat**
they-ERG that Cakrondhima INV-asked REP you pig-feces chicken-feces pull-pull

he Hecchakuppa **bak-khɨ wa-khɨ**   **sat-sat** **mɨ-ma?** **yɨŋma i-sena** **nimaŋ.**
or Hecchakuppa pig-feces chicken-feces pull-pull do-INF QUOTE INV-asked REP

They asked Cakrondhima: "Shall we drag you through pig and chicken shit or shall we drag Hecchakuppa through shit?" they asked her.

99. **iŋka-lo** **budhi-kok-ma**   **Hecchakuppa** **i-sawa** **yaʔ-aŋ-ko,** **khoko**
I-TOP old.woman-old.person-f Hecchakuppa his-strength be-IPFV-NML that.one

wa-khɨ   **bak-khɨ** **sat-sat-ne,** **iŋka-lo** **doli-da-ŋka**   **ne,** **yɨŋma** **mo**
chicken-feces pig-feces pull-pull-OPT I-TOP palanquine-LOC-ABL OPT QUOTE that

Cakrondhima-ʔa lo-ci **nimaŋ.**
Cakrondhima-ERG tell:3P-ns REP

"I am an old woman; Hecchakuppa is strong, he may be dragged through pig and chicken shit, I shall go in a palanquine," Cakrondhima told them.

100. **munkiyalo moko Cakrondhima-lo i-ketta** **kiya bhererewa sat-yaŋ-sa** **i-khatta**
and.then that Cakrondhima-TOP INV-tied SEQ (sound) pull-IPFV-SIM INV-took

Hecchakuppa unco-chɨchawa-lo **doli-da-ŋka** **i-khatta** **nimaŋ.**
Hecchakuppa their-nephew-TOP palanquine-LOC-ABL INV-took REP

Then they tied Cakrondhima and took her, dragging her along; their nephew Hecchakuppa they took in a palanquine.

101. **khim-da** **ɨm-khatt-u-ci** **kiya kok-wa**   **saw-wa** **ɨm-pɨ-ci** **nimaŋ.**
house-LOC INV-take-3P-ns SEQ boiled.rice-liquid meat-liquid INV-give:3P-ns REP

They took them home and gave them rice soup with meat.

102. **munkiya khat-ma-wo** **bela-da unco-chɨchawa-lo** **bəddhe** **khannu-wo**
and.then go-INF-NML time-LOC their-nephew-TOP more be.good-NML

khannu-wo **cama.cam-ci** **khabasam-ci** **i-pakta-khaisa** **nimaŋ kiya khadda**
be.good-NML food-ns wealth-ns INV-put.in-V2:SENT REP SEQ where

am-nɨwa **nu** **khadda sɨŋsa-ʔa** **tɨ-sɨ moda** **ŋa** **oko nant-u** **kiya**
your-liking good where hunger-INST 2-die there EMPH this lean.against-3P SEQ

---

[10] The *m* in the prefix is conditioned by the nonsingular patient (cf. *i-khatta* 'they took him' in 100)

hoŋs-e, i-lowa-khaisa nimaŋ.
open-OPT INV-told-V2:SENT REP

When it was time to go they put more good food and wealth for their nephew and told him: "Wherever you like, wherever you feel hungry, there you may rest (= lean your back-basket against sth.) and open it."

103. moko Cakrondhima-lo maksa saksiŋma-ci i-pakta-khaisa kiya khadda
that Cakrondhima-TOP bear tiger-ns INV-put.in-V2:SENT SEQ where

am-kima khat-ko khodda nant-u oko am-camawo co! i-lowa-khaisa nimaŋ.
your-fear go-NML there rest-3P this your-food eat:3P INV-told-V2:SENT REP

For Cakrondhima they put bears and tigers. "Wherever you feel afraid, there rest and eat this food!" they told her, sending her away.

104. khunkiya moci khara-ŋa-ci khara-ŋa-ci-hidalo Cakrondhima-lo khakhutt
and.then they went-IPFV-d went-IPFV-d-TEMP Cakrondhima-TOP night

ta-khara-wo bela i-kima kara kiya moko i-khaja hoŋs-u nimaŋ-talo
came-V2:WENT-NML time her-fear feel SEQ that her-tiffin open-3P REP-TEMP

moko saksiŋma-ci-ʔa i-ca-khatt-a nimaŋ.
that tiger-ns -ERG INV-eat-V2:TOOK REP

So they went and went, and at the time the night came, Cakrondhima felt afraid, and when she opened her tiffin the tigers ate her.

105. Hecchakuppa-lo ikta khannu-wo thampuŋ-da ta.la kiya moda nanta-
Hecchakuppa-TOP one be.good-NML land-LOC arrived SEQ there leaned.against-

ncin kiya i-cama.cam-ci hoŋs-u-ci nimaŋ-hidalo səbəy səbəy khabasam-ʔa
REFL SEQ his-food-ns open-3P-ns REP-TEMP all all wealth-INST

bhukt-u-khatt-u kiya moda ŋa khimnam mia kiya yuŋa nimaŋ.
bury-3P-V2:TAKE-3P SEQ there EMPH settlement did SEQ stayed REP

When Hecchakuppa came to a good land and rested there and opened his food and things, he was covered with wealth, and he settled and stayed there.

Hecchakuppa sends out animals to find his sisters

106. modaŋka ik-len hiwa-len-ci-da-lo i-chekuma-ci mitt-u-lott-u-ci nimaŋ.
thereafter one-day two-day-ns -LOC-TOP his-sister-ns think-3P-V2:INCH-3P-ns REP

After some time he started to think of his sisters.

107. isari misari iŋ-na-ci Taŋwama Khiyama-ci yaŋa-ci-wo ye, yiŋma
like.this like.that my-e.sister-ns Tangwama Khiyama-ns was-d-NML PART QUOTE

mitt-u-ci nimaŋ.
think-3P-ns REP

"Whatever, there were my sisters Tangwama and Khiyama," he thought of them.

108. han saŋ-ʔa   iŋ-chekuma-ci   hanlap-ma   tat-ma   ri-ci[11]?   yiŋma
     now who-ERG   my-sister-ns   look.for-INF bring-INF   can:3P-ns   QUOTE

     sen-u-ci-hidalo   ikta   sit-ʔa: iŋka-ʔa ri-ŋ,   yiŋa nimaŋ.
     ask-3P-ns-TEMP   one   louse-ERG I-ERG   can:3P-1s said REP

     "Now, who can look for my sisters and bring them?" he asked them, and a louse said: "I can."

109. moko sit   khara kiya Taŋwama   Khiyama-ci   yuŋa-ŋa-ci-wo-da
     that louse went SEQ Tangwama Khiyama-d   remained-IPFV-d-NML-LOC

     ta.la   kiya ŋew-u-lott-u-ci   nimaŋ.
     arrived   SEQ bite-3P-V2:INCH-3P-ns   REP

     The louse went and came to where Tangwama and Khiyama were staying and started biting them.

110. moci-ʔa   kha[ŋa]-c-u: sit ye rəchə!   yiŋma kiya sera-khaisa-c-u   nimaŋ.
     they-ERG looked-d-3P   louse FOC MIR   QUOTE SEQ killed-V2:SENT-d-3P REP

     They looked at it: "It's a louse!" they said and killed it.

111. moko sit   man-la.ban-kiyalo   kippa-ʔa iŋka-ʔa lam-u-ŋ-tar[12]-u-ŋ-c-iŋ,
     that louse NEG-return-TEMP   flea-ERG I-ERG   seek-3P-1s-bring-3P-1s-ns-[copy]

     yiŋma   kiya khara nimaŋ.
     QUOTE   SEQ go   REP

     When the louse didn't come back the flea said: "I will look for them and bring them,"
     and it went.

112. moko kippa-ʔa chaŋ isa   ŋew-u-lukt-u-ci   nimaŋ-hida mo   chaŋ
     that flea-ERG also like bite-3P-V2:FINISH-3P-ns REP-TEMP   that also

     i-sera-khaisa[13]   nimaŋ.
     INV-killed-V2:SENT   REP

     When the flea bit them, they killed it also.

113. munkiya pheri ikta sekba khara nimaŋ.
     and.then again one bedbug went REP

     Then a bedbug went.

114. moko chaŋ   i-sera-khaisa   nimaŋ.
     that also   INV-killed-V2:SENT REP

     It was also killed.

115. munkiya lupmi khara nimaŋ   kiya mosa-ʔa dhuw-u-lukt-u-ci   nimaŋ.
     and.then needle went REP   SEQ s/he-ERG poke-3P-V2:FINISH-3P-ns REP

     Then the needle went and it pricked them.

---

[11] ri- must be a transitive verb; note that in the next clause the subject is in the ergative.
[12] The second verb is not desemanticized, as is otherwise common in compound verbs.
[13] In the dual it should be (i-)sera-khaisa-c-u (cf. 110).

116. moko chaŋ ɨ-sera-khaisa.
that also INV-killed-V2:SENT

It was also killed.

117. ɨkta walapma: ɨŋka khat-ŋa, yɨŋma kiya khara nimaŋ.
one feather I go-1s QUOTE SEQ went REP

A feather said: "I go," and left.

118. moko-lo phinta-lukta-hida ɨ-lawa-c-u kiya ɨ-hɨtta-khaisa-c-u nimaŋ.
that-TOP jumped-V2:FINISHED-TEMP INV-caught-d-3P SEQ INV-burned-V2:SENT-d-3P REP

As it stopped jumping around, the two caught it and burned it.

119. ɨŋka khat-ŋa, yɨŋma kiya ɨkta wa khara nimaŋ.
I go-1s QUOTE SEQ one rooster went REP

"I will go," said the rooster and off he went.

120. moko wa-lo moda ta.la-kiya okta-lonta nimaŋ.
that rooster-TOP there arrived-SEQ crowed-V2:INCH REP

The rooster arrived there and started to crow.

121. hona saŋ-ko wa ye lo? oda ta kiya ok-yaŋ, yɨŋ-sa wen-yaŋ-sa
oh! who-GEN rooster FOC PARThere came SEQ crow-IPFV say-SIM beat-IPFV-SIM

ɨ-thila-c-u nimaŋ.
INV-chased-d-3P REP

"Oh, who is that rooster, he came here and is crowing," they said and they chased him, beating him.

122. moko wa-lo yani yani thin-c-u-khan-c-u,[14] *pheri* la.ban[15]-yaŋ-sa
that rooster-TOP across across chase-d-3P-pursue-d-3P again return-IPFV-SIM

ok nimaŋ; lak lutt-u-ci nimaŋ.
crow REP dance perform:APPL-3P-d REP

They chase away the rooster, chase and pursue him, but he keeps coming back and crows; he performs a dance for them.

123. yani yani thin-yaŋ-sa khan-c-u la.ban nimaŋ.
across across chase-IPFV-SIM pursue-d-3P return REP

Chasing him away, they pursue him, but he comes back.

124. moko wa thin-yaŋ-sa thinyaŋsa khatta-ŋa-c-u khattaŋacu-hidalo
that rooster chase-IPFV-SIM [repet.] pursued-IPFV-d-3P [repet.] -TEMP

---

[14] Not a past form; cf. (*ɨ-*)*thila-c-u* 'they chased him' in (121).
[15] Lexicalized compound < *la + ban* 'arrive+come (across)'; cf. also *ta.la* (< come+arrive) 'arrive'.

mosa-?a-lo   unco-cheiwa   Hecchakuppa-wo   khim-da ye   tar-u-lo-ci
s/he-ERG-TOP   their-brother   Hecchakuppa-GEN   house-LOC FOC   take-3P-V2:ARRIVE:3P-ns

niman.
REP

When they went after the rooster, chasing it, it finally took them to their brother Hecchakuppa's house.

Reconciliation

125. **moci-?a-lo   unco-cheiwa-lo   sia-khara   kiya khumta-da-c-u-wo-lo**
they-ERG-TOP   their-brother-TOP   died-V2:WENT   SEQ buried-V2:PUT-d-3P-NML-TOP

khaysa kiya o-da   isari   khimnam mia kiya   yuŋ-yaŋ, mina-ci niman.
how   SEQ this-LOC like.this settlement made SEQ   stay-IPFV thought-d REP

Their brother having died and they having buried him, how could he build a settlement like this and live here? they thought.

126. **unco-cheiwa-nin   cep-ma   unco-_laja_   kara   man-cep-paŋ   yuŋa-yakta-ci**
their-brother-COM   speak-INF   their-shame   was.felt NEG-speak-CONV stayed-CONTV-d

niman.
REP

They felt ashamed to talk to their brother and they remained without speaking.

127. **unco-cheiwa-?a   dem   dem   cep-ma   lapt-u-ci chaŋ   man-cep-paŋ**
their-brother-ERG   how.much how.much speak-INF try-3P-ns also   NEG-speak-SIM

yuŋa-yakta-ci niman.
stayed-CONTV-d REP

No matter how much their brother tried to talk to them, they remained silent.

128. **mosa-?a   lak   lott-u-ci   cham lott-u-ci   chaŋ man-cep-da-ci**
s/he-ERG   dance   perform: APPL-3P-ns song perform:APPL-3P-ns also NEG-speak-AUX-d

niman.
REP

He performed a dance for them, he sang for them, but still they didn't speak.

129. **mosa-?a   balam thukt-u-ci   kiya hoptaŋ   kiŋs-u-pi-ci   niman.**
s/he-ERG   pole   erect-3P-ns   SEQ bacon   hang-3P-V2:GIVE:3P-ns REP

He set up a pole and hung up a bacon for them.

130. **mutna   hoptaŋ kiŋs-u-pi-ci   kiya lak   lott-u-ci   cham**
so.much bacon   hang-3P-V2:GIVE:3P-ns SEQ dance   perform:APPL-3P-ns song

lott-u-ci   kiya   chaŋ man-yi-da-ci   man-cep-da-ci niman.
perform: APPL-3P-ns SEQ   also NEG-come.down-AUX-d NEG-speak-AUX-d REP

No matter how much meat he hung up for them, how much he danced and sang for them, they still didn't come down and they didn't speak.

131. munkiyalo suncukwa-ci   im-kiŋs-u-pi-ci   nimaŋ.
     and.then   sour.fruit-ns   3p-hang-3P-V2:GIVE:3P-ns REP

Then sour fruit was hung up for them.

132. moko suncukwa   i-khaŋa-hidalo   unco-thetma.wa   lonta   nimaŋ kiya
     that   sour.fruit   INV-saw-TEMP   their-spittle   came.out REP   SEQ

     yiya-ci   kiya i-phutta-ca-c-u   nimaŋ.
     came.down-d SEQ INV-plucked-V2:ATE-d-3P REP

When they saw the sour fruit their saliva came out, and they came down and plucked and ate it.

133. modaŋkalo   ye   moci-ʔa unco-cheiwa   lak   lotta-c-u   lak lottacu nimaŋ.
     thereafter   PART they-ERG   their-brother   dance performed-d-3P [repet.]   REP

Thereafter they performed a dance for their brother.

134. modaŋkalo   Taŋwama-nin Khiyama-ʔa: iŋkan-lo   isa .isa lis-in-ko
     thereafter   Tangwama-COM Khiyama-ERG we$_{pe}$-TOP   like.like become-1/2pS/P-NML

     ye,   yiŋma cham lama   lotta-c-u   nimaŋ.
     PART QUOTE song through performed-d-3P REP

Later Tangwama and Khiyama expressed through a song: "Such and such happened to us."

135. khaysakiya dukha   im-tokta-wo moci lo-pa   im-mia nimaŋ.
     how   grief   3pS-felt-NML they   tell-REC 3pS-did REP

They told each other how grieved they felt.

136. unco-papa-mama-ci   im-khara-lowa   kiya   unco-makanchi-ʔa   dukha   pi-ci-wo
     their-father-mother-ns   3pS-went-V2:?   SEQ   their-stepmother-ERG pain   give:3P-d-NML

     Hecchakuppa sakuyumba-ʔa   khatt-u-wo-ci   səpəy səpəy   lo-pa   im-mia nimaŋ
     Hecchakuppa   hunger-INST   take-3P-NML-ns all   all   tell-RECIP 3pS-did REP

That their father and mother went away, that their stepmother gave them pain and that Hecchakupa suffered from starvation, everything they told each other.

137. Hecchakuppa-ʔa chaŋ khoko   khaysari thinta-lonta kiya dukha tokta khaysari
     Hecchakuppa-ERG   also that.one how   woke-V2:UP   SEQ pain   saw   how

     i-kiyaŋpa-ci-ʔa   i-dhira   khaysari Cakrondhima sia   yiŋma   i-chekuma-ci
     his-mat.uncle-ns -ERG INV-found how   Cakrondhima   died QUOTE   his-sister-ns

     khaŋ-mett-u-ci nimaŋ.
     see-CAUS-3P-ns   REP

Hecchakuppa also revealed to his sisters how he woke up and what trouble he had, how his maternal uncles found him and how Cakrondhima died.

138. moci im-khawa niman; khap-pa im-mia niman.
they 3pS-wept REP weep-REC 3p-did REP

They wept, they wept for each other.

139. Hecchakuppa-?a khaysari moko khaba.chenbi-ci dhir-u-wo-ci khan-mett-u-ci
Hecchakuppa-ERG how that wealth-ns find-3P-NML-ns see-CAUS-3P-ns

niman
REP

Hecchakuppa showed them the wealth he had found.

140. khaysari unco-cheiwa-?a unco-chekuma-ci han-lapt-u-ci niman,
how their-brother-ERG their-sister-ns send-try-3P-ns REP

yinma lo-ci niman.
QUOTE tell-d REP

He told them how he, the brother, tried to send for the sisters.

141. mundankalo moda na mo lenta-da cheiwa chekuma lak
thereafter there EMPH that day-LOC brother sister dance

lu-sa cham lu-sa cep-sa im-yuna niman.
perform-SIM song perform-SIM speak-SIM 3p-stayed REP

That day brother and sisters stayed together, dancing, singing and talking.

Thulung

2. Jaw, Khliw, Khakcalap

narrator: Phure, from Mukli
recording: N.Allen, analysis: K.H.Ebert

The owl eats Khliw

1. **Jaw KhliwKhakcilik su-le   ba-mḍi.**
    Jaw Khliw Khakcilik   three-CL be-3p:PT

    Jaw, Khliw and Khakcilik, three there were.

2. **ma mörmiŋ[1]-ka cakthö Jaw-nuŋ Khliw-nuŋ-ka: ici-ri   sen-cima   lëë-ci,**
    and those-ERG   later   Jaw-COM Khliw-COM-ERG our$_{di}$-sibling kill-d   and   go-d

    roa-becci.
    say-do:PT:d

    And later they, Jaw and Khliw, said: "Let's kill our brother and go."

3. **mökotimaKhakcilik uci-ri-kam ...   bon-kam   u-*sarup bane*cci ma**
    thereafter Khakcilik their$_d$-sibling-GEN gourd-GEN his-effigy make:PT:d and

    demci[2] ma secci.[3]
    stamp:d and kill:PT:d

    So they made an effigy of their brother Khakcilik out of a gourd and trampled him to death.

4. **secci, mökotima lë-m-belaka[4] Jaw-ka u-loak   Khliw-*lāi* gana**
    [repet] thereafter go-NML-TEMP Jaw-ERG her-y.sibling Khliw-DAT you

    ŋaddo lëksa!   b-üü-r-ü.[5]
    first   go:IMPER do-[ü]-PT-3s>3 (= told her)

    They killed him; then, when they set off, Jaw said to her younger sister Khliw: "You go first."

5. **me'e, gana ŋaddo lëksa!   büürü-lone, u-loak   mi-bi.si[6]-wama u-wa**
    no   you   first go:IMPER told-TEMP   her-y.sibling NEG-obey-IRR and her-e.sister

---

[1] *mörmim*; *mö-r-mim* (that-[r]-pl)
[2] Some stems ending in *r, l, m, n* have no past marker with the dual suffix *-ci*.
[3] *secci* =*set-* (past stem) + *-ci*. Past t is realized as *ḍḍ* before a vowel: *seḍḍü* (or set+T+ü??) and assimilated to certain stems (*mallü*, 9).
[4] Nepali *belā* 'time' + *-ka* is a common device for embedding temporal clauses; cf. also 20, 33, 36. The subordinator *belaka* follows a nominalizer. Temporal expressions are optionally topicalized; I do not separate the topicalizer in the glosses (*-belaka* = *-belakane*).
[5] *büürü*: *be-* 'do; tell' + *T* + *ü*; cf. introduction to Rai languages, fn. 8.
[6] *bisi* 'obey' is lexicalized. The origin in two verbs is apparent in *mi-bi-**n**-si-**na*** 'you don't obey' (29).

cahĩ   **huḍḍa ma   lës-ta.**
CONTR.FOC   fly:PT and   go-PT

"No, you go first" Khliw told her, and as the younger sister did not obey, the elder sister flew away.

6. **u-loak   misiŋa   par-jöll-ü.**
   her-y.sibling behind   leave-V2:PUT:PT-3s>3

She left her younger sister behind.

7. **ma cakthö** *pherile*-**a   mö   u-loak   reb-ḍa   rok-ta-lone u-loak-ka**
   and later   again-PART that her-y.sibling look-PURP come-PT-TEMP her-y.sibling-ERG

   bobop *khij*-**ü-r-ü   rëcha.**
   owl   mock-[ü]-PT-3s>3 MIR

Later when she came back to look for her sister, she found that her sister had mocked an owl.

8. **bobok-ka këk-t-ü   ma   seḍḍ-ü.**
   owl-ERG   peck-PT-3s>3 and   kill:PT-3s>3

The owl had pecked her to death.

9. **seḍḍü ma, cakthö rok-ta ma   mall-ü-lone   me-loaas-ü-ya.**
   [repet] and later   come-PT and search:PT-3s>3-TEMP NEG-see-3s>3-IRR

Now, when she came in search of her, she did not find her.

10. **hama bobop: riw   *jethá* ottha a-loak   me-loaa-na-wa, roak-ta-lone, go-ne**
    and.so owl   in.law e.son here my-y.sibling NEG-see-2s-IRR say-PT-TEMP   I-TOP

    me-law-wa, roak-ta.
    NEG-see:1s-IRR say-PT

When Jaw said to the owl: "Brother-in-law, have you not seen my sister?" he said "I haven't seen her."

11. **me'e, gana asiŋa baṭ-pa, gana a-loak   loa-m *parcha,* büürü-lo**
    no   you   here stay-AP you my-y.sibling see-INF must   told-TEMP

When she said: "But you live here, you must have seen her,"

12. **hunu lëksa   ma *ṭoḍkā*-no rebḍa,   büürü ma**
    across go:IMPER and hole-levLOC look:IMPER told and

he told her: "Go over there and look in the hole in the tree."

13. **mal-to   mal-to   lëks-ta-lone, bobok-ka këk-t-ü   ma seḍḍ-ü   ma**
    search-SIM search-SIM go-PT-TEMP   owl-ERG   peck-PT-3s>3 and kill:PT-3s>3 and

    u-sö   *jati* p-ü-leaḍḍ-ü;
    her-meat   all   eat-[ü]-V2:TAKE:PT-3s>3

As Jaw went searching, searching, the owl pecked her to death and ate all her flesh;

14. u-ser   koŋŋa bay-ra.
her-bone only   be-PT

Only her bones were left.

15. ma mö u-ser-mim khobḍ-ü   ma, *jammā baṭul-ü-r-ü*   ma, kurwabet-to
and that her-bone-p collect:PT-3s>3 and all   collect-[ü]-PT-3s>3 and (ritual) make-SIM

kurwa betto hadiboŋ-kahot-to   büürü-lone u-loak   ŋos-ta.
[repet.]   gourd-INST sprinkle-SIM said-TEMP   her-y.sibling wake-PT

And having collected her very bones she made them join, and when she spoke, invoking the ritual
and sprinkling with the gourd, her younger sister woke up.

16. uloak ŋosta, hamko   chöm re ëŋ-ŋuro,   roak-ta-lone,
[repet]   how.much very FOC sleep-1sS:PT say-PT-TEMP

Her sister awoke, and when she said: "I must have slept very deeply,"

17. ā   ëm-na, bobok-kakëë-na ma gana seṭ-na ma pen-na-m;
PART sleep-2s owl-ERG   peck-2s and you   kill:PT-2s and eat:PT-2s-NML

(her sister said): "So you slept, did you? Owl pecked you and killed you and ate you.

18. go phëë-ni-m   ḍe, büürü.
I   awaken-1>2-NML FOC told

I have just brought you to life again," she told her.

19. gana lilumla   me-ber-ü-cö.[7]
you   instruction? NEG-make-3s>3-child

"You are unobedient child.

20. gana ŋaddo lëksa!   roa-ŋḍo-m-belaka me-lëë-na-wa;
you   first   go:IMPER say-1sS:PT-NML-TEMP NEG-go-2s-IRR

When I said 'Go first!' you did not go.

21. ma atha *pherile* bobok-ka seṭ-na ma   a-sin-ḍa   go phëë-ni-ma   re.
and now again   owl-ERG   kill:PT-2s and this-place-LOC I   awaken-1>2-NML FOC

Owl killed you, but it is me who resuscitated you right here."

The sisters separate

22. athane lëë-na re? büürü-lone, lë-ŋu,   roak-ta ma
now   go-2s FOC told-TEMP   go-1sS   say-PT   and

When she asked her "Will you go now?" she said "I'll go";

23. wa   ŋaddo Luwale-ra lës-ta-m bay-ra, möram *pheri*, mö u-loak
e.sister first   (place)-LOC go-PT-NML be-PT   that.one CONTR   that her-y.sibling

---

[7] This is not a common expression; cf. footnote in Allen (1975:331).

Khliw   ayu   *pheri* Wayecaptü lës-ta.
Khliw   down   CONTR (place)   go-PT

and as the elder sister had gone (north) to Luwale first, the other one, the younger sister Khliw
went south, down to Wayecaptü.

24. **Wayecaptü lësta, hucci ma lëkci.**
[repet]   fly:PT:d and go:PT:d

She went down to Wayecaptü; both flew away.

25. **lëkci-m-*pachi* diphu Jaw-ka halalaŋ-ka suna-buŋ   samse-buŋ   khole**
[repet]-NML-after   later   Jaw-ERG beak-INST   suna-flower samse-flower all

södd-ü   ma yok-ta.
bring.down:PT-3s>3 and come.down-PT

Later Jaw came south bringing all sorts of mountain flowers in her beak.

26. **ayu-lam u-loak-ka   Khliw-ka khawa-buŋ *masi*-buŋ khole-buŋ**
down-MED her-y.sibling-ERG Khliw-ERG cotton-flower lentil-flower all-flower

khedd-ü   ma hanu Jawaji-no   ghröm-ci.
bring.up:PT-3s>3 and across (place)-levLOC meet-d

From below her sister Khliw brought up cotton-seed, lentil-seeds and the like, and they
met over at Jawaji.

27. **Jawaji-no, ici-ri   secci *bhanera* Jawaji-no   ghröm-ci ma doa becci.**
[repet]   our$_{di}$-brother kill:PT:d QUOTE   (place)-levLOC meet-d   and loom make:PT:d

Thinking that they had killed their brother, they met at Jawaji and set up a loom.

Khakcilik fishes a stone

28. **doa becci-lone, cakthöne mö Wayeluŋma[8]-kam u-maŋ-ku   — nëŋ**
[repet]   -TEMP   later   that Wayelungma-GEN her-mother-GEN   name

go me-cëk-pu —   Wayeluŋma-ku u-maŋ-ka:
I NEG-know-1s>3:NPT Wayelungma-GEN her-mother-ERG

Later, Wayelungma's mother — I don't know her name — Wayelungma's mother said:

29. **Wayeluŋma, go roa-ŋu-mim   ganame-thöö-na *rëcha,* mi-bi-n-si-na   *rëcha*;**
Wayelungma I say-1sS-NML:NPT you NEG-hear-2s MIR   NEG-listen-2s-REFL-2s MIR

"Wayelungma, you don't listen to what I say, you don't obey.

30. **gana ku jub-da   lëksa!   büürü u-cö.**
you water jump-LOC go:IMPER told   her-child

Go and jump in the water!" she told her child.

---

[8] *Waye-luŋ-ma*: the water- (*wa*) stone- (*luŋ*) female.

31. ma ku jub-ḍa lës-ta-m-ne mö-yu *silā* düs-ta-ma bay-ra.
and water jump-LOC go-PT-NML-TOP that-loLOC stone become-PT-NML be-PT

And gone into the water, she had became a stone and stayed down there.

32. kuḍḍ-yu *silā* düstama bayra, mökotima mö Khakcilik paluŋ-cö bay-ra.
water-loLOC [repet.]   thereafter that Khakcilik fisher-child be-PT

She had turned into a stone down in the water, meanwhile Khakcilik had become a fisherman.

33. Khakcilik paluŋcö bayra, paluŋ ob-ḍa lës-ta-m-belakane mö luŋ ḍe
[repet]   fishernet cast-PURP go-PT-NML-TEMP that stone FOC

paluŋ-ḍa geḍḍa.
fishernet-LOC come.up:PT

When he went to cast his net, that same stone came up in the net.

34. ma möram thas-t-ü ma ghrok-t-ü.
and that.one take.out-PT-3s>3 and throw-PT-3s>3

He took it out and threw it (back).

35. parr-ü, *pheri* thama *arko daphā* obḍ-ü-lo *pheri* mö luŋ-ŋa geḍḍa.
throw:PT-3s>3 again later other second cast:PT-3s>3-TEMP again that stone-EMPH come.up:PT

When later he cast a second time, that same stone came up again.

36. *pheri*-ŋŋa parr-ü ma *pheri* obḍ-ü-m-belaka *pheri* mö luŋ-ŋa
again-EMPH discard:PT-3s>3 and again cast:PT-3s>3-NML-TEMP again that stone-EMPH

geḍḍa.
come.up:PT

Again he threw it away; and again when he cast his net, that very stone came up.

37. luŋŋa geḍḍa mane,*e* oram-ne go lë-m ma yo-nuŋ khorsay-nuŋ düm-khop
[repet]   PART INTJ this.one-TOP I go-INF and salt-COM chili-COM grind-LP

düm-luŋ re *bane*-m *paryo*, roak-ta ma u-*jābi*-ra kurr-ü ma
grind-stone FOC make-INF must say-PT and his-bag-LOC carry:PT-3s>3 and

kheḍḍ-ü.
bring.up:PT-3s>3

The stone came up; "well, I should take it and use it as a grinding stone for salt and chilli," he said and carried it up in his bag.

38. ujābira kurrüma kheḍḍü ma chörcü-ra jüll-ü.
[repet]   and basket-LOC put:PT-3s>3

Having brought it home in his bag, he put it in a storage basket (hanging from the beams).

39. chörcüra jüllü ma *pheri* paluŋ ob-ḍa lës-ta.
[repet]   and again fishernet cast-PURP go-PT

Having put it in the basket he went fishing again.

Wayeluŋma (the girl turned into a stone) is discovered and stays with Khakcalap

40. paluŋ obḍa lësta-lone mö chörcü-ra-m luk-ta   ma mö Wayeluŋma-ka-ne
       [repet]   -TEMP that basket-LOC-ABL come.out-PT and that Wayelungma-ERG-TOP

luk-ta   ma u-*bhansā-kunsā* pomu-ḍuumu khole baya-niya b-üü-r-ü
come.out-PT and his-cooking-ECHO   food-drink   all   floor-ECHO make-[ü]-PT-3s>3

ma thës-ta.
and hide-PT

When he went off fishing again, Wayelungma came out of the basket, cooked food, prepared
food and drink, swept the floor, and then went into hiding.

41. *pherile*[9] mö chörcü-la   lës-ta ma mö-la-ŋa   bay-ra.
       again   that basket-hiLOC go-PT and that-hiLOC-EMPH stay-PT

Again she went up into the basket and remained up there.

42. hanu rok-ta-m-belakane, mö Khakcilik rok-ta-m-belakane khole pomu-ḍuumu
       across come-PT-NML-TEMP   that Khakcilik come-PT-NML-TEMP all   eat-drink

ṭhikka b-ü-jüll-ü,   khole baya-niya chi-m-jül-ma   bay-ra.
ready   make-[ü]-V2:PUT:PT-3s>3 all   floor-ECHO sweep-[m]-V2:PUT-NML be-PT

When he came, when Khakcilik came, she had prepared food and drink, the floor was swept.

43. hamane:akom go o ricukupa-kam a-pomu re-pa, a-krüm   re-pa, a-kora
       later   PART I thisorphan-GEN my-food look-AP my-hunger look-AP my-thirst

re-pa, sü bu-na, ganaottha[10] roka   po-ci, büürü-lone,
look-AP who be-2s you here   come:IMPER eat-d   told-TEMP

He said to himself: "Poor me, the food-bringer of this poor orphan, the one who takes care of my
food, who takes care of my hunger, who takes care of my thirst, who are you? come here, let's eat!"

44. mö u-*chimek*-ḍa   kole ŋaami   bay-ra e,   mö ŋaami-ka:
       that his-neighbourhood-LOC one-CL old.woman be-PT REP that old.woman-ERG

There was an old woman in his neighbourhood, and that old woman said:

45. go re *bābu*, āmai i-krüm-kora   re-pa, i-pomu-ḍuumu
       I   FOC ADDR INTJ your-hunger-thirst look-AP your-food-drink

i-cape-ḍupe[11] be-pa-ne, go re, roak-ta.
your-food-drink make-AP-TOP I   FOC say-PT

"It's me, babu! The one caring for your hunger and thirst, the one caring for your food and drink,
it's me."

---

[9] *pherile* is used here in the same way as *pheri* (< Nepali).
[10] *o* PROX + *tha* DIR; cf. *möttha* in sent. 52.
[11] *pomu-ḍuumu* '(eat:INF-drink:INF) = *cape-ḍupe*; *ca-* is the common Kiranti root for 'eat'.

46. hala gera po-ci mima, büürü ma geḍḍa ma pe-thal-ci.
up come.up:IMPER eat-d grandmother told and come.up:PT and eat-ITER-d

"Come up, let's eat, grandmother," he said to her, and she came up and they ate together.

47. nëk *khep* su *khep* möm-saka[12] pecci *rëcha*.
two times three times that-from eat:PT:d REP

Two or three times after that they ate together.

48. hamane *pheri* mö-bhare-m kole /.../ waŋ-miŋ-ka-ŋa roa-mḍi:
later again that-around-NML one other-p-ERG-EMPH say-3p:PT

Later another neighbor ... some others said:

49. ima-ne o ŋaami-ne, ima i-pep-saṭ-pa koŋŋa.
your-TOP this old.woman-TOP your your-eat-V2:BEN-AP only

"This old woman of yours, she is only the one who eats from you.

50. ima i-cape-ḍupe be-pa, ima i-krüm-kora re-pa, i-baya-niya
your your-food-drink make-AP your your-hunger-thirst look-AP your-floor-ECHO

i-plan-komsi be-pa-ne *arko* re bu, chörcü-ra re bu.
your-bedding-pillow make-AP-TOP other FOC be basket-LOC FOC be

The person who takes care of your meals, who takes care of your hunger and thirst, who sweeps the floor and lays out the bedding, she is another one, she is in the storage basket.

51. ma gana paluŋ kura ma ŋo ob-ḍa lëë-na-mim-belaka lëk-pa
and you fishernet carry:IMPER and fish cast-PURP go-2s-NML:NPT-TEMP go-AP

lisa ma lamcaka laptiper yacapim jera ma *kunā*-ra
pretend:IMPER and door winnowing.fan broom hold:IMPER and corner-LOC

thëësa ma baya.
hide.REFL:IMPER and stay:IMPER

Pick up your net and at the time when you usually go fishing, pretend to go, but take a winnowing fan and a broom, hide in the corner and stay there.

52. thama mö i-cape-ḍupe be-pa möttha lu-mim-belaka möraŋ-ka
later that your-food-drink make-AP there come.out-NML:NPT-TEMP that.one-ERG

yacapim mal-ü, yacapim mal-to bi-mim-belaka gana möḍḍa
broom search-3s->3 broom search-SIM beg-NML:NPT-TEMP you there

cümḍa ma
catch:IMPER and

Later, at the time when your food-and-drink preparer comes out, when she searches for the broom, when she asks for the broom, catch her and say:

53. *āmai!* gana-neakom a-krüm-kora re-pa, a-plan-komsi be-pa, go ricukupa-
INTJ you-TOP PART my-hunger-thirst look-AP my-bedding-pillow make-AP I orphan-

---

[12] *-saka* (< converbal *-sa* + ABL? *-ka*) is not transparent any more; cf. *hesaka, homsaka* in 63, and the rare sequential converb in *-saka*.

kam khole a-krüm-kora   re-pa-ne ganare *rëcha*,roaka   ma   cümḍa
GEN all   my-hunger-thirst look-AP-TOP you FOC MIR   say:IMPER and catch:IMPER

***hai!* büürü *rëcha*.**
INTJ told   REP

'So it's you who cared for my hunger and thirst, who made my bedding, who looked after me, the poor orphan, who cared for my hunger and thirst turned out to be you!' say it and catch her, okay?" they told him.

54. büürü   ma, yacapim jeḍḍ-ü   ma laptiper-ka   khrems-ta ma
[repet]   and broom   hold:PT-3s>3 and winnowing.fan-INST cover:REFL-PT and

***kunā-ra* thës-ta   mane bay-ra-m-belakane thamane mö**
corner-LOC hide:REFL-PT and stay-PT-NML-TEMP   later   that

chörcü-laŋ-ka-ne   jus-ta *rëcha*.
basket-MED-ABL-TOP jump-PT REP

And when he took the broom and covered himself with the winnowing fan and hid in the corner and waited, she jumped down from the basket.

55. chörcülaŋka justa ma mö yacapim mal-to   lës-ta-lone, mö-no   mö
[repet]   and that broom   search-SIM go-PT-TEMP that-levLOC that

laptiper-ka   khrems-ta-m   go-no /.../ hoak-t-ü-m-belakane
winnowing.fan-INST cover:REFL-PT-NML inside-levLOC open-PT-3s>3-NML-TEMP

mö-go-ra   ḍarr-ü   mane *thyāppai* cüm-ḍ-ü-m-belakane,
that-inside-LOC meet:PT-3s>3 and (sound)   catch-PT-3s>3-NML-TEMP

When she jumped from the basket and went to search the broom, he opened the fan inside which he was covered, and he met her and caught her.

56. *āmai!* ganasü   re, gana sü-na? büürü-lone,
INTJ   you who FOC you   who-? told-TEMP

"You - who is it? who are you?" she asked him.

57. *āmai!* a   go Khakcilipa-kamakom a-krüm   re-pa   a-kora   re-pa,
INTJ PARTI   Khakcilikpa-GEN PART my-hunger look-AP my-thirst look-AP

a-plan-komsi   be-pa, khole baya-niya be-pa-ne   ganare   *rëcha*,büürü ma
my-bedding-pillow make-AP all   floor-ECHO make-AP-TOP you FOC MIR   told   and

cüm-ḍ-ü-lone
catch-PT-3s>3-TEMP

"It's me! Khakcilipa's ... my cook, the one who looked after me, who made my bed and cleaned the house, it wasyou!" he said and when caught her [she said]

58. me'e, go me'e; ganapaluŋ   ob-ḍa   lëë-na-m-belaka i-paluŋ-ḍa
no   I no   you fishernet cast-PURP go-PT-2s-NML-TEMP your-fishernet-LOC

ge-ŋɖo   ghro-ŋɖi   ottha par bëk-ta.
come.up-1sS:PT throw-2>1s:PT here sore rise-PT

"No, not me! When you went fishing I came up in your net, you threw me back; it is swollen here.

59. arko daphā pheri op-na-m-belaka ge-ŋɖo-lone   gana i-jābi-ra
other second again throw-2s-NML-TEMP come.up-1sS:PT-TEMP you your-bag-LOC

kur-ŋiri   ma   kheṭ-ŋiri   chörcü-ra jül-ŋiri-m.
carry-2>1s:PT and bring.up-2>1s:PT basket-LOC put-2>1s:PT-NML

When you threw me back a second time and when I came up again, you carried me up [home] in your bag put me in the storage basket.

60. gana möm-saka   go me-doak-pa,ham /.../ atha o doaa-ŋi   ma, büürü-lo
you that-from   I NEG-want-AP what   now this want-2>1s PART told-TEMP

You did not want me then, do you want me now?" she asked him.

61. me'e, gana-ne khup doaa-ni-mim, gana khole a-plan-komsi   be-pa,
no   you-TOP much want-1s>2-NML you all my-bedding-pillow do-AP

a-krüm-kora   re-pa, gana re rëcha, büürü ma bacci.
my-hunger-thirst look-AP you FOC MIR   told and stay:PT:d

"No, no, I want you very much. It's you who made my bed, the one who cared for my hunger and thirst, it is you," he said and they settled down.

The house-building

62. bacci, hamane cakthöne: lu! Wayeluŋma-ka roak-ta, nebdi-khibdi
[repet] later   later   INTJ Wayelungma-ERG say-PT house-ECHO

bane-ci ma bu-ci, roak-ta.
make-d and stay-d say-PT

One day Wayelungma said: "Let's build a house and live in it."

63. lone ma he-saka   nebdi-khibdi bane-mu? mö Khakcilik-ka roak-ta-lone,
then PART what-from house-ECHO make-INF that Khakcilik-ERG say-PT-TEMP

hom-saka   nem bane-m basi.
how-from   house make-INF must

Then: "From what to make a house?" asked Khakcilik. "How shall I build a house?"

64. gana ghocā ghārā phël-la lëksa!   büürü ma, ghocā phël-la
you pole stake cut-PURP go:IMPER told and pole   cut-PURP

lës-ta-lone u-mina   /.../ kāpe manthim reɖɖ-ü   rëcha.
go-PT-TEMP its-what's.it   fork without look.for:PT-3s>3 REP

"Go to cut poles and stakes," she told him, and when he went to cut poles he only looked for - what's it - non-branching ones.

65. **ukāpe** **manthim reḍḍü, mömlone: o** **hopma-ne me'e, hopma-ne**
[repet] that.time this like-TOP not like-TOP

me'e, hopmam ḍe *cahed*-**ü-m,** **büürü-lone**
not like FOC be.necessary-3s>3-NML told-TEMP

When he came with non-forked poles she told him: "Not like this, not like this. We need like this."

66. **go-ne me-theṭ-pu,** **hepmam ma? roak-ta-lo, hayu nömli rebḍa**
I-TOP NEG-understand-1s>3:NPT what.sort PART say-PT-TEMP down (bird) look:IMPER

la, hayu nömli-ku mer loa-na, büürü.
PART down (bird)-GEN tail see-2s told

"I don't understand. What sort do you mean?" - "Look, that Nömli bird down there, you see its tail?" she told him,

67. **ma nömli rebḍ-ü-lone** **nömli-kam-ne hopmam** *hāge* **rëcha u-mina** **u-mer.**
and (bird) look:PT-3s>3-TEMP (bird)-GEN-TOP like branch MIR its-what's.it its-tail

When he looked at that Nömli, the Nömli's was like a branch, its - what's it - its tail was.

68. *hāuhā,* **hem be-pa** **ren-mu** *hai*! **büürü ma,** *lu,* **roak-ta ma lës-ta ma**
INTJ such do-AP collect-INF INTJ told and INTJ say-PT and go-PT and

mepmam u-*kāpe* **baṭ-pa** *ghōca* /.../ **reḍḍ-ü;**
that.sort his-fork be-AP pole look.for:PT-3s>3

"You must collect one that does like this," she told him, and he said "okay," he went and looked for that sort of forked poles.

69. **mökotima krok-ci-m-belakane** /.../ **mö Wayeluŋma-kam u-cö** **bay-ra** *rëcha.*
thereafter plant-d-NML-TEMP that Wayeluŋma-GEN her-child be-PT REP

When they planted the pole ... there was Wayelungma's child.

70. **mö ucö bayra** *rëcha, pherile* **mö Khakcilik-ka ayu** **krok-si mi-theḍ-ba.**
[repet] again that Khakcilik-ERG down ram-MAN NEG-understand-IRR

Now, that Khakcilik did not understand how to ram (the pole) into the earth.

71. **kroksi mitheḍba-lone, u-cö** **phep-thaḍḍ-ü** **ma lës-ta ma mö-yu**
[repet] -TEMP her-child hold.in.arm-V2:TEL:PT-3s>3 and go-PT and that-loLOC

ghocā **kroo-mu sinḍ-ü-lone** **u-cö** **ḍisok-t-ü.**
pole plant-INF teach:PT-3s>3-TEMP her-child lay.down-PT-3s>3

Wayelungma took the child in her arm and went, and when she taught him (how) to plant the pole, she lay down the child.

72. **ucö ḍisoktü ma mö** *ghocā*-**ka mö-gu-yu** **ḍocci** **ma secci u-cö.**
[repet] and that pole-INST there-inside-loLOC beat:PT:d and kill:PT:d her-child

She lay the child down, they beat the pole down and killed the child.

73. ḍoccimasecci, mökotima athaldika nem b-i-yi-m-belaka kole
[repet] thereafter nowadays house make-[i]-1pi-NML-TEMP one

jhar-mu basi po-ka.
sprinkle-INF must chicken-INST

Nowadays, when we build a house, we must sprinkle with (the blood of) a chicken.

74. poka jharmu basi — mömlo-ŋa u-ḍümla gës-ta-m.
[repet] that.time-EMPH its-custom originate-PT-NML

— At that time the custom [of blood sacrifice] originated.[13]

75. poka jharmu basiṭ-pa, u-nem düm-ku-mim-*pachi* /.../ guku po-ka
[repet] must-AP his-house finish-1nse-NML-after we_pe chicken-INST

jhar-ku. —
sprinkle-1nse

The one who has to sacrifice, after we finish his house we sacrifice a chicken. —

Khakcalap sends out animals to find his sisters

76. ma möm-saka bacci.
and that-from stay:PT:d

From then on they stayed there.

77. mane cakthöne Wayeluŋma-ka roak-ta: *lu* i-rii-mi hamko bu-mi,
INTJ later Wayelungma-ERG say-PT INTJ your-sibling-p how.much be-p

ban-thö lë-mḍi-m bu-mi, büürü ma hila büürü-lone,
where-DIR go-3p:PT-NML be-3p told and question said-TEMP

One day when Wayelungma asked him: "How many siblings of yours were there and where are they?"

78. a-rii-ci *dui bahini* Jaw-nuŋ Khliw-nuŋ bacci, *tara* mörcip-ka go
my-siblings-d two y.sister Jaw-COM Khliw-COM be:PT:d but that:d-ERG I

set-ŋiri-ci ma ano lëkci.
kill:PT-3>1s:PT-d and across go:PT:d

"I had two sisters, Jaw and Khliw, but they killed me and went off.

79. bante lëkci, ko-le Luwale lës-ta, ko-le Wayecapt-yu lës-ta-m bu,
where go:PT:d one-CL (place) go-PT one-CL (place)-loLOC go-PT-NML be

roak-ta *rëcha* Khakcilik-ka.
say-PT MIR Khakcilik-ERG

Where they went? One went to Luwale, one down to Wayecapt," Khakcilik said.

---

[13] The Camling explain the Thulung custom of blood sacrifice with an incident (offering their sister) during the migration (cf. the text "Escaping from Khowalung").

80. mömlone:*lu* **mal-mu basi, u-mocü Wayeluŋma-ka   roak-ta-lo,**
that.time INTJ search-INF must his-woman Wayelungma-ERG say-PT-TEMP

ma heka mal-mu ma, roak-ta.
PART how   search-INF PART say-PT

Then his wife Wayelungma said: "We must look for them." "But how to search?" he asked.

81. *lu,   upiyã* **re   thür-ci, roak-ta ma— Jawaji-no   mömlo bacci —**
INTJ flea FOC send-d say-PT and (place)-levLOC that.time be:PT:d

upiyã **re   thür-ci, roak-ta ma**
flea FOC send-d say-PT and

"Well, let's send the flea." — The two sisters lived at that time over at Jawaji. — "Let's send the flea."

82. *upiyã thürci,* **ma prok-to prok-to lës-ta ma ḍoa becci-m-belaka mö**
[repet]   and jump-SIM jump-SIM go-PT and loom do÷PTd-NML-TEMP that

*upiyã-***ka ciriri   khreḍḍ-ü-lone,**
flea-ERG (sound) bite:PT-3s>3-TEMP

Off it went, jumping along, and when it found the sisters working at the loom, it bit them.

83. *āmai* **sü-kam, u-hamsüma   re, aki-ri-ne   make si-leaḍḍa- m**
INTJ who-GEN his-what's.it.called FOC our_pe-sibling-TOP long.ago die-V2:GO:PT-NML

sü-ku u-mina   re oram ham *ho,* roak-ta ma möram w o khrecci ma
who-GEN its-what's.it FOC this what be say-PT and that also bite:PT:d and

secci.
kill:PT:d

"Ouch! Whose is this ...what's-it-called? Our brother died long ago. What is this about?" they said. So they bit it also and killed it.

84. hamane cakthö *pheri* **po   thürci, grokpu.**
then   later   again chicken send:d rooster

After that they sent the chicken, the rooster.

85. po thürci e   ma möram ok-to ok-to ok-to lës-ta,
[repet]   EMPH and that.one crow-SIM crow-SIM crow-SIM go-PT

Jawaji-no ok-to   lës-ta-lone ḍoa bet-to lecci-m   bay-ra.
(place)-levLOC crow-SIM go-PT-TEMP loom do-SIM busy:PT:d-NML be-PT

They sent the rooster and off he went, crowing, crowing, crowing, and when he came to Jawaji, crowing, the sisters had set up a loom.

86. lës-ta ma: këkërika Khakcilípobaŋpá!   roak-ta.
go-PT and (sound) Khakcilik go.between say-PT

"Kokorika Khakcilipo, bangpa!" it crowed.

87. — mömlo-ŋa   baŋpa   gës-ta-m   kole. —
that.time-EMPH go.between originate-PT-NML one

— At that time one of the marriage intermediaries originated. —

88. baŋpa   roak-ta-lone: *āmai* **sü-ku   *cokṭā,*   aci-ri   me-baṭ-pa,**
go.in.between say-PT-TEMP   INTJ   who-GEN   cursed   our_d-sibling   NEG-be-AP

roakci   *rëcha* ma mina-ka -   *thuri*-ka   ghrokci.
say:PT:d   REP   and what's.it-INST   shuttle-INST   throw:PT:d

When he said "bangpa", they said: "Whose is this cursed bird? Our brother doesn't exist."
they said, and they threw the - what's it - the shuttle at him.

89. *thuri*-ka   ghrok-to ghrok-to op-to   op-to   phicci-lone   u-ri
shuttle-INST   throw-SIM throw-SIM aim-SIM   aim-SIM   bring.across:PT:d-TEMP   3POSS-brother

Khakcilik-ku   neb-ḍa   mö *bhāle*-ka reṭ-phaḍḍ-ü,   grokpu-ka.
Khakcilik-GEN   house-LOC   that   cock-ERG   bring-V2:COME:PT-3s>3   rooster-ERG

While they were bringing him across, throwing and aiming the shuttle, the rooster led them
to Khakcilik's house.

90. grokpuka reṭphaḍḍü; reṭphaḍḍü-m-*pachi*ne   mörcip-ne uci-*lāji*
[repet]   -NML-after   that:d-TOP   their_d-shame

lüü-ra ma   hucci   ma   lëkci.
feel-PT and   fly:PT:d   and   go:PT:d

After he led them there, they were overcome by shame and flew away.

91. huccima lëkci, huccima lëkci-m-*pachi*-ne   mörcip gojü-mi bacci,
[repet]   -NML-after-TOP   that:d   pregnant-p   be:PT:d

u-khoacep-nuŋ-ma bacci   *rëcha* e   niphi-ŋa.
its-belly-COM-NML   be:PT:d   REP   EMPH   both-EMPH

Now, they were pregnant, they were both with belly.

92. hamane he   bo-mu, ham bo-mu *ta*   roak-ta Khakcilik-ka-ne roak-ta-lone
later   what be-INF   what be-INF   PART say-PT   Khakcilik-ERG-TOP   say-PT-TEMP

u-mocü   Wayeluŋma-ka:
his-woman   Wayelungma-ERG

Later Khakcilik was wondering what to do, and his wife Wayelungma said:

93. *lu*,   guci   dukci   be-pa ba-ci.
INTJ   they_d   hot   do-AP be-d

"Well, those two like hot food (as pregnant women).

94. *lu*   kheli-nuŋ rici-nuŋ   agora tam-mu   basi, ottha roo-ci!
INTJ   (plant)-COM (plant)-COM here   add.water-INF must   here   come-d

roak-ta Wayeluŋma-ka.
say-PT   Wayelungma-ERG

We must take a preparation from Kheli and Rici plants and they will come, Wayelungma said.

95. **hama kheli-nuŋ rici-nuŋ tamci-lone mö *aba* dukci be-pa-ka**
then (plant)-COM (plant)-COM add.water:d-TEMP that now hot do-AP-ERG

möram peb-ḍa jukci, jukci ma *aba* dika-cakthö ba-mḍi.
that.one eat-PURP jump:d jump:d and now tomorrow-later stay-3p:PT

When they soaked the two herbs, the hot-food-eaters came down to eat it; they jumped down and now they stayed.

96. **dika-cakthö lëë-mu-belaka: ici-ri-ne guci-ne secci-m *ho*.**
tomorrow-later go-INF-TEMP our_di-brother-TOP we_di-TOP kill:PT:d-NML be

Later, when it was time to go, they thought: "This brother of ours, we have killed him.

97. ***aba* ici-ri-ne *jiũdo* areka (iki-) ici-ri-ka mal-saḍḍa-m-*pachi***
now our_di-brother-TOP alive PART our_pi- our_di-brother-ERG search-V2:BEN:PT-NML-after

guci ham goa-m-jöl-mu *ta*, roa-becci-lone,
we_di what give-[m]-V2:PUT-INF PART say-V2:DO:PT:d-TEMP

Now that our brother is alive, after our brother searched for us, what are we going to give him?

98. ***lu* guci soa goaa-ci — athaldika *bihā*-ra-m soa möram**
INTJ we_di vessel give-d nowadays marriage-LOC-NML vessel that.one

luk-ta-m wo —
come.out-PT-NML also

"Let's give vessels." — That is where the bride-price comes from in today's weddings. —

99. **soa goaa-ci, roa-becci ma, Luwale lëk-pa-kakole nële sule blële ŋole**
vessel give-d say- V2:DO:PT:d and (place) go-AP-ERG one two three four five

rule soa, rule goak-t-ü,
six vessel six give-PT-3s>3

"Let's give vessels," they said and the one who went to Luwale gave one, two, three, four, five, six bride-price vessels.

100. **ayu Wayecapt-yu lëk-pa-ka yatle goak-t-ü.**
down (place)-loLOC go-AP-ERG seven give-PT-3s>3

The one who went down to Wayecapt gave seven.

101. **soa goakci möm-saka phëk-ci ma u-soa goak-jöl-ci.**
vessel give:PT:d that-from raise-d and his-vessel give-V2:PUT-d

They collected the contributions and presented the vessels.

102. **mökotima mörcip hucci ma lëkci.**
thereafter that_d fly:PT:d and go:PT-d

Then those two flew away.

103. **huccima lëkci-m-*pachi*, mökotima soa goak-jöl-ci ma hucci ma**
[repet] -NML-after thereafter vessel give-V2:PUT-d and fly:PT:d and

guci lëk-leak-ci.
they_d go-V2:GO-d

They gave the vessels and parted for good.

104. mökotima Wayeluŋma-nuŋ u-ri Khakcilik-nuŋ-kaguci-ka möttha
thereafter Wayelungma-COM her-sibling Khakcilik-COM-ERG they_d-ERG there

nebdi-khibdi *banecci ma/.../ uci-jiupālā* möḍḍamma becci ma
house-ECHO make:PT:d and their_d-subsistence from.then make:PT:d and

bacci-m *ho*.
stay:PT:d-NML be

After that Wayelungma and her brother Khakcilik built their house and supported themselves, and stayed there.

105. mökotiŋa go cëk-pu *aba*, möḍḍamma *cahĩ* go me-cëk-pu.
then I know-1s>3:NPT now from.then CONTR.FOC I NEG-know-1s>3:NPT

This is what I know, other things I don't know.

4. The territorial dispute[1]

narrator: Karbari, from Lokhim
recording: N. Allen; analysis: K.H.Ebert

The 4 Kiranti brothers[2]
jeṭhā	first-born son	Camling
mahilā	the second son	Ombu
sahilā	the third son	Kulunge
kānchā	the youngest son	Phulüku-cö (=Thulung)

1. luk-ta   e   ma   *cār bhāi   jamma* düm-miri   e   MajuwaDiktel-no,
come.out-PT REP and four brother all   become-3p:PT REP (place)-levLOC

Majuwa Diktel-la[3] *jamma* düm-miri e.
(place)-hiLOC   [repet]

2. dümmiri e ma o   iki-*jaggā*   /.../   ṭhāü mal-si-mḍi   e.
[repet]   and EMPH our_pi-plot   /to settle/   place look.for-REFL-3p:PT REP

And they looked for our plot ... for a place to settle down.

3. ma, u-*jeṭhā*-ka   roak-ta e: Majuwa Diktel go buŋu,   roak-ta e;
and his-1st.son-ERG say-PT   REP (place)   I stay:1s:NPT say-PT   REP

And the first son said: "I will stay [at] Majuwa Diktel ," he said.

4. *mahilā*-ka roak-ta, *sahilā*-ka   roak-ta e: go-o!   roak-ta e, *mahilā*-ka roak-ta:
2nd.son-ERG say-PT   3rd.son-ERG say-PT REP I-EMPH [repet]   2nd.son-ERG [repet]

go! roak-ta, *kānchā*-ka   roak-ta: go! roak-ta.
I say-PT   youngest.son-ERG [repet]

The second said, the third said: "It is me!" he said, the second said "I!", and the youngest said "I!"

5. mömlo u-*jeṭhā* Camliŋ-ka: me'e, roak-ta e,   guku ŋaacökaḍe, go ḍe   taba,
then   his-1st.son Camling-ERG no   say-PT REP we   e.child FOC I FOC self

roak-ta e,   me'e go ḍe! /.../
say-PT REP no   I FOC

Camling, the first-born, said: "No, we are the oldest, so it is <u>me</u> [who stays here], no, it's me!" he said /and they quarreled/.

6. ma: a-loak-ni[4]   iki-ye   ḍö-si /.../
and my-y.sibling-? our_pi-FOC decide-INF:NPT

---

[1] I have left out some of the many repetitions and some passages in Nepali.
[2] The Rai people generally refer to sons by Nepali terms. For the girls the old terms are still in use, e.g. Caml. *tuŋma* first-born daughter, *poke* 2nd daughter etc.
[3] Majuwa Diktel is UP if seen as the goal of the ancestor's ascent; from today 's Thulung territory it would be DOWN.
[4] *aloak-ci*? (cf. 13, 16)

"My younger brothers, our decision is due," he said.

7. **misimma: lau, roa-mḍi   e   ma   *sallā*   be-mḍi   e.**
   and.then INTJ say-3p:PT REP and counsel make-3p:PT REP

"Alright," they said and they held a counsel.

8. ***sallā* be-mḍi e ma heka ḍö-mu   /.../ u-*mahilā* Ombule: /.../ iki-ye**
   [repet]   and how decide-INF   his-2nd.son Ombule   our_pi-FOC

   ḍö-si   khājā-bhuja   p-iy.
   decide-INF:NPT snack-ECHO   eat-1pi

Now how to decide? Ombule, the second son, suggested: "To make a decision let's eat some *khaja* (snack)."

[So they ground some flour, and Camling asked: "Where do you want your land?" The other could not speak because his mouth was full of flour, all he said was "om-om-om."]

9. **mömlone: e Ombu doaa-na, büürü e   mane /.../ Ombu-ŋa   doaa-na*rëcha*,**
   the   eh Ombu want-2s   said REP then   Ombu-EMPH want-2s MIR

   roak-ta, lëksa   mane   goak-t-ü   e.
   say-PT   go:IMPER then   give-PT-3s>3 REP

Then: "Oh, Ombu you want," he said, "so it turned out to be Ombu you want," he said, "Go!" and he gave Ombu to him.

10. **misinḍa *pheri tin bhāi   rahyo*,   /.../ *jeṭhā*-ka-o   mi-ḍit-wa,**
    then   again three brother remainded   1st.son-ERG-EMPH NEG-let.go-IRR

    ***sahilā*-ka-o   mi-ḍit-wa,   *kānchā*-ka-o   mi-ḍit-wa;**
    3rd.son-ERG-EMPH [repet]   youngest-ERG-EMPH [repet]

Now three brothers were left /and the three brothers quarreled/; the first son would not let go [of the place], the third son would not let go, the youngest son would not let go.

11. **mö MajuwaDiktel-ye jöpa   bayra e   ma   mösimma gumi ṭhulo /.../**
    that (place)   FOC beautiful was REP and therefore they big

Majuwa Diktel was good land and therefore they /staged a big quarrel/.

13. **mö *jhagarā* düs-ta *rëcha* mane: *lau* a-loak-ci-o,   iki-caŋma thir-i,**
    that quarrel begin-PT PART then INTJ my-y.sibling-ns-EMPH our_pi-earth invoke-1pi

    ala iki-pari-o   thir-i;
    above our_pi-heaven-EMPH invoke-1pi

When they began to quarrel [Camling said]: "Okay, my younger brothers, let us call on our earth, let us call on our heaven.

14. **pari-lam /.../ uhem ḍëk-sa,   ago-yu   iki-caŋma-ka uhem tuk-sa**
    heaven-ABL   such cover-3>1pi down-loLOC our_pi-earth-ERG such reply-3>1pi

möram-*cahî*-ka-o   MajuwaDiktel *rāj* bo-mu s ö *bhanto gare.*
that.one-FOC-ERG-EMPH (place)   king be-INF who

Who will be covered from heaven, whom our earth will reply from below, he shall be the ruler of Majuwa Diktel."

15.**su-sule *liŋgo*,   tin *bhāi*-ka   sule *liŋgo*   kro-mḍi   e .**
RED-three bamboo.pole   three brother-ERG three bamboo.pole   ram.in-3p:PT REP

The three brothers rammed each a bamboo pole, three poles they rammed in.

16.**misinḍamma: *lu*   thir-i   a-loak-ci!   büürü e .**
and.then   INTJ invoke-1pi my-y.sibling-ns told   REP

Then he said: "Well, let's invoke, my brothers!"

17.**gukucuḍe: thi-si   mi-then-cuku   hesaka thir-i,   roak-ta e .**
we$_{de}$ FOC invoke-INF:NPT NEG-know.how-1de how   invoke-1pi say-PT REP

But we (the Thulung and the Kulung) said: "We two do not know how to invoke, how do we invoke?"

18.**Camliŋ u-*jethā*-ka   siḍḍ-ü-ci   e: Sola PājaMajuwa Diktel ama s ö,**
Camling his-1st.son-ERG teach:PT-3s>3-d REP (name) (place)   mine speak

ama s ö,   roak-ci ma ayu   koa-yu   yal-ci! büürü-ci e .
mine speak say-d   and below ground-loLOC strike-d told-d   REP

Camling, the oldest, taught them: "Sola Pãja, Majuwa Diktel is mine, [speak that] it is mine! - say this and then strike on the ground," he told them.

19.**agu-yu   cëkpu-ku cö bu-la   ḍe je   ma MajuwaDiktelama roak-ci   ma**
down-loLOCbird-GEN child be-COND FOC sound and (place)   mine say-d   and

boak-boak! becci   e-lone   me-jesa-wa   e .
(sound)   do:PT:d REP-TEMP NEG-sound-IRR REP

"If there is a bird['s young] below then it will squeak and Majuwa Diktel will be mine," [he thought], and when the other two clapped boak-boak! there was no answer.

20.**Majuwa Diktel ama-ŋa   roak-ci e   ma ala   *liŋgo halle*cci-lo   ku**
(place)   mine-EMPH say-d   REP and above pole   shake:PT:d-TEMP water

mi-yok-wa   e .
NEG-come.down-IRR REP

"Majuwa Diktel is mine," the other two said, but when they shook the pole above, no water came down.

21.***mahilā*-ka-o [5]   mö-ŋa   büü-r-ü,   *kānchā*-ka-o möŋa büürü, miyokwa.**
2nd.son-ERG-EMPH that-EMPH do-[ü]-PT-3s>3 y.son-ERG-EXCL [repet]

The second son did like this, the youngest did like this, nothing came down.

---

[5] Probably it should be *sahilā,* the third son, as *mahilā* already went to Ombu.

22. *jethā*-ka mödḍamma: *lahai* a-loak-ci-o   go thi-pu /.../
1st.son-ERG thereafter INTJ my-y.sibling-ns-EMPH I invoke-1s>3s

Then the eldest [Camling] said: "Okay, my brothers, I will invoke now.

23. Sola Pãja MajuwaDiktel ama sö,   roak-ta e   ma bhoak-bhoak-bhoak büürü e,
(name)   (place)   mine speak say-PT REP and (sound)   said REP

möm-lo mö cëkpu-ku cö-ka   cya.cya.cya.cya roak-ta ma yes-ta   e.
that-TEMP that bird-GEN child-ERG (sound)   say-PT and sound-PT REP

"Sola Pãja Majuwa Diktel is mine , speak [thus]!" he said and clapped bhoak-bhoak! and now
the bird squeaked cya-cya-cya-cya!

24. *pheri:* a-loak-ci-o   thöccí[6] büürü e, tööcco-ko, roak-ci e.
again my-y.sibling-ns-EMPH hear:PT:d:Q said REP hear:PT:d-1e say-d REP

Then he asked: "My brothers, did you hear?" — "We heard it," they said.

25. *lahai pheri*-o   *liŋgo hall*-ü-r-ü   e-lone/.../ gu-yu ku   phik-t-ü-m
INTJ again -EMPH pole shake-[ü]-PT-3s>3 REP-TEMP up-hiLOC water put.in-PT-3s>3-NML

bayra, mö ku *halle*-düs-ta e-lone yok-ta   ma jiṭ-miri e,
was   that water shake-begin-PT REP-TEMP come.down-PT and wet-3p:PT REP

tin bhāi   jamma oŋkagën-miri-m.
three brother all   ?   sit-3p:PT-NML

And when he shook the pole ... the water he had put up there, when he shook, that water fell
down and wet them, the three brothers sitting there.

26. misinḍamma hila   büürü-ci e: a-loak-ci-o   gaci thöccí,
and.then   question said-d REP my-y.sibling-ns-EMPH you_d hear:PT:d:Q

thöcco-ko, roak-ci e.
hear:PT:d-1e say-d REP

Then he asked them: "My brothers, did you hear?"— "We heard it," they said.

27. niphi-ka thöccí,   niphi-ka thöcco-ko.
both-ERG hear:PT:d:Q both-ERG hear:PT:d-1e

"Did you both hear it?" — "We both heard it."

27. *lu* mömma-la-o MajuwaDiktel-ka go doa-ŋḍi-m   *rĕcha,* ama *rĕcha,* roak-ta
INTJ that-if-EMPH (place)-ERG I favor-1sP:PT-NML MIR   mine MIR   say-PT

e ma gu-ŋa   ras-ta.
REP and there-EMPH claim-PT

"Well, if it is so, it turned out that Majuwa Diktel gave it to me, it is mine," he said and laid claim
to it.

---

[6] Question intonation is indicated by a high accent in Allen's texts.

28. guŋa rasta e, misimma: *lau*   a-loak-ci-o,   iki-*ṭhāū̃*-ka   pripcika
    [repet]   then   INTJ   my-y.sibling-ns-EMPH   our_pi-place-ERG   ECHO?

    subuka go-ŋa   doa-ŋḍi   *roje*   be-ŋḍi   *rëcha,*   gaci mal-sik-ci   *hai !*
    ECHO? I-EMPH   favor-1sP:PT select   make-1sP:PT   MIR   you look.for-REFL-d   INTJ

    büürü-ci   e .
    said-d   REP

    Then: "Well, my brothers, our place favored me, it has selected me, look for your own!" he told t
    them.

29. *lau,* roak-ci e   ma   *mahilā*-ka   ano   *Arun   khola* khlëk-t-ü   ma
    INTJ say-d   REP   and   2nd.son-ERG   up   Arun   river   follow-PT-3s>3   and

    Salewa Luŋkhim khuŋ-ḍa   e .
    (place)   reach-PT   REP

    "Okay," they said and the second son followed up the Arun river and reached Salewa Lungkhim.

30. *kānchā*-ka: go-o   mal-sim   *paryo,*   roak-ta e   ma   *Dudh Kosi*
    youngest-ERG I-EMPH   look.for-INF:NPT   must   say-PT REP and   Dudh river

    khlëk-t-ü   e   ma   ala hala Phulüku-la   geḍḍa   e ,   Mukli-del-no.
    follow-PT-3s>3   REP   and   up up   (place)-hiLOC come.up:PT   REP   (place)-village-levLOC

    The youngest thought: I must also look for a place ," and he followed the Dudh Kosi and came
    up to Phulüku, over to Mukli.

31. Phulüku-la geḍḍa e ma   tatásöm mal-si-mḍi   ma   be-mḍi   ma ba-mḍi-pe-mḍi
    [repet]   and   each   look-REFL-3p:PT   and   make-3p:PT   and live-3p:PT-eat-3p:PT

    rëcha.
    REP

    And each looked for a place for himself and they settled and lived there, it is told.

5. Baginanda, the flying shaman

narrator: Phure, from Mukli
recording: N.Allen; analysis: K.H.Ebert

1. **Baginanda-kam   go   then-mu-ne mi-theṭ-pu   kiki thötöwa loa**
   (name)-GEN   I   know-INF-TOP NEG-know-1s>3NPT little hearsay words

   mātrai go theṭ-pu,   möram go thö-w-to-m   *jati*   go sö-w.
   only   I   know-1s>3NPT that   I   hear-1s>3PT-NML that.much I   tell-1s>3NPT

   What I know of Baginanda, I know only a little from hearsay; what I have heard, that much I
   will tell.

2. **Baginanda   make   nokcho   bay-ra.**
   (name)   of.old   shaman   be-PT

   Baginanda was a shaman of old.

3. **mö   nokchobayra-m-belaka[1] phlus-ta-lo   u-mina   (dela) -ḍhol phël-mu-kam**
   that shaman was-NML-TEMP   initiate-PT-TEMP his-what's.it drum[2]   drum cut-INF-GEN

   lāgi u-*deutā*-mim   yeḍ-ḍ-ü-lo   u-*deutā*-ka anu   Baŋdel roaa-ma-no
   for   his-god-p   call-PT-3s>3-TEMP his-god-ERG across   (place) say-PP-levLOC

   mö   *ḍhol*-ku u-sëŋ   goak-t-ü   *rëcha* e.
   that drum-GEN its-wood   give-PT-3s>3 MIR   REP

   During his initiation time, when he had to make his - what's it - drum, he called his gods, and
   his gods gave him a tree for his drum across [the Dudh Kosi river] at a place called Bangdel.

4. **hama ottha   u-*ḍhole*-mi   kole-nële opcö-mimkhob-ḍ-ü   ma mö *ḍhol***
   and.so there   his-drummer-p   one-two   assistent -p collect-PT-3s>3 an d that drum

   phël-la   lë-mḍi.
   cut-PURP   go-3p:PT

   And so he gathered his drummers, one or two assistants, and they went to cut the drum.

5. **mö-no-m[3]   Baŋdile-ku   u-*bāri*-ra   *rëcha*, phël-la   lë-mḍi-lo,**
   that-levLOC-NML (person.from.B)-GEN its-garden-LOC   MIR   cut-PURP   go-3p:PT-TEMP

   Baŋdile-ka: hawma phël-ni-mim? roa-mḍi-lo
   (person.from.B)-ERG why   cut-2p-NML   say-3p:PT-TEMP

   It turned out to be over in a garden of one of the Bangdiles, and when they went to cut, the Bandile-
   people said: "Why have you come over to cut [here]?"

---

[1] See fn4 to Thulung text 2.
[2] The Thulung word for drum is *dela*.
[3] According to Allen -*m* is an ablative; he glosses "across-there+from". I think *mönom* is a nominalized
form attributed to Bangdile; cf. also *mögoram, oram* (PROX+LOC+NML) 'this'.

6. **orama-*guru*-ka goa-ŋḍi-m *ḍhol* phël-la bik-to-ko-m, roak-ta e**
this my-guru-ERG give-1sP:PT-NML drum cut-PURP come.over-PT-1e-NML say-PT REP

"This is the drum my tutelary spirit gave me, we have come over to cut," he said.

7. **hama thama phël-miri ma mö *ḍhol* ki-mḍi.**
and.so later cut-3p:PT and that drum stretch-3p:PT

So they cut it and stretched [hides over] it.

8. ***ḍhol* ki-mḍi ma thama mö-no-m Baŋdile-ka mat be-mḍi ma**
[repet.] and later that-levLOC-NML (place)-ERG plan do-3p:PT and

After that the Bangdile people made a plan.

9. **oramnokchohamko-kam rëcha, iki *bāri* sëŋ phël-la bik-pa,**
this shaman how.much-GEN PART our$_{pi}$ garden wood cut-PURP come.over-AP

thama iki neb-ḍa.
later our$_{pi}$ house-LOC

"How much of a shaman is he, the one who comes to cut wood in our garden? Maybe later in our house.

10. **oramnokchojem-ber-i, jemberima *mārikana* yals-i, roa-mḍi e.**
this shaman perform-make-1pi [repet] and murderously beat-1pi say-3p:PT REP

Let's make this shaman perform, let's make him perform, and then we will give him a good beating," they said.

11. **ma thama *ḍhol* kii-mu düm-miri-m[4]-*pachi:* lu akima - ama neb-ḍa**
and later drum stretch-INF finish-3p:PT-NML-after INTJ our$_{pe}$ my house-LOC

gana *cintā* me-be-saka lëk-si mi-nü, be-mḍi ma *thune*-mḍi
you seance NEG-make-CONV go-INF:NPT NEG-good do-3p:PT and hold.back-3p:PT

rëcha.
REP

When they had finished the drum, they [the people from Bandile] said: "You must not leave without having made a seance our - in my house," and they held him back.

12. ***thune*mḍi ma thama gumi-ka mat be-mḍi ma**
[repet] and later they-ERG plan make-3p:PT and

They held him back and later they made a plan.

13. **möram nokcho-mimmö lëk-pa mücü-mim-*lāi* puwaŋ-kusö reṭ-miri**
that shaman-p that go-AP man-p-DAT (bird)-GEN meat bring-3p:PT

ma banthöm seṭ-miri ma reṭ-miri ma oram goak-i, roaa-be-mḍi
and where.from kill-3p:PT and bring-3p:PT and this give-1p say-do-3p:PT

---

[4] The speaker says *düm-miri-mim-pachi*, but later admits that this was a slip of the tongue, cf. Allen 1995:145.

ma   gumi-ka   *sallāh*   be-mḍi.
and   they-ERG   plan   do-3p:PT

For the shaman's people who came they brought the meat of the puwang-bird, they killed it and brought it, "let's give this to him," they said and made a plan.

14.   mökotima thama   mö   puwaŋ-ku s ö   kho-mḍi   ma   puwaŋ-ku sö-nuŋ   jam-nuŋ
thereafter   later   that   (bird)-GEN   flesh   cook-3p:PT   and   (bird)-GEN   flesh-COM   rice-COM

goa-mḍi.
give-3p:PT

Then they cooked the bird's meat and gave them the meat with rice.

15.   goa-mḍi-lo   Baginanda-ka   roak-ta e   — basiyā   u-yuŋ-ka   loas-ledḍ-
give-3p:PT-TEMP   B.-ERG   say-PT   REP   already   his-magic-INST   see-V2:COMPL:PT-

ü   — ma   Baginanda-ka   roak-ta e:
3s>3   — and   B.-ERG   say-PT   REP

When they gave it, Baginanda said — he had already seen through them with his magical power — Baginanda said:

16.   oramguy   puwaŋ-ku s ö   goak-saḍḍa-mi   mi-pi-mim   s ö   goak-saḍḍa-mi.
this   we_pi   (bird)-GEN   meat   give-V2:BEN:PT-p   NEG-eat-NML   meat   give-V2:BEN:PT-p

"They gave us puwang meat, meat that is not eaten they gave us.

17.   pe-pa   li-n-siṭ-ni   ma   ama   a-*bhāg*-ḍa   o   puwaŋ-ku s ö   *cālī*   phii-ni
eat-AP   lie-2p-V2:REFL-2p   and   my   my-portion-LOC   this   (bird)-GEN   meat   FOC   pour-1>2

hai!   roak-ta-m   bayra   e   ma
INTJ   say-PT-NML   was   REP   and

Pretend to be eating and pour the puwang meat on my portion!" he said.

18.   thama   pe-pa   li-m-si-mḍi   ma   uma   *bhāg*-ḍa   *jammā*   be-m-
later   eat-AP   lie-3p-V2:REFL-3p:PT   and   his   protion-LOC   all   do-3p-

sa-mḍi,   khole   uma   *bhāg*-ḍa   be-m-sa-mḍi,
V2:BEN-3p:PT   all   his   portion-LOC   do-3p-V2:BEN-3p:PT

So later they pretended to be eating and put all on his portion, they put all on his portion.

19.   ma   thama   pe-pa   li-m-si-mḍi,   u-miksi - khole-kam   miksi   *chal*-ü-
and   later   eat-AP   lie-3p-V2:REFL-3p:PT   his-eye   all-GEN   eye   distract-3s>3-

thaḍḍ-ü   Baginanda-ka   pe-pa   li-m-si-mḍi   waŋ-ka.
2:TAKE:PT-3s>3   B.-ERG   eat-AP   lie-3p-V2:REFL-3p:PT   other-ERG

They pretended to eat; his eye - everyvody's eyes he distracted, Baginanda, the others pretended to eat.

20.   mökotima/../   mö   puwaŋ-ku s ö   *jāg*-üü-r-ü   ma   *jiūdo*   *ban*-üü-r-ü
thereafter   that   (bird)-GEN   meat   resurrect-[ü]-PT-3s>3   and   alive   make-[ü]- PT-3s>3

ma thok-t-ü *rëcha* e.
and join-PT-3s>3 MIR REP

Then he resurrected the bird, made it alive and joined it together.

21. thoktü rëcha e, thama: (oram go) oram ŋoo-si beṭ-pu;
[repet] later this I this arise-INF:NPT make-1s>3:NPT

o puwaŋ go ŋoo-si beṭ-pu ma *ani* guy yal-sa-mi *rëcha*.
this (bird) I arise-INF:NPT make-1s>3:NPT and then they beat-1nsiP-p PART

He resurrected it and [he said]: "I shall make it rise; I shall make this puwang bird rise, and then they will beat us.

22. o puwaŋ go ŋoosi beṭpu ma thama puwaŋ! roa ma hun-mim-belaka
[repet] later (sound) say and fly-NML:NPT-TEMP

g ohaha! roak-to oram khat-to lëk-pu.
I (sound) say-SIM this pursue-SIM go-1s>3:NPT

I shall make the bird rise and it will say puwang! and when it flies up, I will go after it, shouting haha! and pursuing it.

gani *dui-paṭṭi*-m ḍhol-la ce-n-siṭ-ni wo, roak-ta e.
you_p two-side-ABL drum-LOC hang-2p-V2:REFL-2p also say-PT REP

Hang yourself also on both sides of the drum," he said.

24. hamanethamane po-mu düm-miri-m-*pachi* *cintā* bayra bayra.
and.so later eat-INF finish-3p:PT-NML-after seance was was

Then later, after they finished eating, there was a seance.

25. *cintā* bayra-m-*pachi*-ne thamane hanu-lam athö-lam mö-go-ra-m mücü
[repet] -NML-after-TOP later across-ABL this.side-ABL that-in-LOC-NML man

kho-m-si-mḍi ma ko-kole *laurā* jet-miri ma yal-mu-kam *lāg i*
gather-3p-V2:REFL-3p:PT and one-one stick hold-3p:PT and hit-INF-GEN for

tayār ba-m-si-mḍi-lone
ready be-3p-V2:REFL-3P:PT-TEMP

When after that the people gathered from all sides, and each held a stick and they were ready for beating.

26. basi puwaŋ-kusö goa-mḍi ma puwaŋ *jāg*-üü-r-ü ma puwaŋ!
already (bird)-GEN meat give-3p:PT and (bird) resurrect-[ü]-PT-3s>3 and (sound)

roak-ta-lone Baginanda-ka haha! roak-ta ma khat-to pakha-nu phlö
say-PT-TEMP B.-ERG (sound) say-PT and pursue-SIM outside-levLOC suddenly

luk-ta.
come.out-PT

and when the bird-meat that he had already given them, the bird that he had resuscitated said puwang! Baginanda shouted haha!, and he came suddenly outside following it.

27. **mömlo** **ḍe** **mö** **Baginanda** **yal-mu-kam** *lāgi* **mö-go-nu-m** **mücü-ka**
that.time FOC that B. beat-INF-GEN for that-inside-levLOC-NML person-ERG

laurā **jeṭ-miri** **ma** **khaṭ-miri-lone** **huḍḍa** **ma** - **huḍḍa** **ma** **ala** **geḍḍa.**
stick hold-3p:PT and pursue-3p:PT-TEMP fly:PT and [repet] and up.here come.up:PT

At that moment when the men over there held their sticks, ready for beating Baginanda, and pusued him, he flew off and - he flew off and came up.

28. **geḍḍa** **ma** **mö-belaka** **u-*ḍhole*-miŋ-ka** **hanu-lam athö-lam** (**dela-ra** **cem-**)
[repet] and that-time his-drummer-p-ERG across-ABL this.side-ABL drum-LOC hang

mö *ḍhol*-**la** **ce-m-si-mḍi** **ma** **cemsimḍi-lo mö** *ḍhol*-**ka** **huḍḍ-ü**
that drum-LOC hang-3p-V2:REFL-3p:PT and [repet]-TEMP that drum-ERG fly:PT-3s>3

ma **hala mina** **ge-mḍi** **e.**
and up what's.itcome.up-3p:PTREP

He came up and at that time his drummers hung themselves to either side of the drum, and when they hung onto it the drum flew them off and they came up here to what's it?

29. **o** - **go** **plaw-to,** **o** *Rawa Khola* **athö-humbu möram** *cālī* **plaw-to**
this I forget-1s>3:PT this (river name) this.side-bank that FOC forget-1s>3:PT

go /.../
I

I forgt, this side of the Rawa Khola, I forgot ...

30. **ma** **mela** **ḍe** *ḍhyaŋrā* **jes-ta** **e.**
and up.there FOC drum sound-PT REP

And up there the drum sounded.

31. **mela** **khat-to** **ge-mḍi-lone** *pheri* **o** **Birajura-ra** [sic!]**ge-mḍi,**
up.there pursue-SIM come.up-3p:PT-TEMP again this (place)-LOC come.up-3p:PT

huṭ-miri **Biraju-ra ge-mḍi** **e.**
fly-3p:PT (place)-LOCcome.up-3p:PTREP

When they [the others] came up there in pusuit, they [Bagiananda's helpers] came up to Birajura, they flew off and came up to Biraju.

32. **Biraju gemḍi-m-*pachi*-ne** **gumi-ka** /.../ **mö-no** **mina** *pharke*-**düm-miri**
[repet] -NML-after-TOP they-ERG that-levLOC what's.it return-finish-3p:PT

gumio **lë-mḍi ma** **Biraju-nu-m** **huḍḍ-ü** **ma** **u-*ḍhol*-nuŋ** **u-mina-**
they this go-3p:PT and (place)-levLOC-NML fly:PT-3s>3 and his-drum-COM his-what's.it-

nuŋ **u-ŋopcö-nuŋ** **asinḍa neb-ḍa** **phiḍḍ-ü** **ma** **asinḍa** *cintā*
COM his-assistant-COM here house-LOC bring:PT-3s>3 and here seance

b-üü-r-ü **e**
make-[ü]-PT-3s>3 REP

After coming up to Biraju they ... [the others] returned, they went, he flew to
Biraju and and he brought his drum and his assistants home and he held a seance here.

33. ma möram-ka, mö Baginanda-ka /.../ *kãsã* yub-ḍ-ü,
    and that-ERG that B.-ERG bell.metal fabricate-PT-3s>3

    tãbã-mi yub-ḍ-ü, khole *kãsã* yub-ḍ-ü-m.
    copper-p fabricate-PT-3s>3 all bell.metal fabricate-PT-3s>3-NML

And he, that Baginanda, used to fabricate bells, he worked copper and bell metal.

34. mö Sakhle-yu kole *jhyãli* bu, Baginanda-ka yub-ḍ-ü-m.
    that (place)-loLOC one cymbals is B.-ERG fabricate-PT-3s>3-NML

Down at Sakhle there are the cymbals Baginanda made.

35. sën-kaŋ-ŋa mina b-üür-ü - *ḍhol* sën-kaŋ-ŋa yub-ḍ-ü-m
    wood-GEN-EMPH what's.it make-[ü]-PT-3s>3 drum wood-GEN-EMPH fabricate-PT-3s>3-NML

    bu/.../ Baginanda-ka u-yuŋ-ka yub-ḍ-ü-m bu, kole sölewap
    is B.-ERG his-magic.power-INST fabricate-PT-3s>3-NML is one long.straight

    bom wo yub-ḍ-ü-m bu.
    gourd also fabricate-PT-3s>3-NML is

And this thing from wood he made, the drum from wood Baginanda has fabricated with the help of
his magical power; also a 'sölewap' gourd he has made.

36. ma guku *aba* cöcö-mancö-ka - gumi-ka makem purkhã-mi-ka u-cö-mi-
    and we_pe now little.children-ERG they-ERG of.old ancestor-p-ERG his-child-p-

    ka cüsi-miŋ-ka roa-mḍi-m go thöwto-m ne.
    ERG grandchild-p-ERG say-3p:PT-NML I hear:1s>3:PT-NML PART

And we children now - I have heard the ancesors, their children and grandchildren telling it.

37. thöwtom *ani* lip-nuŋ, bom, *jhyãli*-ne go a-taaku miksi-ka
    [repet] then pot-COM gourd cymbals-TOP I my-own eye-INST

    lawto-m, athambili o bu.
    see:1s>3-NML nowadays this is

The pot and the gourd and the cymbals I have seen with my own eyes, they are still there today.

38. go akotiŋa thöwto-m *cãhĩ*, akotiŋa cëk-to-ŋa.
    I this.much hear:1s>3:PT-NML FOC this.much learn-1s>3:PT-EMPH

I have heard this much, this much I learned.

Mewahang

1. Somnima's Creation

narrator: Birkha Ram Rai, Bala
recording and analysis: Martin Gaenszle

Somnima and Paruhang

1. **nap-pi-tu   Pa:ruhaŋ cuʔ-a-ne:mo kuʔmu Somnima   cuʔ-a-ne:mo.**
    sky-LOC-hiLOC P.   be-PT- REP   below S.   be-PT-REP

    Up in the sky was Paruhang, down (on earth) was Somnima.

2. **molmaʔa Somnima-ʔa taŋwapa yok-let-a-ne:mo,... *buṛho* yok-kapa.**
    then   S.- ERG   boy   search-V2:INCH-PT-REP husband search-NML

    Eventually Somnima began to search for a boy, searching for a husband.

3. **Somnima na   honan asa -pi-l(e)   khɛʔ-ma-bɯ ?**
    S.   FOC now   who-LOC-EMPH   go- INF-PART

    But now, where should Somnima go?

4. **honan aka na *kuṭumba*- pi   khɛ-ʔaŋ   kas-a-ne:mo.**
    now   I   FOC wife.taker-LOC go-1s   shout-PT-REP

    She called out, „I'll go to the wife-takers."

5. **om-ma:-pi   asa- pi-l(e)   khɛʔ -ma -bɯ ?**
    her-mother-LOC   who-LOC-EMPH   go-INF-PART

    Her mother said (lit. at her mother's place), „Where do you want to go?

6. **am-*māiti*-ci   tɛ: cu:-k- mi.**
    your(s)-parents'.house-ns   only be-NPT-3p

    There is only your parents' house."

7. **hɯʔwapa- pi   khɛ-ʔaŋ-ne: is-u-ne:mo**
    wind-LOC   go-1s-PART   say-3P-REP

    „I'll go to the wind," she said.

8. **hɯʔwapa ko   am-koyeŋ-le   khɛʔ-ma   nu:-na   let-u-ne:mo**
   wind   this your(s)-mother's.brother-EMPH go-INF   be.good-NEG say-3P-REP

„But the wind is your maternal uncle (sic); you're not allowed to go there!" she (i.e. the mother) said.

9. **mupi   khɛ-ʔak   is-u-ne:mo**
   there go-1s   say-3P- REP

„I'll go there!" she said.

10. **moʔo   ŋa   hɯʔwa-cha *acel* mina-ʔa   togu-k-u-ci-ha:**
   those PART wind-child today people-ERG give.birth-NP-3P-ns-3p

Such „children of the wind" (illegitimate children) are still being born oday.

11. **tomaŋ   lɯ   *ḍãḍã*-pi   khed-a-maŋ *suisula*-ʔa   che:t-u-maŋ**
   and.then INTJ mountain-LOC go-PT-SEQ   whistle-INST call-3P-SEQ

mupi   yep-kha.
there stand-V2:look (IMPER)

„Be off, go to the mountain and whistle for the wind to come. Stand there and pay attention:

12. **yebu-k-na-lo   ap -te:ʔ   te:lak-piʔ -lapsɯ   mupi -ŋ(a) khed-aye**
   stand-NPT-2s-TEMP your (s)-dress turn-V2:give-COND   there-EMPH go-IMPER

If he flutters your dress upward, then go there.

13. **ap -te:ʔ   si:keʔwaʔa   lap-ti:-piʔ -lapsɯ   khɛʔ- na -ho   let-u-ne:mo.**
   your (s)-dress tight   grap-V2:TEL-V2:give-COND go-NEG-IMPER   say-3P-REP

But if he makes your dress cling tightly about you, then don't go," she (the mother) said.

14. **molmaʔa   khed-a -ne:-maŋ *sãci*   moʔo hɯʔwapa kag-u-ne:-go   om - te:ʔ**
   then   go-PT-REP-SEQ   really that wind   call-3P-REP-TEMP her-dress

hup-ti:-pit-u -ne:mo.
wrap-V2:TEL-V2:give-3P-REP

When she went there and did summon the wind, he pressed her clothing close aginst her.

15. **aŋ -ma:ʔa   kodo is- u- bɯ,   ma- khɛʔ-ma   *rahecha* min- a- ne:mo.**
   my-mother-ERG thus say-3P-PART NEG-go-INF   EVI   think-PT-REP

„So according to my mother I should not go," she thought.

16. **khɯp - pi   khed -a -ne:-maŋ   ɯŋdo   pɯg-a-bɯ**
    house-LOC   go-PT-REP-SEQ   how   be-PT-PART

When she went back home (her mother asked): „What has happened?"

17. **aŋ-te:?   ku?mu-ba?mu   gune:?-na   ɯce:ta   hup-ti:-pit-aŋ,**
    my-dress   down.here   skirt-EMPH   very   wrap-V2:TEL-V3:give-1sP

    cɛknam   ne: kuiga   khap - tet -aŋ.
    cloth   also   here (dir.)   put.on-V2:BEN-1sP

„My dress, my skirt he pressed very strongly around me, and he also put that cloth on here."

18. **ho   tomaŋ   am -koyeŋ-pi   khɛ?-ma   nu:-na(m)   let-u -ne:mo.**
    INTJ   then   your(s)-mother's.brother-LOC go-INF   be-NEG   say-3P-REP

„Well good, then. You may not go to your uncle," said (her mother).

19. **asa -pi -l(e)   khɛ?-ma   asa -pi -l   khɛ?-ma   kas -a -ne:mo**
    who- LOC-EMPH   go-INF   who-LOC-EMPH   go- INF   shout-PT-REP

„Who should I go to, who should I go to?" she cried.

20. *ta* **asa- pi- l(e)   khɛ-k-na-maŋ-lo   Pa:ruhak-pi   khed-a   let-u -ne:mo**
    so   who-LOC-EMPH   go-NPT-2s-SEQ-TEMP   P. -LOC   go-IMPER   say-3P-REP

„Well, who should you go to? Go to Paruhang," she said.

21. **Pa:ruhaŋ-na   osa-?a   maŋ -khak -tit –u-m   *thiyo are*   modolo-*samma***
    P.-FOC   she-ERG   NEG-V2:see-V2:TEL-3P-NML   be(PT) REP   then-until

Paruhang – well, she had not had a chance to see him so far.

22. **molma?a   *cipurke*   tu:k -si   coks -u -ne:mo**
    then   **Prinia criniger** (bird)   bring-PUR   send-3P-REP

Thereupon (her mother) sent the cipurke bird off to fetch him.

23. *cipurke*-**?a   Pa:ruhaŋ   tu:k-lo -ne:-maŋ   om –*gãṛa*   kodododo   yus -a -ne:mo**
    prinia cr.-ERG   P.   bring-TEMP-REP-SEQ   his-goiter sooo   be-PT-REP

    tin dānā   **cu?- a-ne:mo**
    three pieces   be-PT-REP

When the *cipurke* bird fetched Paruhang, his goiter was sooo big; he had three of them.

24. **tuːk-tɛːt-u -ne: -maŋ Somnima-m(i)** *cheu* **-pi pet-a-ne:-lo**   **ko Somnima**
bring-TEL-3P-REP-SEQ   S.- GEN   place-LOC sit-PT-REP-TEMP   this S.

       tarsa **-lus-a-ne:-maŋ**   **om -lawa -ŋ(a)**   **khɛʔ-da-ne:mo**   *bhāga-leʔ-da-ne:mo*
frighten-VB-PT-REP-SEQ   her-soul-EMPH   go-V2:RELIN-REP   escape- V2:INCH-V3:RELIN-REP

When (the bird) had brought him, (Paruhang) sat down next to Somnima, and Somnima was so terrified that her soul (lawa) escaped.

25. **molmaʔa**   *aba* **ana nuŋa**   **chi:yu-k -pɯ**   **Somnima-ʔa**
then   now you mind   dislike-NP-PART   S. – ERG

Then (her mother said to Paruhang), „Well, Somnima doesn't like you.

26. **khed-ɯ !**   **wasupkha - wahɛpkha**   **mu: -do -ye !**
go - IMPER   drought M+   make-V2:RELIN-IMPV

Go and make the world dry up.

27. **am-lasen**   *cahī* **yaksɯ**   **bakwa -pi**   **weʔ -do –ye**   **let-u-ne:mo**
your (s)-essence FOC   **Colocasia** leaf-LOC   leave-V2:RELIN-IMPV   say-3P-REP

Leave the best part of you on a Colocasia leaf"

28. **moʔo**   **om-chɯ:plɯŋwa** *ni*
this   his-urine   EMPH

- This urine of his, right? –

29. **tomaŋ khɛʔ-da -ne:mo**
then   go - V2:RELIN- REP

Thereupon (Paruhang) returned.

30. **Paːruhaŋ nap -pi - tu**   **hone** *jamma-ŋ* **kɯŋwa sɛk -weʔ-do-ne:mo**
P.   sky -LOC-hiLOC again   all-EMPH   water   dry –V2:leave-V2: RELIN –REP

Paruhang back up in the sky made all the water dry up.

31. **wɛ:ʔma-ʔa**   **ko Somnima heta-heta-ŋ**   **si:ʔ-da -ne:mo**
thirst-INST   but S.   almost -EMPH   die-V2:RELIN-REP

Somnima almost died of thirst.

32. **om –ma:-pi**   **ɯŋkhal duŋ-ma-bɯ**   **ɯŋkhal duŋ -ma -bɯ**   **kas- a- ne:mo**
her-mother-LOC   what   drink-INF-PART   what   drink-INF-PART   shout-PT-REP

She called on her mother: „What should I drink, what should I drink?

33. **wɛ:ʔma -ʔa   si:-khɛʔ-let-aŋ   is-u-ne:-maŋ**
    thirst-INST   die-V2:GO-V2:INCH-1sP   say-3P-REP-SEQ

I'm about to die," she said.

34. **uŋkhal *ta*,   makcha   kak -tɛ:ʔ-ma -lo   nuŋwa   chi:yu–k-u**
    what   PART   son.in.law   call-V2:TEL-INF-TEMP   mind   dislike-NP-3P

„What do you expect? When they bring you a husband, you don't like him.

35. **mosa-ʔa   kuŋwa   chɛk-laks-u   hogo   uŋkhal duŋ-k-u -maŋ -lo**
    that.one-INST   water   lock-V2:COMPL-3P   now   what   drink-NP-3P-SEQ-TEMP

He was the one who held back the water. And now, what will you drink now?

36. **khɯp-choŋ   khɯm -daʔ   khak -kho   *sita* cu:-k-pɯ-lo   let-u- ne:mo**
    house-above   house-below   see-see (IMPV) dew be-NP-PART-TEMP say-3P-REP

Look around uphill from the house, downhill from the house, to see whether there is dew there,"
said (the mother).

37. **molmaʔa *sãci*   khɯp-chok-pitkaʔa khed-a-ne:-lo -l(e)**
    then   actually   house-above-toward   go-PT- REP-TEMP-EMPH

    yaksɯ   bakwa -pi bayayaya[1] ŋet-a -ne:mo,   kuŋwa   gok-tit-a- ne:mo
    Colocasia leaf-LOC   white   look.like-PT-REP   water   fall-V2:CONT-PT-REP

When (Somnima) thereupon went in the uphill direction from the house, there really was something
white of a Colocasia-leaf: water dripped down.

38. **ko:p-let-u -ne: -maŋ   hop-wet-u -ne:mo**
    pluck-V2:INCH-3P-REP-SEQ   slurp-V2:COMPL-3P-REP

She plucked the leaf and lapped up (the liquid).

39. **molmaʔa moʔo-ŋ   *garbha*   bokdi:ma   pɯg-a -ne:mo Somnima   bokdi:ma pɯg-a**
    then   that-EMPH pregnant pregnant   become-PT-REP S.   pregnant become-PT

Then – well – she became pregnant from it. Somnima became pregnant.

40. **sagoŋwa -pi *pahile* na   wachekla:ma-l   tog -u**
    womb-LOC   first   EMPH thorny.creeper-EMPH give.birth-3P

---

[1] < bayappa = 'white'

The first thing born from her womb was the thorny creeper.

41. **wachekla:ma**   **tog - u -ne:-maŋ**   **om -sagoŋ**   **cep -kapa,**
    creeper   give.birth-3P-REP-SEQ   her-womb   tear-NML

    After she gave birth to the thorny creeper her womb was torn apart.

42. *ta*   **ɯŋkhɯ ye:ʔlo**   **ko**   **ak -cha:**   **kodokpɯ tɯtɯŋ-lɯ**   **tok -dhet-u**
    then   what   wonder this   my-child   such   thorn-EMPH give.birth-V2:take.down-3P

    "O my goodness! This child of mine, only such thorns were born!"

43. **is -u -ne:-maŋ**   **om -ma:**   *chakka*   *para*-**lus-a -ne:mo.**
    say-3P-REP-SEQ   its-mother astonished   to.be - PT-REP

    Its mother said in astonishment.

44. **toʔmaŋ** *pheri* **molmaʔa** **Pa:ruhaŋ-loŋ,**   *ta*   *kehi*   *lagena* **tub –a-ci-ne:-maŋ**
    then   again   then   P. -COM   PART something was.not meet-PT-d -REP-SEQ

    Then eventually, no matter what, she met Paruhang again.

45. *pheri* **ne:** *garbho* **ta**   **khin-a-ne:mo.**
    again also pregnancy PART   carry-PT-REP

    And again she became pregnant.

46. **molmaʔa** *pheri* **Pakpahaŋ** **tog -u -ne:-pho,**   **hako**   *gope*
    then   again Pk.   give.birth-3P-REP-EMPH this   **Cephalostachyum capitatum**

    After that she gave birth to Pakpahang, this small bamboo.

47. *pheri* **om -ma:**   **theiya ɯŋkhɯ ye:ʔlo,**   **kodokpɯ tɛ:**   **ak -cha:**
    again his-mother INTJ   what   wonder such   only my-child

    cha: wɛd-a -bɯ
    child go.pregnant.with-PT-PART

    Again his mother (said): "My goodness, no! My children, the childrend I bore, are only like this!"

48. **i-saʔa**   **nyen -a -ne:m,**
    say-CONV   become.angry-PT-REP

    Saying (this) she became angry.

49. *pheri garbha*   *ta*   *lagatai*   *hune* **pɯg-a -ne:mo**
    again pregnant PART incessantly   be   be -PT-REP

But soon she became pregnant again.

50. *pheri* **Lalahaŋ** *po*   hako *mālbãs*   *po*   *janmyo are*
    again L.   PART this **Bambusa nutans** PART was.born REP

And so Lalahang was born then, this thick bamboo.

51. *mālbãs* **tog-u-ne:-maŋ**   *pheri*
    bamboo give.birth-3P-REP-SEQ again

She gave birth, again, to the thick bamboo and (said):

52. **honan ma-puɯk-na-m,**   **honan ati**   **Pa:ruhaŋ-loŋ**   **ne: cu:-(k)-ci -na-ho**
    now   NEG-to.be-2s-PART   now   EMPH P. -COM   also sit-NPT-ns-NEG-IMPER

"Now, you are a failure. Well, it seems Paruhang and I should not come together!"

53. **let-u -ne:m   om-ma: -ʔa**
    speak-3P-REP his-mother-ERG

his mother told him.

54. *abo yo   ekdam   taltal pheri* **ne:** *uttikai*   **thu:-khɛ-k-ci -ne:mo**
    now these very   horny again also that.much mix −V2:GO −NPT-d-REP

But these (two) were very horny and again they had intercourse as before.

55. **tog -u -ne:mo   modo-ha:-ci-ŋ**
    give.birth-3P-REP such-3p-ns-EMPH

And (again) she gave birth to such (creatures).

56. **molmaʔa dɛkpi-lɯ   moʔo** *tinwata* **tok -we-ci-ne:mo,**
    then   later-EMPH that   three   give.birth-V2:COMPL-ns-REP

Eventually then she had given birth to those three,

57. *tin bhāi*   **mici ne: wathak-wathakpa -ŋ**   *bhayo are.*
    three brothers those also male.person (REDUP)-EMPH were   REP

Three brothers, so these were all male persons.

58. **molmaʔa** *pheri* **kuɯ:puɯ tog -u-ne:mo,**
    then   again tiger   give.birth-3P-REP

After that, again, she gave birth to Tiger.

59. **ko?o-mi na   om -laŋ om -hu? cu: om -ŋace ɯŋdo ŋet-a -bɯ,**
    this-GEN FOC   his-leg his-hand be   his-face how be-PT-PART

    Though he had legs and hands, his face looked quite ugly.

60. *pheri* **ne: om –bokpi-na   hone modo-ŋ   *nāni*-ŋ   khin-ne:mo,**
    again also her-belly-FOC   now such-EMPH child-EMPH carry-REP

    And again, now she carried another such child in her belly.

61. *pheri* **tog -u -ne:mo   ma:ksɯ <...>**
    again give birth-3P-REP   bear

    And she gave birth to Bear.

Tiger and Bear kill their mother

62. *abo* **cigippa narappa o:ci   hɯ?-paŋ   *dāju bhāi***
    now bear M* tiger M*   they(d)   two-(persons)   brothers

    Now these two, Bear and Tiger, were brothers.

63. *jeṭhā*   **kɯ:pa *kāncha*   ma:ksɯ**
    elder.brother tiger   younger.brother bear

    The elder brother was Tiger, the younger brother was Bear.

64. **molma?a** *abo* **icin   thapna-pi   khɛ?ɛ-k-ci,**
    then   now we(i) jungle-LOC go- NPT-d

    Eventually (they said): "Now, we two, let's go to the jungle!

65. **icim   ma: ɯŋkhal pi? -ma -bɯ,**
    our(di) mother what   give-INF-PART

    What shall we give to our mother?

66. **om-dudu duŋ –u-m   is –a-c-u -ne:-maŋ**
    her-milk drink—3P-p>3P say-PT-d-3P -REP- SEQ

    We have drunken her milk," they said.

67. **aka-n** *ta* **ɯŋkha ne: sa: se? -hɯ:-ŋa-na (...)**
    1s -PART PART what   also meat kill-V2:can-1s-NEG (NPT)

    "I couldn't catch any game."

68. *ani* kɯ:pa-ʔa lo hai a:m-o   *abo* iciga   khɛʔɛ-k-ci-ga bu:bu -loŋ
    then tiger-ERG INTJ mother-VOC now we(dex)   go –NPT-d-ex brother-with

Then Tiger (said): "All right, mother, now we two, my brother and I will go,

69. *abo* kodo   hɯŋ-let –a-ci-ga   aka-ʔa dibɯŋwa mu:-ʔaŋ
    now this.much raise-V2:INCH-PT-d-ex 1s -ERG game   do -1s

You have raised us to be (grown-ups) like this now. I will bring you game.

70. lap -chokpi ka: -ʔaŋ-go   lap -pendakpi yog-u-ye
    path-hiLOC shout-1s -TEMP path-loLOC   search-3P-IMPER

When I am shouting above the path, look for it below!

71. lap -pendaʔ ka: -ʔaŋ-lo   lap -chokpitkaʔa yok -co -ho
    path-loLOC shout-1s -TEMP path-hiLOC (dir)   search-V2:eat-IMPER

When I am shouting below the path, look for it above!"

72. leʔ -do -ne:m   *thiyo are*, om -ma:
    speak-V2:RELIN-REP was REP his-mother

he spoke to his mother.

73. om-ma: moʔo-ŋa   bokdi:ma cuʔ-a-ne:m
    his   this-EMPH pregnant   be -PT-REP

His mother, she was pregnant.

74. moʔo-ŋa ak -cha: *abo* khed-a, ɯŋdo ŋe:-k -pɯ
    that-EMPH my-child now go -PT how be-NPT-PART

But she (said): "My child has gone now, what shall I do?"

75. khokwabɯ wɯ:-loŋ, khɛʔɛʔ-baka-ne:-bɯ
    sickle   attach-SIM go -V2:PRETEND-REP-PART

She stuck her sickle (into her belt) and pretended to go.

76. ma:ri   *garja*-lus-a -lo
    suddenly roar-VB -PT-TEMP

Roaring suddenly (Tiger said):

77. **aka   khɛʔɛ-ʔaŋ-maŋ   ka: -mɯ   yakwe-k-u-ŋ-maŋ   tɛ: dab -aho**
    I   go -1s -SEQ   shout-INF finish-NPT-3P-1s -SEQ only come-IMPER

"When I have left, come only after I have finished shouting."

78. **leʔ -do -ne:-bɯ -lɯ.**
    speak-V2:RELIN-REP-PART-PART

He spoke to her.

79. *chārai*   **kha(ŋ)-kha(ŋ)-ma   mit -u -ne:-maŋ   phin-a -ne:m   na   om-ma:.**
    quickley   look (REDUP) -INF   think-3P-REP-SEQ jump-PT-REP   FOC his-mother

But immediately his mother curiously wanted to look and came jumping.

80. **moʔo   hɛluwa-ʔa   sed -u -ne:-lo   ko   om-ma -l   *dui tukra***
    that   blood -INST intoxicate-3P-REP-TEMP this his-mother-PART two pieces

    ŋek-set-u-ne:m
    bite-V2:kill-3P-REP

Intoxicated from this (game's) blood (Tiger) bit his own mother in two pieces and killed her.

81. **molmaʔa ho?numaŋ moʔo hɛluwaʔa seʔ-ma   yakwet-u -ne:-maŋ**
    then   later   this blood-ERG intoxicate-INF finish-3P-REP-SEQ

Lateron, when the blood stopped intoxicating him, (he said):

82. **aŋ-ma: ɯkpa:palo, lap-pentakpimgaʔa yok-co-ho   leʔ -da -k -pɯ,**
    my-mother   my.goodness path-loLOC (dir)   search-V2:eat-IMPER speak-V2:RELIN-1s-PART

 "O my mother, my goodness, I told you to look below the path,

83. *sidha -ŋ   ta   abo*   **ɯŋkha-l   mu:-ma-na-bɯ   kha:p-tit -a -ne:mo,**
    straight-EMPH PART now what-PART do-INF-2s-PART   cry –V2:CONT-PT-REP

But (you went) straight... Now what shall I do with you?" He kept on crying.

84. **se ta   seʔ-wet -u,**
    kill PART kill-V2:COMPL-3P

He had in fact killed her.

85. **molmaʔa ma:ksɯ lo   *kāncho*   ana-ʔa   ikim-ma: khu-meʔ   let -u -ne:m**
    then   bear   INTJ younger.brother you -ERG our(i)-mother dig/bury-V2:CAUS speak-3P-REP

Then he said "Hey Bear, younger brother, you go and bury our mother!"

86. **maksa-ʔa na   moʔo** *dinbhar* **chɯk-tit -u -ne:mo,**
    bear -ERG FOC   that   all.day   carry-V2:CONT-3P-REP

    But Bear carried her (body) around all day long.

87. **chek** *abo thikɯ* **om-ma: wak-apa** *khāṛal*-**loŋ   ma-yoktok-ne:mo**
    INTJ now well his-mother fit-NML hole -COM   NEG-find -REP

    "Damn it!" He could not find a hole into which his mother would fit

88. **ɯbom khopcɯ cuʔ-a-ne:-ba -pi   nɛk -tit -u -ne:mo**
    one   cavity   be-PT-REP-NML-LOC bury-V2:CONT-3P-REP

    so he buried her at a place where there was a small cavity.

89. **maŋ-waks-u -ne:mo dɛ:t -a -ne:mo**
    NEG-fit –3P-REP   be.evident-PT-REP

    When he realized that she did not fit

90. **molmaʔa** *abo* **maŋ-waks-u is-u -ne:-maŋ co:-ne:-pho   om-ma:**
    then   now NEG-fit –3P say-3P-REP-SEQ eat-REP-EMPH his-mother

    he said to himself: "Well, she doesn't fit" and ate from his mother.

91. *ādhi* **co:-wet -u-ne: -maŋ   mopaŋ   nɛg -u -ne:m,**
    half   eat-V2:COMPL-3P-REP-SEQ following.that bury-3P-REP

    When he had eaten up half of her he buried her.

92. **koʔo op-kɛk -pi   na   taŋa-ŋɯ bis -a -ne:m om-ma:-mi,**
    this   his-tooth-LOC FOC   hair-EMPH stick-PT-REP his-mother-GEN

    But at his teeth stuck a hair of his mother.

93. **moʔo** *pheri mālbãsa* -**loŋ   hako** *gope*-**ʔa   khak-tok-a-c-u-ne:m,**
    that   again big bamboo -COM this   small.bamboo-ERG see-achieve-PT-d-3P –REP

    And that was seen by the big and the small bamboo.

94. **ikim -ma: ca:-kapa   kici,   ɯbom se:-kapa ɯbom ca:-kapa,**
    our(i)-mother eat -NML   these.two one   kill-NML one   eat –NML

    They have eaten our mother, one has killed her, the other has eaten her!

95. **lɯ   seʔ -weʔ -ma-ci   is-a-c-u-ne:-maŋ.**
    PART kill-V2:COMPL-INF-d say-PT-d-3P-REP-SEQ

Come on! Let's kill them off!" The two said.

96. **molmaʔa   mica -ʔa   ta,   oːci   dhānu kã̄ḍ   āphoi   puɨg-a-ci -neː-maŋ**
    then   those.two-ERG PART they   bow   arrow themselves become-PT-d-REP-SEQ

So then they turned into bow and arrow

97. **moʔo   kuɨːpa-loŋ maːksuɨ seʔ-ma   iː-loŋ   sed-a-c-u -neːmo.**
    that   tiger-COM   bear   kill-INF   say-SIM   kill-PT-d-3P-REP

And saying: "Let's kill this Tiger and Bear!" they killed them.

98. **mopaŋ   hillasi   moʔo kuɨːpa-ʔa hillasi mus –a-c-u**
    following.that bad.death.spirit that   tiger-ERG   spirit   make-PT-d-3P

As a result of that they created the Bad Death Spirits from Tiger (and Bear)

99. **om-ma: ma:maksi,   moʔo   bhitrayum garbha chanu,**
    his-mother mother.spirit that   inner   womb   foetal.spirit

His mother became the Mother Spirit, that inside of her womb (became) the Foetal Spirit

100. **tin   tālā tyahã̄, tin   thari puɨg-a-mi-neː-maŋ**
    three levels there three kinds become-PT-3p -REP-SEQ

Three levels, three kinds came into existence.

101. **mo-ŋa   aceli̇̄   koʔo ma:maksi   hillasi,   chanu**
    that-EMPH nowadays this   mother.spirit bad.death.spirit foetal.spirit

Those still (exist) nowadays, these Mother Spirits, Bad Death Spirits and Foetal Spirits

102. **mopaŋ   puɨg-let -a -neːm,**
    from.that become-V2:INCH-PT-REP

They began to originate from this.

103. **tyahi Somnima-paŋ   tyahã̄-dekhi uṭhiyo,   yo   na-jāti na-jāti-harū.**
    there S. –ABL   there-from   originated these no-good (REDUP)-p

There, from Somnima, from there they originated, these beings which are no good.

3. & 4. Ancestral Migration and Settlement

narrator: Birkha Ram Rai, Bala
recording and analysis: Martin Gaenszle

Coming up from the place of origin

1. **khowaluk-paŋ   aptok   *thau*-pi-l   ked-in-ne:-lo,   *jeṭhā*   *ra***
    place.of.origin-ABL how.many place-LOC-EMPH come.up-1pi-REP-TEMP elder.brother and

    ***mailā*,   *jeṭhā*   lamlo   ked-a-ne:-bɯ.**
    younger.brother elder.brother ahead   come.up-PT-REP-PART

    When we came up from Khowalung, the elder and the second brother, the elder one went ahead in front.

2. **lap-pi   cino ne   hako bohori   *kerā*   khoŋ-sa   ked-a-ne:mo.**
    path-LOC sign also   this **Reevesia pubescens** banana cut-CONV come.up-PT-REP

    Cutting a sign on this banana tree he came up.

3. **lo   aŋ-bu: kutga   ked-a-m   *rahecha* min-loŋ   ikin-ʔa**
    INTJ my-elder.brother up.here come.up-PT-NML REP   think-SIM we(i)-ERG

    tɯŋ-u-m-ne:mo.
    follow-3P-p>3-REP

    Thinking "So, my elder brother came up here!" we followed him.

4. **ikim   phoba-ʔa   tɯŋ-u-ne:mo.**
    our(i) grandfather-ERG follow-3P-REP

    Our grandfather followed him.

5. **koʔo makluŋ-na mecha na *kordi ta   kordi   nai ho.***
    these (name)-FOC little FOC leprous EMPH leprous EMPH is

    These Maklung (name of the Kulunge) are a bit like lepers (i.e. bad).

6. **moʔo   dɛŋ-dɛŋ   tɯŋ-a-ŋ-ne:maŋ**
    that   after-after follow-PT-1s-REP

    "He will come after me."

7. **mo?o** *kerā* **ne** *abo* **khoŋ-laŋ-loŋ** **ɯ-*cina*-ŋ** **kodo** **be?lo**
   that banana also now cut-V2:TEL-SIM one-moment-EMPH like.this long

   le:-khɛ-k.
   come.out-V2:GO-NPT

   If one cuts the banana it immediately becomes long like this.

8. **bohori** **khoŋ-loŋ makthorokke hoŋ pɯ-khɛ-k.**
   Reevesia pubescens cut-SIM black now become-V2:go-NPT

   After cutting the banana it turns black at the same moment.

9. **yuŋ-da-bɯ** **khaŋ-k-u-ne:mo.**
   put-V2:RELIN-PART see-NPT-3sP-REP

   He (the younger brother) saw the remains.

10. *purāno* **cu?-a-ne:mo.**
    old be-PT-REP

    It was old.

11. **hadem** **lo khɛ?-da-bɯ** **min-sa?a** **modo-ŋ** **ked-a-ci-ne:mo.**
    when be go-V2:RELIN-PART think-CONV like.this-EMPH come.up-PT-ns-REP

    Thinking "How long is it ago? He has gone!" they came up.

12. *pheri* **hako** *chatra*-**pi** **tub-a-ci-ne:m,** *pāri-patti* *pāri-vāri.*
    Again this Chatra-LOC meet-PT-ns-REP other.side-side other.side-this.side

    They met again at Chatra, one on that the other on this side.

13. **molma-?a tɯ** **bu:bu** **ana ɯŋkha** *pāra* *tāra*-**lɯ:-ma** **ɯŋ-*pāra*-lo**
    Then PART elder.brother you which manner cross-VB-INF which-manner-is

    is-u-ne:mo.
    say-3P-REP

    Then he said: "Hey, elder brother, how did you manage to cross?"

14. **hoina ikim** *celi*-**mi** **om-hɯkchomma-pi hɛg-u-ŋ-ne:**
    no our(i) sister-GEN his-little.finger-LOC cut-3P-1sA-REP

    amliso-?a **tomaŋ** *bhok* **pit-u-ŋ-maŋ** **aka-n** *tāra*-**lɯs-a-ŋ.**
    (type of grass)-ERG then sacrifice give-3P-1sA-SEQ I-EMPH cross-VB-PT-1s

let-u-ne:mo om-bu:-ʔa   *cahī* **makluŋ-ʔa**
say-3P-REP   his-elder.brother-ERG   FOC   (name)-ERG

"Well, I cut the little finger of our sister and after sacrificing (it) with *amliso* leaves I crossed," said the elder brother, this Makluŋ.

15. **tomaŋ** *sãci* **peṭāro-yu**   **cuʔ-a-ne:-bɯ**   **om-*celi*.**
then   indeed   basket-levLOC   be-PT-REP-PART   his-sister

But in fact his sister was in the carrying basket.

16. **moʔo ɯb-ɯbom has-ci-ne:mo Khambuhang-ʔa ɯbom Mewahaŋ-ʔa ɯbom**
that   one-one   divide-ns-REP   Kh.-ERG   one   Mew.-ERG   one

Meʔnahaŋ-ʔa ɯbom Meche-ʔa ɯbom.
Me.-ERG   one   Mec.-ERG   one

They divided them up one by one: Khambuhaŋ got one, Mewahaŋ got one, Meʔnahaŋ got one and Meche got one.

17. *cār* **bahini-*celi* ɯb-ɯbom has-ci-ne:mo.**
four   sister   one-one   divide-ns-REP

They divided up the four sisters one by one.

18. **la:-len-loŋ**   **om-*kānchi-aulo* hɛk-pit-u-ne:-maŋ**   *bhok*   **pit-u-ne:m**
pull.out-V2:come.out-SIM   her-little-finger   cut-V2:give-3P-REP-SEQ   sacrifice   give-3P-REP

thiyo are.
was   REP

After taking her out (of the basket) he cut her little finger and sacrificed it.

19. **tomaŋ** *ḍeli*-**pi**   **ma-ti:-pa-ŋ**   **si:-k-da-ne:-pho**   **om-*celi***   **ikim-mi**
then   basket-LOC   NEG-put-NML-EMPH   die-NPT-V2:RELIN-REP-EMPH   our-sister   our(i)-GEN

But when he was about to put her back into the basket his sister died, our sister.

20. **Makluŋ-mi** *cahī* *kālo jureli*-**ʔa**   **lɯ**   *bhok*   **pit-u-ne:mo** *rahecha are.*
(name)-GEN FOC   (type of bird)-INST   PART   sacrifice   give-3P-REP   EVI   REP

Makluŋ, it turned out, had given a *kālo jureli* bird as sacrifice.

21. **sip-tis-a-ne:**   **bara-ʔa-ŋ**
deceive-V2:TEL-PT-REP   purpose-INST-EMPH

He had deceived us, on purpose.

22. **hi:wa mus-u** *hola* *nahi*
    curse make-3P   probably EMPH

    It seems he spelled out a curse.

23. ***tān-tāra*-lɯ-khed-a-mi-ne:mo**
    cross (redupl.)-VB-V2:GO-PT-3p-REP

    And they crossed the river.

24. **molmaʔa** *ta* **o:ci Dudh Koshi tɯŋ-loŋ**   **khed-a-mi-ne:mo**
    then   EMPH they (river)   follow-SIM   go-PT-3p-REP

    Then they followed up the Dudh Koshi River.

25. **lɯ**   **ana**   **kuiga**   **khed-aho let-loŋ** *pheri* **om-bu:-ʔa-ŋ**
    INTJ   you   over.here   go-IMPER say-SIM again   his-elder.brother-ERG-EMPH

    koʔo **Khambuhaŋ-ʔa-ŋ Arun tɯŋ-ma**   **hak-***āyo***   *are*
    this   Kh.-ERG-EMPH   (river) follow-INF   send-PT   REP

    "Hey, come over here!" said his elder brother, this Khambuhang and sent him up the Arun River.

26. *pheri* **ikin Aruna**   **tɯ:-khet-u-m-ne:-maŋ**   **ked-in-ne:mo**
    again we(i) (river)   follow-go-3P-p>3-REP-SEQ   come.up-1pi-REP

    So we followed the Arun and came up.

27. **molmaʔa lɯ**   **hapiʔ lo lɯ**   **ta:-in-ne:-lo**   **muiga om-bu:**   *kacur*
    then   PART where be PART   come-1pi-REP-TEMP   there his-elder.brother root

    weŋ-a-ne:mo
    cut-PT-REP

    Eventually when we came to where-was-this-place, there was his brother and cut the *kacur* root.

28. **lou aŋ-necha-loŋ**   **hone tubu-k-ci-ga-m**   *rahecha* **tupma** *jeṭhā*
    INTJ my-younger.brother-COM   now   meet-NPT-d-e-NML   EVI   meet   eldest.brother

    ma-miŋ-a-bɯ   **is-u-ne:m**
    NEG-think-PT-PART say-3P-REP

    "So then, I meet again my younger brother, but I don't like this!" the elder brother said.

29. **molmaʔa** *sãci* **kuttu hapal-ko** *simanā*-**tu**   **miʔduŋ** **tɯŋ-sa**   **tɯŋ-sa**
    then   EMPH up   where-GEN boundary-hiLOC ashes   follow-CONV   follow-CONV

khɛʔ-da-ne:-ha:-ci
go-V2:RELIN-REP-3p-ns

Then, up there at the boundary, they went around burning down the jungle.

30. *bhāsme*   **hub-a-ci-ne:mo** *wāri*   *pāri*
    burn.down slash-PT-ns-REP   over.here over.there

    They practice slash-and-burn agriculture, here and there.

31. **kuiga**   **ikin-ʔa** *cahī makai* **khawa** **tis-u-m-ne:mo** **tis-a-ne:mo** **ikim** **phoba**   *cahī*
    over.here we(i)-ERG FOC   maize   millet put-3P-p>3-REP put-PT-REP   our(i) grandfather FOC

    Over here we, our forefatheres, we planted maize and millet.

32. **o:ci-mi**   *cahī khāli* **hako** *latte latte*   **tɛ:** **he:-ci-ne:mo**
    they-GEN   FOC only   this   nettle **Amaranthus** (rep.) only sow-ns-REP

    They, for their part, planted only this nettle.

33. **ikim**   *khāja cahī* **khawa-mi** **saruwa di:** **kathuwa-paŋ**   **khi-khet-u-ne:mo**
    our(i)   snack FOC   millet-GEN draught beer wooden.container-ABL   carry-V2:take-3P-REP

    Our drink was draught millet beer, which we carried in a wooden container.

34. **o:-mi**   *cahī latte*-mi   *huṛe*   **muiga**   **khaŋ-be:yu-k-u-ne:mo**   **om-bu:-ʔa**
    he-GEN FOC nettle-GEN   brew over.there see-V2:apply-NPT-3P-REP   his-elder.brother-ERG

    Theirs was fermented spinache brew, which his elder brother showed over there.

35. **ɯ-*ceta*-ŋ**   **chaklakwa-ʔa** **duk-co-k-u**   *din-piche*
    one-moment-EMPH   gurgle-INST   drink-V2:eat-NPT-3P   day-after

    It made a gurgling sound while they drank, taking the whole day.

36. **o:-mi**   *ta*   **boblowa-paŋ** **duŋ-k-u-ne:mo**
    he-GEN EMPH   gourd-ABL   drink-NPT-3P-REP

    He drank his (beer) out of a calebash.

37. **ghoklok ghoklok pugu-k-ne:mo** **kuŋ-kuŋ-na-ne:mo**
    plurp (onomat.)   be-NPT-REP   go.down (redupl.)-NEG-REP

    It made plup plup and (the beer) didn't go down.

38. **wɛʔma-ŋ**   **si:ʔ-na-ne:mo** *jeṭhā*-mi   *cahī*
    thirst-EMPH die-NEG-REP   eldest.brother-GEN FOC

The elder brother couldn't quench his thirst.

39. **se:ma   nɯ   dab-a-ne:-maŋ   *abo* ɯ-*thāũ*   hone icim   kharɯkhom   pug-a**
next.day EMPH come-PT-REP-SEQ now one-place now our(di) fields be-PT

lɯ   icin   ici-mi   *khāja* lɛc-ca:-ma   is-u-ne:m
INTJ we(di) we(di)-GEN snack exchange-eat-INF say-3P-REP

When he came the next day he said: "Now we have our fields in one place, so, let us exchange our drinks."

40. **lo-ye   *ta*   is-u-ne:-maŋ *kāṭhuwa*   muiga om-bu: pit-u-ne:mo**
is-EMPH EMPH say-3P-REP-SEQ wooden.container over.there his-elder.brother give-3P-REP

"Okay then" he said and gave the wooden container to his elder brother over there.

41. **mo?o boblowa kuiga   om-bu:-?a   pit-u-ne:m**
that calebash over.here his-elder.brother-ERG give-3P-REP

Over here his elder brother gave him that calebash.

42. **muiga om-bu:-?a   ɯ-*ceta*-ŋ   mo? *dina* nɯ   *majja-le***
there his-elder.brother-ERG one-moment-EMPH this day EMPH pleasure-ERG

duk-co:-ne:mo
drink-V2:eat-REP

His elder brother over there drank it in one moment with great pleasure that day.

43. **kuiga   om-necha-go   mo?o boblowa-paŋ mo?o *latte*-m   *huṛe***
over.here his-younger.brother-EMPH that calebash-ABL that nettle-GEN brew

dollo dollo duŋ-k-u-ne:m
piece (rep.) drink-NPT-3P-REP

Over here his younger brother drank that nettle beer from that calebash drop by drop.

44. **ghoklok ghoklok huk-khɛ-k-u-ne:mo   temmaŋ   ma-kuŋ-ne:mo**
plurp (onomat.) close-V2:GO-NPT-3P-REP just NEG-go.down-REP

Making plup plup it got stuck, it just did not go down.

45. **molma?a thɯkka   ko?o aŋ-bu: kodokpɯ *rahecha* min-a-ne:mo**
then spit (onom.at.) this my-elder.brother like.this EVI think-PT-REP

So then he thought: "Spit on him! So my elder brother is like this!"

46. **tomaŋ khɯp-pi   na   *ho* bu:b-o   koʔo am-di:wa-nɯ   maŋ-kuks-a-pho**
    then   house-LOC PART is elder.brother-VOC this your-beer-EMPH NEG-go.down-PT-EMPH

    asin   i-saʔa om-bu: piʔ-wet-u-ne:mo
    today   say-CONV his-elder.brother give-V2:COMPL-3P-REP

    Then at home he said: "Hey, elder brother, your beer didn't go down today" and gave it to his elder brother.

47. **boblowa-paŋ duŋ-u-ne:mo**
    calebash-ABL drink-3P-REP

    He drank from the calebash.

48. **ɯŋkhama-l maŋ-duŋ-u-bɯ   *ta*   let-u-ne:mo**
    why-EMPH NEG-drink-3P-PART EMPH say-3P-REP

    "Why can't you drink then?" he (Kulunge) asked.

49. **maŋ-kuk-pɯ   ana-ʔa   duŋ-u-lo-n   kuks-a   aka-ʔa tob-u-ŋ-lo -na**
    NEG-go.down-PART you-ERG drink-3P-TEMP-EMPH go.down-PT I-ERG   touch-3P-1s-TEMP-FOC

    maŋ-kuŋ-ne: is-u-ne:
    NEG-go.down-REP say-3P-REP

    "It doesn't go down: when you drink it goes down, but when I touch it it does not go down," he (Mewahang) said.

50. **molmaʔa koʔo boblowa kodokpɯ-ŋ   i-saʔa   yaŋkhet-u-ne:mo**
    then   this calebash like.this-EMPH say-CONV   take-3P-REP

    So he thought: "This calebash is like this!" and took it with him.

51. **khɯp-pi   ta:-ne:-maŋ   isin bu:bu:-loŋ   *khāja* lɛmma   is-u-maŋ**
    house-LOC come-REP-SEQ today elder.brother-COM snack exchange say-3P-SEQ

    lɛn-a-c-u-ga-bɯ   *laṭṭe*-m   *huṛe* ɯbom ne: maŋ-kuŋ
    exchange-PT-d-3P-e-PART   nettle-GEN brew one also NEG-go.down

    aka-n isin si:-khɛʔ-let-a-ŋ   ne: wɛʔma-ʔa   is-u-ne:-maŋ
    I-PART today die-V2:GO-V2:INCH-PT-1s also thirst-ERG   tell-3P-REP-SEQ

    When he came home (to his wife) he said: "Today I exchanged drinks with my elder brother, but this nettle beer just did not go down. I was about to die of thirst."

52. **ɯŋkhama lɛn-a-c-u-p   to ɯŋkhama lɛn-a-c-u-bɯ   lap-pi-ŋ**
    why   exchange-PT-d-NML PART why   exchange-PT-d-3P-PART path-LOC-EMPH

modo loŋ   is-u-pa-loŋ   ma-lɛmma   *parne*
such nonsense- tell-3P-AP-COM NEG-exchange must

om *jahān-ʔa* let-u-ne:-maŋ   nyen-a-ne:mo
his wife-ERG   say-3P-REP-SEQ   get.angry-PT-REP

"Why did you exchange, why did you do exchange? You should not have made an exchange with such an idiot on the way," his wife said and got angry.

53. **molmaʔa   dɛksaŋ dɛksaŋ-lɯ *pheri ta***
    then   after   after-PART   again PART

    ikim necha-ʔa   mu:-k-u-bɯ-ŋ   kharukhom ikin-ʔa   ne:
    our   younger.brother-ERG   make-NPT-3P-PART-EMPH agriculture   we(i)-ERG   also

    mu:-ma is-u-ci-ne:-maŋ   o:ci-ʔa   ne: *makai* khawa ti:-let-a-mi-ne:mo
    make-INF tell-3P-ns-REP-SEQ they-ERG also maize millet sow-V2:INCH-PT-3p-REP

    Then later on again they said: "We should do agriculture just as our younger brother is doing it," and they also started to grow maize and millet.

54. ***jeṭhā*-ci   ne: *na-bhāe pahile* o:ci *laṭṭe* tɛ: dɛk-pi   *jāhũ* tis-a-mi-ne:mo *gāhũ***
    elder.brother-ns   also NEG-were first   they nettle only after-LOC barley sow-PT-3p-REP   wheat

    So the elder brother, who first had grown only nettles, eventually grew barley and wheat.

55. **molmaʔa *pheri makai*   ti:-let-a-mi-ne:mo**
    then   again maize   sow-V2:INCH-PT-3p-REP

    And they also started to grow maize.

56. **honan koʔo *laṭṭe* ma-ti:-ma   ikin ne: ikim   necha-to-ŋ**
    now   this   nettle NEG-sow-INF we(i) also our(i) younger.brother-like-EMPH

    mu:-ma i:-loŋ   ikim phoba-ʔa   *pheri* cam le:ʔ-let-u-ne:mo
    do-INF   say-SIM our(i) grandfather-ERG again   rice   plant-V2:INCH-3P-REP

    As they said: "So we will no longer grow this nettle, we will also do like our younger brother," our grandfather started to plant rice.

57. **moʔo khaŋ-u-ci-ne:mo *pheri* o:ci ne: le:ʔ-let-a-mi-ne:m   *jeṭhā* ne:**
    that see-3P-ns-REP   again they also plant-V2:INCH-PT-3p-REP elder   also

    As they saw that then the elder brother also started to grow (rice).

58. **molmaʔa *dekha-sekhi hoina* kosa-ʔa *abo*   chutti-ŋ   ikin-ʔa   mu:-k-u-pɯ**
    then   imitation   isn't.it this-ERG now   everything-EMPH we(i)-ERG   do-NPT-3P-PART

kamai mu:-let-u
work do-INCH-3P

Thus, by imitation, isn't it, this one began to do all farming work just like we did.

59. *abo* ikin duɯp-sɛk-in *rahecha* is-u-ne:mo
now we(i) be.pained-V2:be.exhausted-1pi EVI say-3P-REP

"Now, it seems we are defeated and outnumbered," she (= Mewahang's wife) said.

60. tomaŋ ana mupi ɯ-*thāū* kharukhom ma-mu:-ma-pho
thus you here one-place farming NEG-do-INF-IMPER

"Therefore you should not farm here in one place.

61. iyak-nɯ *najik najik* pugu
yesterday-EMPH near near was

The other day you were too close,"

62. khɯp-pi mi:mcha-ca-ʔa is-u-ci-ne:-maŋ nyen-a-mi-ne:mo
house-LOC woman-ns-ERG say-3P-ns-REP-SEQ get.angry-PT-3p-REP

said the women at home and got angry.

63. molmaʔa dɛksaŋ dɛksaŋ-pi go *jeṭhā*-ŋ koŋ-let-a-ne:mo
then after after-LOC PART elder-EMPH win-INCH-PT-REP

Eventually, however, the elder brother turned out as the winner.

64. kharukhop-pi ne: koʔo *bastu* ɯŋkha huɯŋma-pi ne: o:ci-ŋ koŋ-let-a-mi-ne:mo
harvest-LOC also this animal what raise-LOC also they-EMPH win-V2:INCH-PT-3p-REP

In farming as well as in raising all kinds of animals they became the winners.

65. *pahile* khipabi maŋ-cu:-ne:-ha: makluŋ-ci ɯbom ne: ta ikim *gāū*-pi
first around.here NEG-be-REP-3p Kulunge-ns one also PART our village-LOC

First these Maklung did not exist around here, not even one was in our village.

66. *abo* o:ci-mi muiga Mahakuluk-pi cuʔ-a-mi-ne:mo ko iki-pi-na
now they-GEN over.there Mahakulung-LOC be-PT-3p-REP this we(i)-LOC-EMPH

ma-cuʔ-a-ha:-ci-ne:-po
NEG-be-PT-3p-ns-REP-PART

Now, their (fields) were over there in Mahakulung, whereas on our (territory) there was none of them.

67. **dɛk-pi   modo pɯk-let-a-mi-ne:-maŋ-po   kupi   cha: let-a-ha: muiga-paŋ**
   after-LOC like.this be-INCH-PT-3p-REP-SEQ-PART here   child come.out-PT-3p   there-ABL

   dab-a-ne:-ha:
   come-PT-REP-3p

   But later they began to show up here like this and had children, so they came over from there.

68. **kupi iki-pi?-na   mina-ŋ   ma-cu:-ne:-ha:-ci-po   *are   paile-nai***
   here our(i)-LOC-PART   people-EMPH   NEG-be-REP-3p-ns-PART   REP   first-EMPH

   Here on our (territory) there had been no (= not many) people in the beginning.

Khaling

2. Kakcalâp* - The orphan

recording: S.Toba
analysis: K.H.Ebert

The sisters bury Khakcalâp and separate

1. **tu hâs-po   u-cö   suh-pu mo-t-nu e.**
   one person-GEN his-child three-CL be-PT-3p REP

   A person had three children.

2. **mana mä hâs-po   u-cö   yahki mo-t-nu-lo   ŋa   mis-tä-na u-cö-po**
   then   that person-GEN his-child small be-PT-3p-TEMP EMPH die-PT-LINK his-child-GEN

   u-häri   mä-piŋ   go-tä e.
   his-full.grown NEG-come be-PT REP

   That person died while the children where still small, the children had not grown up.

3. **läsbä-po *cây*   sah-pu beŋmä mü-yi-t-i, mäsu *cây* ghölä bhör-i-t-i-na**
   boy-GEN FOC   two-CL sister be-[i]-PT-d they$_d$ FOC many grow-[i]-PT-d-LINK

   yoŋkhi khak-bi khös-t-i   e.
   spinach hoe-PURP go.away-PT-d REP

   The boy had two sisters; when they grew up, they went to hoe spinach.

4. **manane mä us-wä   yo: mu-khöc-e! lu-tä-su-lo   mu-ghaŋ-wä e**
   then   that their$_d$-sibling also   NEG-go-IMPER tell-PT-3d>3-TEMP NEG-obey- IRR REP

   And although they told their brother: "Don't go!" he did not obey.

5. **mana mä melsem-su-po us-nâŋ   tu-po Grom tu-po Las.**
   then   that girl-d-GEN   their$_d$-name one-GEN Grom one-GEN Las

   The girls' names, one's was Grom and one's was Las.

6. **mä Grom Las-su-ä lu-tä-su   e: reskâp mu-khöc-e! äjä-ne   so-ä**
   that Grom Las-d-ERG tell-PT-3d>3 · REP orphan NEG-go-IMPER later-TOP hunger-INST

   i-mây kümin-ä i-mây.
   2-die thirst-INST 2-die

   Those two, Grom and Las, said: "You orphan, don't go! Later you will die with hunger and thirst.

---

* I use <a> for Toba's <aa> [a], <â> for Toba's <a>, which represents a back vowel. According to Toba (1984) Khaling distinguishes two tones, but no tones are marked in his texts.

7. maŋ i-jä   maŋ i-tüŋ-ü?   lü-tä-su-lo   mu-ghaŋ-wä e.
what 2-eat:3sP what 2-drink-3sP tell-PT-3d>3-TEMP NEG-obey- IRRREP
Then what will you eat, what will you drink?" they said, but he did not obey.

8. mana khös-tä-nu   e.
then   go.away-PT-3p REP

And so they went away.

9. manane achaŋa äjä-ne   so-ä   mâttü[1]-na u-wä-su-ä-ne   yoŋkhi
then   truly   later-TOP hunger-INST (?)-LINK   his-sibling-3d>3-ERG-TOP spinach

kak-tä-su   e.
hoe-PT-3d>3 REP

And really later he was starving, and his sisters hoed spinach.

10. mä läsbä-po u-nâŋ   Khakcalâp e.
that boy-GEN   his-name Khakcalâp REP

That boy's name was Khakcalâp.

11. manane Khakcalâp-ne u-wä-bi   khaja phik-bi khös-tä-lo:yaka Las-bi
then   Khakcalâp-TOP his-sibling-LOC snack beg-PURP go-PT-TEMP across Las-LOC

bha-ye!   lü-tä e   Las-bi bha-tä-lo: yaka Grom-bi bha-ye!
go.across-IMPER tell-PT REP Las-LOC go-PT-TEMP across Grom-LOC go.across-IMPER

lü-tä-na   mesaŋ äjä-ne   mis-täe.
tell-PT-LINK thus   later-TOP die-PT REP

And when Khakcalâp went to his older sister to beg for a little food, she said: "Go over to Las!"
and when he went there, she said: "Go over to Grom!", so at last he died.

12. jö-nä mämthusombä-ä   khwat-tä-naneGrom-koloLas-su-ne thakây chük-i-t-i-
eat-INF without   hunger-INST take-PT-TEMP   Grom-COM Las-d-TOP tired become-[i]-PT-d

-na mämyoŋkhi-po u-saŋ   sür-tä-lo   âmsu-ä-ne: lâw.tigiKhakcalâp-po
-LINK that spinach-GEN its-herb split-PT-TEMP they_d-ERG-TOPINTJ Khakcalâp-GEN

u-solo ŋâlu tür-(r)e!   äs-t-i   e.
his-bone tooth split-IMPER say-PT-d REP

Being without food he got hungry, and Grom and Las got tired, and when the spinach plant split,
they said: "Hey, may Khakcalâp's bone and tooth split!'

13. mana mä go-bi   käphäm   bek-tä-su   e.
then   that inside-LOCbottle.gourd put.in-PT-3d>3 REP

And they put a bottle gourd in there.

14. mä brök-tä-lone: lâw.tigiKhakcalâp-po u-dhoŋ brök-tä, äs-t-i   e.
that break-PT-TEMP INTJ   Khakcalâp-GEN his-head break-PT say-PT-d REP

---

[1] *mâttü* 1. 'must' (see sent. 82) , 2. 'made'. It is unclear which verb is meant here.

15. **Khakcalâp me mü-s-su mana än** *pheri sâllâ* **mü-s-su e.**
Khakcalâp   what do-PT-3d>3 and   now again advice do-PT-3d>3 REP

And then they held counsel what to do about Khakcalâp.

16. *lâw* **än ic-ä   sämsi puŋme khüc-i-na   bher-i, äs-t-i-na** *sâllâ* **mü-s-su-**
INTJ now we_di-ERG Sämsi flower bring-d-LINK fly-d   say-PT-d-LINK advice do-PT-3d>3-

na: u-hem-po täm sämsi puŋme lâm   mä-po *cây* **som** *bâcey* **chu   min**
LINK his-who-GEN this Sämsi flower shoot that-GEN FOC breath live become life

chuk-ki.
become-1pi

"Hey, let's bring the sämsi flower," and when they had counsel together: "Whose sämsi sprouts,
she will live, may we all live long."

17. *lâw* **lüy-i-t-i-na   bher-i-t-i-na   Dikdel khös-t-i e.**
INTJ say-[i]-PT-d-LINK fly-[i]-PT-d-LINK Dikdel go-PT-d   REP

They agreed and flew to Dikdel.

Khakcalâp fishes a stone

18. **Khakcalâp-ne u-so   pâŋ-tä-m** *pâchi* **phük-tä-na** *châkkey* **chük-tä e   sâlpu**
Khakcalâp-TOP his-hunger ?-PT-NML after get.up-PT-LINK surprise become-PT REP bird

se-tä.
kill-PT

As for Khakcalâp, after he had been overcome by hunger, he woke up, startled, and he killed
a bird.

19. **mana yatha-ne** *pheri* **wär   täy-nä   du-mât-tä-lone   anâm-anâm**
then later-TOP again fish.hook let.fall-INF begin-CAUS-PT-TEMP long.ago-long.ago

tu-ba hâs   u-mäm   mâyh-khâ-pä u-non-ä   helâŋ mü-tä e.
one-CL person his/her-mother die-V2:GO-PCPL her-aunt-ERG contempt do-PT REP

And then afterwards, when he began to fish, — well,there was a person long long ago, whose
mother had died, her aunt (on mother's side) was wicked.

20. **mana âm-po u-kera   del-ku   go-bi   mo-tä e.**
then she-GEN her-uncle village-GEN inside-LOC be-PT REP

And she lived in the village of her uncle (on mother's side).

21. **melo mäm Khakcalâp-ä wär   tän-tä-lo   mä wo ŋö heŋ wär-po**
then that Khakcalâp-ERG fish.hook pull-PT-TEMP that PART fish how fish.hook-GEN

u-coŋ-bi khöŋ-tä   e.
its-tip-LOC come.up-PT REP

And when Khakcalâp pulled his hook, she came up on the tip of the hook like a fish.

And when Khakcalâp pulled his hook, she came up on the tip of the hook like a fish.

22. manane mä hâs   luŋ mân-tä-si-na   me mân-tä-si   molo Khakcalâp-ä
then   that person stone make-PT-REFL-LINK so make-PT-REFL but Khakcalâp-ERG

rwap   löp-tä e.
right.away catch-PT REP

And the person turned herself into a stone, but Khakcalâp caught her right away.

23. melo-ne lâŋ   go-tä-na: äci uŋ-a-ne ses-t-aa[2] w o äy-ŋa-lo *utharo* luŋ g o
then-TOP basket be-PT-LINK you_d I-ERG-TOP kill-PT-1s PART say-1s-TEMP ?   stone ?

***râycha,* äs-ta e.**
turn.out say-PT REP

Then there was a basket, and he said: "I thought I killed you, and it turned out to be a stone."

24. mana *pheri* woŋa-de   tän-tä   e melo y o mesâŋ *pheri* y o
then   again other-locNML let.fall-PT REP then also thus   again   also

tän-tä   mesâŋ e.
let.fall-PT thus   REP

And again he fished in some other place, and again it happened in the same way.

25. äjä wo: khörsäy tâp-de   kho-nä *pâro*, äs-tä-na   kür-tä.
later PART chili   pound-locNML take-INF must   say-PT-LINK carry-PT

Later, "I should take this as a pounder to grind pepper," he said and took it.

26. mana u-kâm   khot-tä-na   châsku-bi   bek-tä-na   tü-tä   e.
then   his-house take-PT-LINK (basket)-LOC put.in-PT-LINK store-PT REP

And he took it to his house and put it into the châsku (basket) and stored it.

27. mana *pheri* mesâŋ khös-tä-na ho-tä-lone   u-kâm-bi-ne   yu kway
then   again thus go-PT-LINK come-PT-TEMP his-house-LOC-TOP rice vegetable

mün-pä go-tä e.
make-PCPL be-PT REP

And when he again went and came back, a meal was prepared at his house.

28. sü-ä   mü-tä? äs-tä-na   hway mü-tä.
who-ERG do-PT say-PT-LINK sound do-PT

"Who made this?" he called out.

29. melo-ne tu-ba mächä   melsem-ä: âkhi! lo-tä-na, uŋ-a mu-ŋ-ta-m, äs-tä e.
then-TOP one-CL old.woman woman-ERG INTJ tell-PT-LINK I-ERG do-1s-PT-NML say-PT REP

An old woman said: "I made it."

---

[2] The original text in Toba (1983:35) has *sestä*, but this is probably an error. The dual pronon (*äci* = *eci*) in this sentence seems unmotivated.

30. **ho-ye   jö-yi! jö-s-su   e.**
come-IMPER eat-1d eat-PT-3d>3 REP

"Come, let's eat," and they ate together.

31. **manane ghölä *din* ŋa   mesâŋ jö-s-su   e.**
then   many day EMPH thus   eat-PT-3d>3 REP

And so the two of them ate like this for many days.

32. **tu nöl go-tä tu-ba melsem-ä: mä-ne moo inpo käm mü-pä-ne   woŋa-m mu,**
one day be-PT one-CL woman-ERG that-TOP not   your work do-PCPL-TOP other-NML be

lü-tä-na   nâŋlo-ä   khrwam-si-tä.
tell-PT-LINK basket-INST cover-REFL-PT

And one day a woman said: "That is not your servant, the one who does your work is another one",
and she covered herself with a basket.

33. **mana inpo käm mü-pä i-cend-ü, lü-tä-na, *acha* ŋa   mesa mo-tä-lo   mä âmpo**
and   your work do-PCPL 2-know-3sP tell-PT-LINK INTJ EMPH thus   be-PT-TEMP that her

u-kokcâmluŋ-ä   wo käm mü-tä e.
her-mortar stone-INST PART work do-PT REP

"But you know your servant," she said, "she really was here and worked with her stone pestle."

34. **mana *pakha* läs-tä   yo rwap   löp-tä e.**
and   outside go.out-PT also right.away catch-PT REP

And when she went outside, he caught her right away.

35. **melo wo: âkâkâ tu-le i-grök-a-ta-lo   a-solo a-ŋâlu   tür-tä sah-le**
then   PART INTJ   one-CL 2-catch-1sP-PT-TEMP my-bone my-tooth split-PT two-CL

i-grök-a-ta-lo   a-säl   a-khâr tür-tä-na   mu-grik-a-ye! lü-tä e.
2-catch-1sP-PT-TEMP my-foot my-hand split-PT-LINK NEG-catch-1sP-IMPER tell-PT REP

At this, she said: "Once, when you caught me, my bones and my teeth split, when you caught me
the second time, my foot and my hand split, don't catch me!"

36. **mana lesä-tä-na   bat mü-s-su   e.**
then   release-PT-LINK talk do-PT-3d>3 REP

And he let her go, and they had a talk together.

37. **in   än-ne uŋ-a mu-câkt-u-wa,   lü-tä e.**
you   now-TOP I-ERG NEG-know-1s>3s-IRR tell-PT REP

He said: "I just did not know."

House building

38. **mana mesâŋ âmsu mey dumbu chük-i-t-i-na   kâm *baney* mü-ne-po *lagi***
then   thus   they_d wife husband become-[i]-PT-d-LINK house make   do-INF-GEN for

läsbä *c â y* **khabolwam-bi   khös-tä-loneghara taŋa w o hö-tä-na   u-mey**
boy   FOC beam   catch-PURP   go-PT-TEMP   ?   only PART bring-PT-LINK his-wife

lü-tä   e: äci reskâpä he   gonö i-chük-tä, lü-tä.
tell-PT REP   you_d orphan how PART 2-become-PT tell-PT

And thus the two of them became wife and husband, and when the man went in order to fetch a beam for housebuilding and he brought back only a straight one, his wife said: "Orphan, what's the matter with you?"

39. **he   mât-t-ü-lo   mä-bi tu sâŋ-bi   cäŋrü   sâlpu mo-tä e   mä-po**
    how make-PT-3sP-TEMP that-LOC one wood-LOC black.bird bird be-PT REP that-GEN

    u-mer   naga-kolo go-tä,mä sey-mât-t-ü-na   mä-heŋ ywayh-pä hä-tä   e.
    its-tail fork-COM be-PT that see-make-PT-3sP-LINK that-like look.like-PCPL bring-PT REP

And just then, there was a swallow in a tree and its tail was forked, and when she had shown him this, he brought a beam like that.

40. **mana** *bâllâ* **kâm   mü-s-su-na   müy-i-t-i-na yatha-ne** *maridhani*
    and   INTJ house make-PT-3d>3-LINK be-[i]-PT-d-LINK later-TOP hard rich

    chük-i-t-i-na   u-mey-ä   siŋ-tä e: inpoi-beŋmä-häm mu-mon-wä, ici
    become-[i]-PT-d-LINK his-wife-ERG ask-PT REP your your-sister-p NEG-be-IRR we_d

    thephem hoŋ babcö   chük-i-t-i.
    such-NML king married.orphans become-[i]-PT-d

And with great effort they built their house and later on they became very rich and the wife asked: "Since there were no sisters of yours we became orphan landlords.

Khakcalâp sends out animals to find his sisters

41. **reskâp-ä i-câkt-ü   o tu-he   mu-nu-kho-mim lwam-bi bha-ye!**
    orphan-VOC 2-know-3sP Q one-how be-3p-if-p   catch-PURP go.across-IMPER

    lü-tä e   u-mey-ä.
    tell-PT REP his-wife-ERG

Orphan, do you know if there are any of yours, go over and bring them," his wife said.

42. **melo Khakcalâp-ä lu-tä e "khäbi tu-ba   sah-pu a-beŋmä**
    then Khakcalâp-ERG tell-PT REP where one-CL two-CL 1smy-sister

    müy-i-t-i-m.
    be-[i]-PT-d-NML

To that Khakcalâp said: "Somewhere there were two sisters of mine.

43. **khäbi khös-t-i uŋ-a mu-câkt-u,   lü-tä e.**
    where go-PT-d I-ERG NEG-know-1s>3s tell-PT REP

Where they went I do not know", he said.

44. melou-beŋmä-su-ne Dikdel dhâm-bi müy-i-t-i-na câkâpe-kolo
then his-sister-d-TOP   Dikdel ridge-LOC be-[i]-PT-d-LINK flea-COM

ser-kolo baŋpö   phiŋ-tä-su-na   khös-t-i-lone câkâpe *cây*
louse-COM go.between send-PT-3d>3-LINK go-PT-d-TEMP flea FOC

***chito*khös-tä ser   *cây* wätäka khös-tä.**
fast go-PT louse FOC slowly go-PT

At that time his sisters lived on the Dikdel ridge, and as they sent a flea and a louse as their go-betweens, they went, but the flea went fast while the louse went slowly.

45. câkâpe-ä-ne Khakcalâp-po u-bra cämhö-tä e   ser-ä   mu-cämhöt-wä e.
flea-ERG-TOP Khakcalâp-GEN his-story forget-PT REP louse-ERG NEG-forget- IRR REP

The flea forgot what Khakcalâp had told him, but the louse did not forget.

46. manape câkâpe-ä ser lü-tä e: uŋ-a bra-ne   cämho-t-a wo, lü-tä.
then   flea-ERG louse tell-PT REP I-ERG story-TOP forget-PT-1s PARTtell-PT

And the flea said to the louse: "I forgot," he said.

47. ser-ä   lü-tä e: uŋ kür-a-ye   mana uŋ-a lân-nä, lü-tä.
louse-ERG tell-PT REP I   carry-1s-IMPER and I-ERG tell-1s>2s tell-PT

And the louse said: "Carry me and I will tell you."

48. mana kür-tä-na   ser-ä   lü-tä-na   mesa khös-t-i-lone: ayeye u-cwarpu
and   carry-PT-LINK louse-ERG tell-PT-LINK thus go-PT-d-TEMP   INTJ REL-sacrifice

khäbi-la   gö, äs-t-i-na   se-tä-su-na   mu-wöc-i-wi-yi.
where-PATH be say-PT-d-LINK kill-PT-3d>3-LINK NEG-cut-[i]-IRR-d

And when he carried him and louse told him and they went, they said: "Oh, now where is the offering?" and they killed it, but did not cut it.

49. manane Khakcalâp-ä *pheri bhale* phiŋ-tä-lo *bhale*
then   Khakcalâp-ERG again rooster send-PT-TEMP rooster

thik-bi khös-tä-na hopäs-tä-m *pâchi bhale*-ä   he äs-tä *bhane:*
?-LOC   go-PT-LINK arrive-PT-NML after rooster-ERG how say-PT QUOTE

Then Khakcalâp sent the rooster, and after the rooster arrived, this is what he said:

50. Khakcalâp Wäylâm pokopoko.oo!äs-tä-na   ök-tä e.
Khakcalâp Wäylâm (sound)   say-PT-LINK crow-PT REP

"Khakcalâp Wäylâm, pokopokoo!" he crowed.

51. manane Grom-koloLas u-wä-ne: u-wärphö-ä   maŋ gonö blät-t-ü.
then   Grom-COM Las his-sibling-TOP REL-wild.fowl-ERG what PART tell-PT-3sP

And Grom and Las, his sisters asked: "What did this wild fowl say?

52. anam   go os-celpä   mis-khös-tä-m, äh-to u-hem-po
long.ago PARTour_{de}-brother die-V2:GO-PT-NML say-SIM his-who-GEN

u-ciplepca   wonö, äs-t-i-na   bâysâŋ-ä   öp-tä-su   e.
his-bird.offering PART say-PT-d-LINK lease.rod.of.loom-INST throw-PT-3d>3 REP

Long ago our brother died", and "whose could the bird-offering be?" they said and they threw the lease rod of the loom.

53. melone *bhale*-ä-ne   tu-ba atha bâŋpä u-pheso wo tät-ü-t-ü   e.
then   rooster-ERG-TOPone-CL very nice his-feather PARTlet.fall-[ü]-PT-3sPREP

54. manane äyeye u-cwarpu-ne   hebe   bâŋpä wonö, äs-t-i süŋ-tä-su   e.
then   INTJ his-sacrifice-TOP how.much nice PART say-PT-d pick.up-PT-3d>3 REP

And: "Oh, how pretty is the bird offering", they said and picked it up.

55. *pheri bhale* meŋ   äs-tä e; âmsu-ä sâŋ suŋ-to   suŋ-to
again   rooster like.that say-PT REP they_d-ERG wood collect-SIM

khös-t-i e.
go-PT-d REP

Again the rooster said the same, they went, collecting wood as they went.

56. mesamesâŋ us-celpä-po   us-kâm   hopäs-tä-nu-nane
thus thus   their_d-brother-GEN their_d-house arrive-PT-3p-TEMP

us-celpä   thö-t-su-lone us-khan   lo-tä-nane dhâm-tü bher-i-t-i-e.
their_d-brother see-PT-3d>3-TEMP their_d-shyness feel-PT-TEMP ridge-hiLOC fly-[i]-PT-d REP

And so they came to their brother's house, and when they saw their brother, they were ashamed and flew up to the ridge.

57. manane Khakcalâp-ä jujur häm-tä-na mä-bi jhük-i-t-i-na
then   Khakcalâp-ERG sour dry-PT-LINK that-LOC run.away-[i]-PT-d-LINK

us-celpä-ä: mana eci a-beŋmä-su i-jhük-i.
their_d-brother-ERG and you_d my-sister-3d>3 2-run.away-d

And Khakcalâp dried some sour herb where they had ran away and said: "My two sisters run away.

Reconciliation

58. ocu i-wä-delme-kolo   hoŋ   chük-u-t-u.
we_d your-sibling-sister.in.law-COM couple.of.orphans become-[u]-PT-1de

We two, I and your sister-in-law have become a couple of orphans.

59. eci beŋmä-su uŋ-a *biha* bi-n-su äy-ŋa-na *bhale* lök-bi   phi-ŋa-m,
you_d sister-d   I-ERG wedding give-INF-d say-1s-LINK rooster find.out-PURP send-1s-NML

lü-tä-su e.
tell-PT-3d>3 REP

I was thinking to marry you two sisters and I sent the rooster to find out," he told them.

60. mana *biha* **bi-s-su   e.**
and   wedding give-PT-3d>3 REP

And he gave them into marriage.

61. yu kway   khip-tä-nu e.
rice vegetables cook-PT-3p REP

They cooked a meal.

62. mana Grom-ä bwap phok-tä-na   chöm-tä e.
and   Grom-ERG wing spread-PT-LINK dance-PT REP

And Grom shook her wings and danced.

63. Las yo bwap phok-tä-na   chöm-tä-na yu   kway   jü-t-nu e.
Las also wing spread-PT-LINK dance-PT-LINK rice vegetable eat-PT-3p REP

And Las shook her wings and danced and they ate the meal.

64. mana bran   thän-tä-nu e.
and   relationshiop break-PT-3p REP

And then they separated.

65. mana okpo *riti*   **râdâm tä-bi-ka   khöŋ-tä   e.**
and   our_e custom custom this-LOC-ABL come.up-PT REP

And our custom comes from this.

66. baŋpö   mü-nä *biha* **mü-nä kâm mü-nä än-nu-na blät-nu**
go.between do-INF wedding do-INF house do-INF say-3p-LINK say-3p

câkpä *purkha*-**häm-ä.**
wise   ancestor-p-ERG.

When they think of go-between, of wedding, of house building, they recite thus, the knowledgeable men, the priests do.

67. uŋ-a yo tib.tibi   blät-t-u-m.
I-ERG also some.some say-PT-1s-NML

I myself have recited a little bit too.

68. okporâdâm-hodâm tephem gö sü.
our_e custom -ECHO like.this be PART

Our customs are like this.

Housebuilding II

69. wäylâm-ä khakcalâp lü-tä: reskap-ä   mämä kâm *bâney* mü-nä äs-tä e.
Wäylâm-ERG khakcalâp   tell-PT orphan-VOC ?   house ready do-INF   say-PT REP

Wäylam said to Khakcalap: "Orphan, we should build a house."

70. kâm mü-tä-lo u-dumbu phiŋ-tä e   khabolwam-bi bha-tä.
house do-PT-TEMP her-husband send-PT REP beam   catch-PURP go.across-PT

When building the house, she sent her husband, he went to search for a beam.

71. suri   lom   taŋa hä-tä   e.
straight beam   only bring-PT REP

He brought back only a straight beam.

72. haga-kolo-m mü-höt-wä e.
fork-COM-NML NEG-bring-IRR REP

He did not bring back one with a fork.

73. mebena wälâm u-cö-kolo   mo-tä.
then   Wäylâm her-child-COM be-PT

Wäylam was there with her child.

74. mana send-ü mä-tü   maŋ-bi   khe-nä-na   *sida*   taŋa hö-ther-tä.
and   see-3sP that-hiLOC what-LOC put.on-INF-LINK straight   only bring-HAB-PT

And she looked up where to hang things, and he kept bringing straight beams only.

75. mana tu nöl cäŋrü sâlpu bher-tä-na cäŋrü-po u-mer hag-pä   gü.
and   one day (bird) bird   fly-PT-LINK (bird)-GEN its-tail be.forked-PCPL be

Then one day a cängrü bird flew by – and the cängrü's tail is forked.

76. mä   hagasey-mät-tä-na: tukum heŋam   haga-kolo-m hotä!   lü-tä e.
that   fork see-make-PT-LINK up.there like.what fork-COM-NML bring:IMPER tell-PT REP

She showed him that forked tail and said to him: "Bring one with a fork, like that one up there".

77. mebena w o Khakcalâp-ä hö-tä   e   mäm u-haga-kolo-m.
then   PART Khakcalâp-ERG bring-PT REP that its-fork-COM-NML

After that, Khakcalap went and brought one, that is, one with a fork.

78. mebena mä-tü   khöleŋ thok lâyh-ki-lo   nü-pä.
then   that-hiLOC   all   thing put.on-1pi-TEMP be.good-PCPL

Then it is okay to put everything up there.

79. mä-bi khabo khân-tä-lo   khakcalâp-ä anek khân-tä y o moo mu-cäp-wä e.
that-LOC beam ram-PT-TEMP khakcalâp-ERG many khân-PT even no NEG-can-IRR REP

When Khakcalap tried to ram the beam there, even ramming it many times he could not do it.

80. mä-lo   Wäylâm-ä   u-cö   kür-de-tä-na   phlök-bi bha-tä-lo
that-TEMP Wäylâm-ERG her-child carry-V2-PT-LINK help-PURP go.across-PT-TEMP

mä khabo then-tä-lo   mä   gob-ü   u-cö   solo öŋ-khös-ta.
that beam   push-PT-TEMP that   inside-loLOC her-child bone break?-V2:GO-PT

Then Wäylam, who carried the child, went over to help, and when she pushed the beam, the child's bones broke.

81. mana   mä   khabo mä-yu   läsü-su-lo   mä   u-cö   mä-yu-ŋ
and   that beam   that-loLOC withdraw-d-TEMP that her-child that-loLOC-EMPH

khlö-tä-na   mis-tä.
crush-PT-LINK die-PT

And when the two of them let go of the beam, the child was crushed to death down there.

82. mäm-po   minä   bhok jütäm äntâsâba y o   kâm   *bâney* mü-ka-lo
that-GEN INTJ   ?   ?   nowadays even house ready do-1pe-TEMP

s ö   sen-nä   mâttü.
flesh kill-INF must

And because of all this, even today, when we build a house, we have to kill an animal.

Shaman praying to Naïma

The Shaman Nirempa (right)